RICHARD WEBSTER

THE ENCYCLOPEDIA OF SUPERSTITIONS

Llewellyn Publications
Woodbury, Minnesota

The Encyclopedia of Superstitions © 2008 by Richard Webster. All rights reserved. No part of this book may be used or reproduced in any manner whatsoever, including Internet usage, without written permission from Llewellyn Publications except in the case of brief quotations embodied in critical articles and reviews.

First Edition
First Printing, 2008

Art direction by Lynne Menturweck
Book design by Steffani Sawyer
Cover design by Kevin R. Brown
Interior art ©: Art Explosion
             Desk Gallery
             The Image Club DigitalArt
Llewellyn is a registered trademark of Llewellyn Worldwide, Ltd.

Library of Congress Cataloging-in-Publication Data for *The Encyclopedia of Superstitions* is on file at the Library of Congress.

  ISBN: 978-0-7387-1277-2

Llewellyn Worldwide does not participate in, endorse, or have any authority or responsibility concerning private business transactions between our authors and the public.

  All mail addressed to the author is forwarded but the publisher cannot, unless specifically instructed by the author, give out an address or phone number.

  Any Internet references contained in this work are current at publication time, but the publisher cannot guarantee that a specific location will continue to be maintained. Please refer to the publisher's website for links to authors' websites and other sources.

Llewellyn Publications
A Division of Llewellyn Worldwide, Ltd.
2143 Wooddale Drive, Dept. 978-0-7387-1277-2
Woodbury, Minnesota 55125-2989, U.S.A.
www.llewellyn.com

Printed in the United States of America

Other Books by Richard Webster

Amulets & Talismans for Beginners

Aura Reading for Beginners

Color Magic for Beginners

Creative Visualization for Beginners

Dowsing for Beginners

Gabriel

Magical Symbols of Love & Romance

Michael

Miracles

Palm Reading for Beginners

Pendulum Magic for Beginners

Practical Guide to Past-Life Memories

Praying with Angels

Raphael

Soul Mates

Spirit Guides & Angel Guardians

Uriel

Write Your Own Magic

For two special friends,
Harley and Lillian Pope

CONTENTS

INTRODUCTION

Whenever Dr. Samuel Johnson (1709–1784), the English lexicographer, critic, and author, walked down a street he touched every wooden post he passed. He also stepped out of a door with his right foot first, and avoided all the cracks between paving stones. He believed that if he didn't, something unpleasant would happen.

Niels Bohr, the famous physicist, had a horseshoe hanging above his office door. "Surely you don't believe that will make any difference to your luck?" a colleague asked. "No," agreed Niels, "but I hear it works even for those who don't believe."

Sir Winston Churchill always carried a "lucky" walking stick when he had to travel on a Friday, a day he felt was unlucky. He refused to travel at all on Friday the 13th. He also touched any black cats he came across, as he considered them lucky.

Alfred Gwynne Vanderbilt slept in a bed that had all four legs resting in dishes of salt, in order to protect himself from evil spirits.

Many years ago, a friend of mine deliberately performed a sequence of events on Friday the 13th, in an attempt to disprove the effects of superstitions. He deliberately spilt salt, walked on all the cracks in the sidewalk he could, had the landlord's black cat cross his path, signed a lease agreement, and then walked under a ladder. The next day, his girlfriend left him.

People are as superstitious today as they have ever been. Have you ever knocked on wood or walked around a ladder? Are you happy when you see a pin and pick it up, because you know you'll enjoy good luck for the rest of the day? Have you ever tied a knot in a handkerchief, crossed your fingers, or said "bless you" to someone who has sneezed?

One might think that as scientists uncover more and more about the workings of the universe, superstitions would gradually disappear. In fact, superstitions are still very common. Certain occupations seem to be more prone to superstition than others. You might not expect an accountant to be superstitious, for instance, but you wouldn't be surprised to learn that a gambler, athlete, or actor was. This is because belief in superstition increases as a result of uncertainty. Accountants know that their job will be secure as long as they do good work. But actors can lose a job at any moment, no matter how good they may be. Sports stars live with uncertainty, since in their world a fraction of a second might determine a win or a loss.

Not surprisingly, there are many stories about the superstitions of sports people. A runner, for instance, wins an important race while wearing a certain pair of running shoes. From that point on, the runner is likely to consider those particular shoes lucky, and will insist on wearing them whenever competing in an important race. Nobby Stiles, a former England football star, never tied his bootlaces until he was on the field. George Seifert, former coach of the San Francisco 49ers, had to touch a book before leaving his office. He also had to be the last person to leave the locker room before a game. Jack Nicklaus always carries three pennies with him whenever he plays golf. A survey conducted in New Zealand in 2006 found that 21 percent of men own "lucky" underpants that they wear while playing sports.[1]

While living in Cornwall, England in the 1960s, I occasionally watched a game of cricket. On the first occasion, the score in the game eventually came to 111. The person I was with told me that a score of three "1s" is called "the Lord Nelson," and that the batsman would probably go out (in baseball terms, "strike out") on the next ball. To my amazement, that is exactly what happened. I asked my friend why this was called "the Lord Nelson," and was told, "Lord Nelson had one eye, one arm, and one unmentionable piece of anatomy." I laughed out loud at this explanation, but discovered over the following few months how strong a superstition "the Lord Nelson" was.

Many people have their own personal superstitions created by two events happening almost simultaneously. If a black dog walks in front of you at the same time that someone is telling you a close friend has died, you could easily develop a superstition about black dogs. This is because the two events became connected in your mind.

Learned superstition, as this is called, has been observed in animals as well as humans. B. F. Skinner (1904–1990), the behavioral scientist, published his classic experiment "'Superstition' in the Pigeon" in 1948.[2] Professor Skinner placed pigeons inside a box and gave them a food pellet every fifteen seconds, regardless of what the birds were doing. After a few minutes, the birds developed a variety of idiosyncratic rituals, such as bobbing their heads up and down or walking in circles. This demonstrated that the pigeons appeared to believe that their actions were causing the release of food. Professor Skinner explained that the accidental combination of food arriving while the bird was performing a certain behavior was enough to reinforce that activity. Most superstitions that humans hold begin in the exact same way. The runner won the race wearing a certain pair of shoes, so now has to wear them in every race from now on. It becomes a personal superstition.

In ancient times, almost every occurrence was examined to see if it was a portent, a warning, or an indication of good or bad luck. The flight of a bird, the patterns of clouds, or seeing a specific person or animal was a sign or omen.

In association with this, throughout history people have utilized a system of seemingly irrational safeguards intended to help them survive and live safely in a difficult world. These superstitions depend on the belief that some superior and potentially dangerous power controls the universe. However, by performing various forms of ritual and magic, people feel they can appease this force and maybe even win its blessing. Consequently, even when they know there is no scientific validity to a superstition, people believe in it because it gives them a sense of security and control over their lives.

Dictionaries define superstition as an irrational belief or practice, something that is not based on knowledge or fact, an irrational fear of the unknown, or a blindly accepted belief. Essentially, dictionaries say that superstition is based on fear and ignorance.

The word "superstition" is derived from the Latin *superstes*, which means "outliving" or "surviving." It proved to be a convenient word for describing religious ideas that carried on long after the particular belief system had died.

There are many superstitions connected with religion, and people who belong to one faith are likely to consider people with different beliefs superstitious. Constantine considered paganism a superstition. Tacitus, on the other hand, considered Christianity a pernicious superstition.[3] Martin Luther said that anything that does not center on Christ was superstition.[4] St. Paul also believed this, and told the men of Athens, "I perceive that in all things ye are too suspicious" (Acts 17:22). In the sixteenth century,

Protestants condemned Catholic beliefs as "Popish superstitions." Nineteenth-century Christian missionaries traveled the world to save primitive people from their superstitious beliefs and practices. The Indian scholar Ananda Coomaraswamy wrote, "The Gods of an older religion become the Devils of one that supersedes it."[5]

Many years ago, I conducted an experiment by placing a ladder against a wall on a busy street. Although it was obvious that no one was on the ladder, almost everyone stepped off the sidewalk to walk around it, rather than under it.

When I lived in Cornwall, one of my neighbors was the seventh son of a seventh son. He was an extremely successful diviner, partly because people believed that his lineage proved he had special abilities.

While writing this book, I arranged a lunchtime meeting with a fellow author. We agreed to meet on a Friday. She was happy with that arrangement until she discovered it was Friday the 13th. She phoned me back to arrange lunch on a different day.

None of these instances are unusual. Education and logic have no place as far as superstitions are concerned, and most people will admit to hanging on to one or two superstitious beliefs. They may touch wood, cross their fingers, or toss a pinch of salt over their left shoulder. They may laugh while doing this, but they still do it, just in case.

One year after World War Two ended, a movie executive called Nick Matsoukas founded the National Committee of Thirteen Against Superstition, Prejudice, and Fear. He was the perfect person to lead this project, as he was born on June 13, his name contained thirteen letters, and he was the thirteenth child in the family. The Committee was founded on Friday the 13th. Its members did everything they could to break superstitions everywhere they went. Nothing adverse happened as a result.

On Friday, August 13, 1948, the First American Exhibition on Superstition, Prejudice, and Fear opened at the American Museum of Natural History in New York. It ran for thirteen days. To get in, visitors had to walk under one of three large ladders. Inside, open umbrellas hung from the ceiling and there were displays of spilled salt and broken mirrors. There was also a proposed thirteen-month calendar, which had a Friday the 13th every month. The purpose of the exhibition was to banish superstition. The event received a large amount of press at the time, but was never repeated.

All of this totally ignores the beneficial aspects of superstition. Superstition can be an effective way of handling the anxieties and stress of everyday life. If people believe a certain action will bring them luck, they'll feel calmer and more at ease. Consequently, they'll be more relaxed, confident, effective—and luckier.

My interest in superstitions began when I moved to Cornwall and discovered the large number, and wide variety, of superstitions practiced there. Within days of arriving, I'd learned several superstitions from my landlady:

> If you visit someone's home and leave without sitting down, you'll never be invited there again.
>
> If a stranger visits your home on Christmas Day, you'll be unlucky for the next twelve months.
>
> If more than one lady pours from the same teapot at a morning tea, one of the guests will become pregnant.
>
> A slice of toast placed in the fork of the biggest tree in an apple orchard ensures a good crop.

Some of the superstitions were rather amusing:

> If your nose itches, one of four things will happen. You'll be kissed, crossed, or irritated. If none of these occur, a fool will shake your hand.
>
> If you pick dandelions, you'll wet the bed.

After several months in Cornwall, I moved to Yorkshire and became fascinated with the superstitions there, especially those practiced by the fishermen. Here are a couple of examples:

> A fisherman's wife must never wash clothes on the day he sets out to sea, for if she does, he'll be washed overboard.
>
> Only men can be on the wharf to see a ship sail, and they cannot say "goodbye." If they do, the crew will not return home.

A few years later, I discovered the treasure trove of superstitions in the Far East. My original intention was to include as many of these as possible in this book. However, the sheer number of superstitions practiced around the world made it impossible. Consequently, in this book I've tried to include superstitions that are widely held in the Western world. For the same reason, I reluctantly and sadly have had to leave out most regional superstitions.

I had to make other decisions, too. Is religion itself a superstition? What about magic? Divination? Many people would classify all of these beliefs as superstition, while others would say all of them are real. Even within Christianity, people belonging to one denomination may consider the practices of another denomination to be superstitious. And when I mentioned to someone that I'd written an entry on Wicca for this book, he was delighted, as he considered Wicca a "pernicious superstition." I consider Wicca to be a religion, rather than a superstition. Nevertheless, I included it in this book, as the history of superstitions contains numerous mentions of witches and witchcraft and I wanted the book to be as complete as possible.

I have also included several entries on different forms of divination. Again, this is for completeness, as I do not consider them superstitions. However, I'm well aware that many people do. A close friend of mine has seen ghosts on several occasions and wasn't happy to learn that I'd included them in the book.

In the end, I've tried to include everything that is pertinent to the subject, rather than limit my selections to my own beliefs and opinions. I've found that people are quick to notice superstitious practices in others, but consider their own superstitions to be facts of life. This is because superstitions address deep-seated emotions, rather than the more logical, conscious mind.

Professor Bruce Hood, Professor of Experimental Psychology at the University of Bristol, doesn't think superstition will ever disappear. "I don't think we're going to evolve a rational mind because there are benefits to being irrational," he said. "Superstitious behavior—the idea that certain rituals and practices protect you—is adaptive. If you remove the appearance that they are in control, both humans and animals become stressed. During the Gulf War, in areas attacked by Scud missiles, there was a rise in superstitious belief."[6]

Francis Bacon wrote, "There is a superstition in avoiding superstition."[7] Because even avoiding a superstition can be superstitious, it seems that we'll always be influenced by superstition.

A

Abracadabra: Nowadays, "abracadabra" is a word used by stage conjurers when performing their magic. However, it has a lengthy history as a protective amulet and lucky charm. Its origin is unknown, but Cabalists were using it in the second century CE to ward off evil spirits. Quintus Serenus Sammonicus, physician to Emperor Severus on his expedition to Britain in 208 CE wrote a poem (*Precepta de Medicina*) about this charm, which included instructions on how to use it.

In the Middle Ages, many people believed wearing parchment amulets with the word "abracadabra" written in the form of an upside-down pyramid would cure fevers, toothache, warts, and a variety of other ailments. It would also protect the wearer from bad luck. The person wrote the word eleven times, dropping one letter each time.

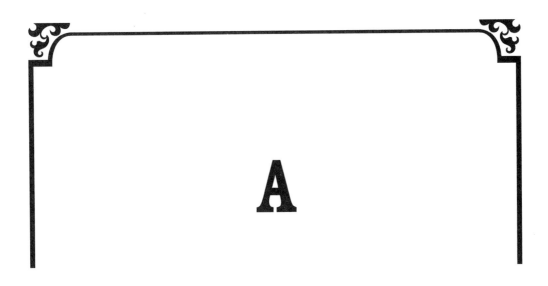

```
A B R A C A D A B R A
A B R A C A D A B R
A B R A C A D A B
A B R A C A D A
A B R A C A D
A B R A C A
A B R A C
A B R A
A B R
A B
A
```

Sometimes, letters would be sequentially removed from each end of each line:

ABRACADABRA
BRACADABR
RACADAB
ACADA
CAD
A

The idea was that as the word vanished, so would the fever. An amulet of this sort was attached to linen thread and worn around the neck. It was usually worn for nine days and then discarded. The best way to do this was to toss it backwards over your left shoulder before sunrise into a stream that flows from west to east. The reason for this is that the left side was believed to be related to the devil. Tossing the amulet into a river that flowed in the direction of the rising sun symbolically banished the evil, and replaced it with the good created by the rising sun that banishes darkness. Daniel Defoe wrote about these charms in his *Journal of the Plague Year* (1722), saying that they were worn to protect people from the plague.

Even saying the word abracadabra out loud was believed to summon powerful supernatural forces. This is probably why magical entertainers still use it as a magic spell today.

The origin of the word is not known. It may come from the Aramaic words *Ab* (Father), *Bar* (Son), and *Ru'ach Acadach* (Holy Spirit). It may come from the Hebrew phrase *abreg ad hâbra* (strike dead with your thunderbolt), or *Ha-b'rakah* (the sacred name). It may even derive from Abraxas, the god of the year whose image appeared on amulets and talismans worn by a Gnostic sect that followed Basilides of Alexandria.

See *amulet, charms, disappearing pattern, left side, warts, words.*

Acorn: As the acorn is the fruit of the sacred oak, it is considered to possess protective powers. Acorn amulets have always been popular, as they are believed to protect the person from illness and disease. Acorns were one of the earliest foods, and the people who ate them believed they provided fecundity and longevity.

An ancient tradition in Britain says that a woman can keep herself forever young by carrying an acorn on her person. This is because oak trees are long living.

Another superstition is the belief that a house will never be struck by lightning as long as at least one acorn is resting on a windowsill. This belief is derived from the Norse story about Thor sheltering from a thunderstorm under an oak tree.

An acorn is a charm that you can carry with you to attract good luck and a long life.

See *amulet, charms, oak, umbrella.*

Actors and Actresses: Actors and actresses are traditionally superstitious people and a huge collection of superstitions has devel-  oped around the theater. Many actors carry lucky charms and have a definite system of preparation before each performance. Whistling backstage is considered bad luck, and anyone who does this has to leave the room, turn around three times and spit before being allowed back in. This probably dates from the days when scene changes were signalled by a whistle. Clapping backstage is also taboo, because it is believed to cause bad luck. Artificial flowers should be used on stage, as it is considered bad luck to use live flowers. Peacock feathers are also believed to create bad luck and should not be worn on stage. Saying the last line of the play during a rehearsal is considered bad luck.

It is tempting fate to wish an actor good luck before going on stage. In fact, the only thing that can cause bad luck is to say "good luck." Consequently, wishing someone bad luck, such as "break a leg," is actually wishing the person good luck.

No one knows where the expression "break a leg" came from, but it may have come from the fact that the word "leg" can mean the stage curtain. As a play will receive many curtain calls if it is success-ful, this might cause the "leg" mechanism to break.

Two other charming, but false, possibilities are often suggested. The first is that after shooting President Lincoln, John Wilkes Booth jumped onto the stage, breaking his leg as a result. In fact, Booth broke his leg later when his horse fell while he was trying to escape. The second relates to the fact that Sarah Bernhardt, the famous French actress, continued her career after her leg was amputated in 1915.

Many actors refuse to wear the color green. This dates back to the days of lime-light, a brilliant light created by heating calcium oxide, or lime. This cast a greenish glow over the stage. Actors dressed in green became almost invisible under this light.

A good dress rehearsal is considered a bad sign, as it gives a false feeling of confidence. However, it's a good sign if an elderly person purchases the first tickets for the performance.

Many actors have specific rituals they perform before a performance. Jack Lemmon used to say "it's magic time" to himself before walking on stage or doing a take on a film.[8]

Some plays are considered unlucky. These include *Robin Hood*, *Ali Baba and the Forty Thieves*, *Babes in the Wood*, and *Macbeth*. Rather than say its name, Shakespeare's tragedy is often referred to as "that Scottish play." On the other hand, *Cinderella* is considered a lucky play.

There are superstitions relating to the box office, also. It is considered bad luck to allow someone with a free ticket to enter the theater until at least one paying customer has entered. It's also bad luck to open a play on a Friday or on the thirteenth of any month. However, it's good luck to start a performance thirteen minutes late.

See *carnelian, film stars, flowers, Friday, green, horse racing, Macbeth, peacock, theater, thirteen, whistle.*

Adam's Apple: The Bible does not name the forbidden fruit that Eve offered Adam in the Garden of Eden. Although most people assume it was an apple, no one even knows if apple trees grew in the Holy Land at that time.

Despite this, many people believe Adam managed to get a piece of apple stuck in his throat. This is the name of the bulge men have in the front of their necks, called the "Adam's apple." The Adam's apple is the thyroid cartilage of the larynx. Women have an Adam's apple, too, but as it is smaller and less obvious, it is not normally noticed.

See *apple.*

Adder: The adder is the only venomous snake found in the British Isles, and a variety of superstitions  are attached to it. It is considered bad luck even to see one, though this bad luck is averted if you kill it. Reciting the first two verses of Psalm 68 is believed to make the snake harmless. Alternatively, you can draw a circle around it and then make the sign of the cross inside the circle.

A live adder on a doorstep is a sure sign of an imminent death in the household. Leaping over water before the snake disappears was believed to be a cure for adder bites. Gypsy tradition says that killing the snake and rubbing its body over the wound is a sure cure for adder bites. In *The Return of the Native*, Thomas Hardy perpetuated the superstition about curing a bite by rubbing a paste of fried adder fat on the wound.

At one time it was believed that adders were deaf because they lack ears. In fact, they detect sound vibrations on their tongues. People also believed that adders swallowed their young when in danger.

Airplane: Most superstitions are extremely old, but new ones are invented all the time. Airplane superstitions reflect people's subconscious fears of flying. It is bad luck to use any word that might remind people of an air accident. Words such as "crash," "evacuation," or "forced landing" are examples.

It is also considered bad luck to take flowers on board a plane. Flowers are used for celebrations of all sorts, but are also used at funerals, which is why they are not welcome on board.

See *flowers, funerals, words.*

Agate: The ancient Egyptians were mining agate as far back as 3500 BCE. It was used to fashion and decorate rings, seals, beads, and other ornaments. It was thought to make people invisible, and could also avert the evil eye. Pliny the Elder (23–79 CE) recorded a great deal of information about the agate in his *Natural History*. He wrote that holding an agate in the mouth quenched even the fiercest thirst, and that looking at it rested the eyes. Wrestlers who wore agate were believed to be unbeatable.

In the Hebrew tradition, agate provided courage, as it was the color of a lion's mane. When strength and courage were required, a piece of agate or a hair from a lion's mane provided the necessary protection. It's possible that the association of agate with the sign of Leo is derived from this.

Sir John de Mandeville reported in his book of travels, *The Voyage and Travels of Sir John de Mandeville, Knight* (c. 1366), that agate destroyed snakebite venom, and also increased the conversational abilities of anyone who wore it.

Agate is believed to protect the earth, making it a good stone for farmers and gardeners to wear. It was believed that the crops of people who wore agate were more abundant than those of people who did not wear it.

Agate is also believed to cure insomnia and help create pleasant dreams for people born in June. However, it is considered bad luck for people born in other months to wear agate while they sleep.[9]

Agate also provides good luck in love, and a rewarding and happy life. It is sometimes known as the Fire Stone, as it is reputed to invigorate and energize people who are tired or suffering from stress.

See *evil eye, gemstones, June, wedding anniversaries.*

Age: Some people consider it dangerous to share any personal information with anyone outside the immediate family. Consequently, they believe it is unlucky to tell anyone their age, as this information could potentially be used against them.

Air: Air is one of the four elements considered to be the primary forms of matter by the ancient Greeks. Gemini, Libra, and Aquarius are the three air elements in astrology. In Wicca, air is one of the four elemental spirits who energize magic spells and help make them real.

Air symbolizes communication and the mind.

See *astrology, Aquarius, earth, elemental, elements, fairy, fire, Gemini, Libra, spell, wand, water, Wicca.*

Albatross: The albatross has always accompanied sailors on their expeditions, continuing to follow the ships long after all other birds had given up. Sailors kept an eye out for the albatross, considering it a sign of good luck. As the sailors watched the albatross' effortless flight, a legend began that these birds contained the souls of drowned

seamen. This seemed a logical explanation for the way they clung so closely to the ship. Naturally, once this superstition began, it became extremely unlucky to kill an albatross. Samuel Taylor Coleridge (1772–1834) wrote an epic poem, *The Rime of the Ancient Mariner,* which describes what happened to someone who killed an albatross:

> And I had done a hellish thing,
>   And it would work 'em woe.
> For all averred, I had killed the bird
>   That made the breeze to blow.

The dead albatross was hung around his neck, which gave us the expression about "having an albatross around my neck."

See *ornithomancy, sailors.*

Alexandrite: Alexandrite is an unusual gemstone because it is green in daylight, but changes color to a light red in artificial light. Legend says alexandrite was discovered on April 29, 1839, which happened to be the twenty-first birthday of the heir to the throne of Russia, Alexander II. This gemstone was named after him.

Alexandrite is worn as an amulet to attract love and good luck. For best results it should be worn close to the heart.

See *gemstone*.

Almond: Because the al-  mond is enclosed inside a pod, it is considered a symbol of the soul inside its mortal body. In the Western esoteric tradition, the almond signifies something that is hidden, secret, or mysterious. Consequently, eating almonds signifies a person's initiation into the hidden mysteries.

The almond tree flowers in early spring and symbolizes renewal and rebirth. In Greek legend, Phyllis was turned into an almond tree after committing suicide when her fiancé, Demophon, failed to arrive for their wedding. (In fact, he was simply delayed.)

Good luck will come to anyone who finds an almond cooked in a rice pudding. If a guest finds the almond, good luck will smile on everyone sitting at the table.

Aluminum: It used to be thought that any food that came into contact with aluminum would turn to poison. Although this was proven to be false by the United States Public Health Service and the American

Medical Association,[10] many people still refuse to use aluminum saucepans.

See *wedding anniversaries*.

Amber: Amber is the translucent fossil resin of extinct pine trees. It can be found in a variety of colors, ranging from clear to white, yellow, brown, and red. It sometimes contains trapped insects. Legend says that amber is actually the tears of birds who were sisters of the Greek hero Meleager. In Roman times, it was used to ensure that young children maintained good health. It has always been considered lucky, and is used as an amulet to provide protection against nightmares, witchcraft, and the evil eye.

If amber is rubbed vigorously, it develops a magnetic quality that enables it to lift light objects. The Greeks called white amber *electrum* because of this.

Ambulance: Ambulances are a relatively modern invention, but superstitions about them go back at least as far as 1908.[11] The sight of an ambulance made people fear that they might shortly be in one themselves. You could help the person inside

the ambulance by holding your breath and pinching your nose until you saw a black or brown dog. (Over time, the dog gradually was replaced by any four-legged animal.)

You could also avoid the necessity of having a ride in an ambulance by saying a rhyme:

Touch your toes, touch your nose,
Never go in one of those,
Hold your collar, do not swallow
Until you see a dog.

Amen: "Amen" symbolizes confirmation, agreement, and affirmation, and is said at the end of a prayer. It means "so be it." People believed that if the entire congregation said it forcefully, the gates of Paradise would remain open.

William Shakespeare was obviously well aware of this superstition. He had Macbeth say,

But wherefore could I
not pronounce "Amen"?
I had most need of blessing,
and "Amen"
Stuck in my throat.
(*Macbeth*, Act 2, scene 2)

See *Macbeth*.

Amethyst: The ancient Egyptians believed that amethyst prevented people from becoming drunk. The Egyptians associated amethyst with Capricorn, the sign of the Goat. As goats caused enormous damage in vineyards, amethyst was believed to cause damage to the wine, preventing the drinker from becoming intoxicated. The Greeks adopted this superstition also, and named this stone *amethystos*, which means "not drunken." Sometimes, when people had drunk too much wine, water was served to them in amethyst goblets. The amethyst made the water look like wine, and they could continue drinking without becoming more intoxicated.

The Egyptians also associated amethyst with intellect, and Cleopatra wore a signet ring of amethyst for both clarity of thought and sobriety. The ancient Egyptians also carved amethyst into the shape of hearts to protect the dead from evil forces in the afterlife.

The Romans believed that wearing this stone would prevent their partners from straying. Roman soldiers wore it as a protective amulet when they went into battle.

The Hebrews believed the amethyst was a virtuous stone that could induce beneficial dreams. Amethyst was the ninth stone on Aaron's breastplate. Priests in the Middle Ages wore amethyst to symbolize their virtue. It also emphasized their sober habits.

Camillus Leonardus, the sixteenth-century Italian physician to Cesare Borgia, wrote that amethyst increased shrewdness and intelligence, and also removed negative thoughts.[12]

St. Valentine is reputed to have worn an amethyst, which is why it is sometimes called the "stone of love." This also makes it a popular gift for lovers to give to each other. Other names for the amethyst include the Bishop's Stone, the Stone of Healing and the Stone of Peace.

Engraved amethyst amulets are used as protection from nightmares, infidelity, plagues, headaches, toothache, gout, and a variety of other ailments. Amethyst is also an effective amulet that protects the wearer from evil. Amethyst is often used to cleanse other crystals before they are used for healing or divination work.

See *amulet, Aquarius, Capricorn, divination, gemstones, headache, pin, St. Valentine's Day, wedding anniversaries.*

Amulet: Amulets, like charms, are objects that are carried or worn to provide good luck. The main purpose of an amulet is to provide protection from illness, misfortune, danger, and the evil eye. Originally, amulets were natural objects, such as four-leaf clovers or "lucky" rabbits' feet. However, it didn't take long before man-made objects were also used. Jewelry probably originated in the form of amulets, which are often still worn to provide symbolic protection.

See *abracadabra, acorn, alexandrite, amber, amethyst, bay, Bible, cake, carnelian, charms, claw, clover, coral, evil eye, frog, gemstones, gris-gris, heart, jade, jet, knot, ladybug, lapis-lazuli, lodestone, luck, malachite, moonstone, owl, petrified wood, rabbit's foot, ring, rowan, sailors, St. Christopher, scarab, scissors, snake, spider, teeth, tiger's eye, turquoise.*

Ankh: The ankh is an ancient Egyptian symbol that looks like a cross with a loop at the top. It was an extremely popular amulet in Egyptian times. They wore it to protect themselves from sickness, sterility, and evil spirits. It is frequently worn nowadays as an attractive alternative to the standard Christian cross. While Christians wear the ankh to proclaim their faith, many other people wear it as a general good luck charm.

In Wicca, the ankh is known as the *crux ansata*, and is used in spells relating to health and fertility.

See *amulet, spell, Wicca.*

Announcement: It is considered bad luck to announce a forthcoming project until it is completed. Authors, for instance, usually refuse to tell anyone the plot of the book they are currently working on. If they do, they are unlikely ever to finish the project.

Ants: Ants appear to be highly industrious and motivated. In Cornwall, England, ants are believed to be fairies enjoying their last incarnation. Another tradition says they are the souls of ancient Druids 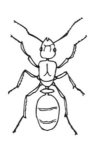 who refused to accept the Gospel. While living in Cornwall, I was told you could eliminate ants from your home by talking to them and asking them to leave. More than twenty years later I remembered this when we moved to a new home and found it infested with ants. I told the ants I didn't want to poison them, but would have to if they didn't leave. To my family's astonishment, the ants left within twenty-four hours.

Another British belief is that it is bad luck to destroy an ants' nest because they are the souls of children who died unbaptized. It is an indication of prosperity if ants build a nest close to your front door. It is considered a sign of bad weather when ants are noticeably busier than usual.

Because ants are so industrious, it is considered bad luck to dream of them.

This is a sign that you are overly concerned with prosperity and material possessions.

See *fairy, weather.*

Aphrodisiac: The Greeks and Romans constantly sought the perfect love potion, and today interest in the subject is just as strong. There are two types of love potions. The first is to attract love, and the second is to stimulate arousal. Many love potions manage to combine both elements in one. If a particular person is desired, a sample of his or her hair, nail clippings, or body fluids is required to create a special potion.

The range of aphrodisiacs is almost unlimited. Foods, such as apples, apricots, artichokes, asparagus, beans, cabbage, carrots, celery, leeks, lettuce, oysters, parsnips, potatoes, strawberries, tomatoes, walnuts, and watercress have all been considered aphrodisiacs. Spicy foods are still considered to have an aphrodisiacal effect. Fish is also considered an effective aphrodisiac because of the huge volume of eggs they produce.

Two hundred years ago, tomatoes were not normally eaten, but grown as

"love apples." The Spaniards, who brought the tomato to Europe from South America, considered it an aphrodisiac. Consequently, tomatoes symbolize love and passion, which explains the old saying, "She's a hot tomato!"

Mandrake, the plant that has a human form, has been credited with a variety of special properties including that of aphrodisiac. Bull testicles, rhinoceros horn, and deer antlers have also been used.

The best-known aphrodisiac is Spanish fly, which is made from the wings of the blister beetle. Spanish fly creates a condition known as priapism in men. This is a long-lasting erection, which sounds good in theory. Unfortunately, Spanish fly removes all sensitivity from the organ, rendering it ineffective. In women, the results are more severe. These include depression, vomiting, inflammation of the kidneys, and even death.[13]

Cures for impotence range from eating the fat from a rabbit's kidneys to creating a brew with mandrake. People also believed that if a woman grew too much lettuce or parsley, she would become infertile.

Celery is still sometimes used as a cure for impotence. Several sticks of celery need to be boiled in a saucepan of water until the celery turns into a pulp. The person with the problem needs to eat this while it is still hot, and can then look forward to a night of successful lovemaking.

An experiment conducted by the BBC in Britain found garlic to be more effective than any of the foods normally considered aphrodisiacal. In the experiment, seven impotent men were given two cloves of garlic twice a day for three months. Six experienced "uplifting" results. Two described the results as "outstanding." The most likely reason for this is that garlic improves the overall blood flow, which has a beneficial effect on the person's circulation.[14]

See *apples, broom, carrots, eagle, elements, fish, garlic, honeymoon, mandrake, mushroom, oysters, parsley, potatoes, sex, tomatoes, unicorn, vervain.*

Apple: The Bible does not actually identify the fruit eaten by Adam and Eve. Eve took "the fruit of the tree which is in the midst of the garden" (Genesis 3:3). This fruit is more likely to have been a fig than an apple, as Adam and Eve both covered themselves with fig leaves after tasting the fruit (Genesis 3:7).

According to Greek legend, Dionysus, god of the fertility of nature, created the apple as a gift for Aphrodite, the goddess of beauty. (This is the opposite of the Bible story, as in this case the man gave the

apple to the woman.) When Zeus and Hera got married, Gaia, Mother Earth, gave the bride golden apples to symbolize fertility. These apples of fertility later became Hercules' eleventh labor, when he had to steal them and bring them back home. These apples provided immortality to anyone who tasted them.

These stories, and others, gave the apple its erotic connotations. Consequently, it's not surprising that Christians considered the apple tree a tree of sin. The phrase "apple of one's eye," which indicates a favorite, well-loved person, may come from this.

The nineteenth-century proverb, "An apple a day keeps the doctor away," may have had its beginnings in Norse legend, because the gods retained their vitality and health by eating apples from the gardens of Asgard.

The ancient custom of wassailing is still practiced in parts of the United Kingdom. The farmer and his family eat hot cakes and drink cider in their apple orchards in the evening, usually on Twelfth Night. This is supposed to be a noisy affair. Pots and kettles are banged together, and the family sing wassailing songs to frighten away any evil spirits. This ensures a bountiful crop.

It is considered bad luck to leave a single apple on a tree after the rest have been picked.

Apple seeds can also be used to determine a future partner's identity. The person asking this has to name a few seeds after possible partners and place them on his or her cheek. The last seed to fall off will bear the name of the future husband or wife.

The apple stalk can also be used, to reveal the first letter of the future partner's first name. The stalk is twisted once for each letter of the alphabet until it snaps off. It will break at the first letter of the person's name.

Yet another method, used in New England, is to count the number of apple seeds. The number of seeds determines the person's future:

One, I love
Two, I love
Three, I love, I say.
Four, I love with all my
heart
And five, I cast away.
Six, he loves
Seven, she loves
Eight, they both love;
Nine, he comes
Ten, he tarries
Eleven, he courts

Twelve, he marries;
Thirteen, wishes
Fourteen, kisses
All the rest little witches.[15]

See *Adam's apple, death, Halloween, St. Swithin's Day, tomato, tree, Twelfth Night, wassailing, wedding.*

April: The weather in April is changeable. The old saying "April weather: rain and sunshine, both together" says it all. William Shakespeare wrote about "the uncertain glory of an April day" (*The Two Gentlemen of Verona*, Act 1, scene 3). He also wrote in *As You Like It* (Act 4, scene 1), "Men are April when they woo, December when they wed: maids are May when they are maids, but the sky changes when they are wives."

Every child knows that "April showers bring May flowers." Farmers want it to rain in April, as this old rhyme attests:

A dry April
Not the farmer's will.
April wet
Is what he would get.

Another April superstition says, "If it rains on Easter Sunday, it will rain on the next seven Sundays."

See *December, Easter, May, rain, weather.*

April Fool's Day: April Fool's Day is celebrated on April 1 each year, and provides an opportunity for people to play practical jokes on each other. The custom began in France, in the late sixteenth century when the Gregorian calendar was adopted. This changed the start of  the New Year from March 25 to January 1. As March 25 coincided with Holy Week, the New Year had traditionally been celebrated on April 1. When the date changed, many peasants paid surprise visits to their neighbors on April 1 to trick them into thinking it was still the start of the New Year. Gradually, the custom spread around the world, and people look forward to this day as an opportunity to play tricks on their friends and colleagues.

It is considered bad luck to attempt to trick someone after noon on April 1. Children born on April 1 are believed to be lucky, except when they gamble. If a man gets married on April 1, his wife will dominate him.

It is also considered bad luck to become annoyed when someone plays a practical joke on you.

If a young lady plays a practical joke on an eligible man on April Fool's Day, it is a sign that they will marry.

In his book *Popular Superstitions* (1925), Charles Platt wrote that April Fool's Day was "rapidly dying out."[16] However, people love having fun, and more than eighty years later, April Fool's Day seems as popular as ever.

See *New Year.*

Apron: It is a sign of good luck to accidentally put an apron on back to front. It is bad luck if an apron falls off. In the case of  a young married woman, an apron falling off means that she will have a baby within a year. If an apron falls off a young single woman it is a sign that she is thinking of her sweetheart. Fishermen believe that seeing a woman wearing a white apron while on the way to their boat is a sign of bad luck. The bad luck is averted if they delay the trip until the next tide.

See *fishermen.*

Aquamarine: Aquamarine is a sea-blue stone that is reputed to give mental clarity, peace of mind, and a stress-free life to people who wear it. Aquamarine has always been considered a good stone to protect travelers of all sorts, but especially people who travel by sea. The ancient Romans believed aquamarine would protect them from any dangers while traveling across the sea. They also thought it provided energy and cured laziness.

Aquamarine is a variety of beryl, and was first called aquamarine in *Gemmarum et Lapidum Historia* by Anselmus de Boodt in 1609. All forms of beryl are believed to help cure problems with the eyes. As it is believed to absorb feelings of love, it makes a popular gift for lovers to give to each other.

Beryl was also used as an oracle crystal in the Middle Ages. The beryl was attached to a piece of thread, creating a pendulum. This was suspended over a bowl of water, which had the letters of the alphabet engraved around the side. The pendulum would move to indicate different letters, and gradually a message would appear. An alternative method was to toss the crystal into a bowl of water and interpret the movements it created on the water's surface.

Dreaming of aquamarine is a sign that the dreamer will climb to a position of honor and importance.

See *gemstones, pendulum.*

Aquarius: Aquarius is the eleventh sign of the zodiac. Its symbol is the water carrier. Its element is air, and its gemstone is amethyst. The keyword for Aquarius is: I know.

Aquarians are believed to be sympathetic, peace-loving, and strong-willed. They are independent, tolerant, broad-minded, intellectual humanitarians. Aquarians are progressive thinkers, and are constantly looking ahead. They sometimes give the impression of being detached or aloof, as they can remove their emotions from everyday events.

See *air, amethyst, astrology, element, gemstone, zodiac.*

Aries: Aries is the first sign of the zodiac. Its symbol is the ram. Its element is fire and its gemstone is diamond. Its keyword is: I am.

Arians like responsibility and enjoy managing and organizing others. They are magnetic and outgoing, inspiring others to action with their drive and enthusiasm. Arians can be tactless and impatient at times. They enjoy taking risks, and often find this stimulation in adventurous, outdoor activities.

See *astrology, diamond, element, fire, gemstone, zodiac.*

Ascension Day: It is considered bad luck to work on Ascension Day. If you do, you are likely to have an accident. In Lincolnshire, it was believed that hanging out sheets to dry or air on this day indicated someone in the family would die before the year was over.

Ash: The ash has always been considered a magical tree, which is why it plays such an important role in the mythologies of the Greek, Roman, and Nordic people. In Norse mythology, Yggdrasil, the World Tree, which joins heaven and hell, is an evergreen ash. The roots are in hell, the trunk on the earth, and the branches in heaven. Its leaves are the clouds in the sky, and its fruit are the stars. Odin hanged himself from an ash tree to gain enlightenment and knowledge of the runes.

Ancient shepherds used crooks made of ash, and even today ash is the most favored material for walking sticks. Centuries ago, midwives in Scotland fed newborn babies a drop of ash sap to protect them against witchcraft.

The ash is one of the sacred trees of Wicca, and is referred to in the blessing "by oak, and ash, and thorn."

It is an indication of a good summer if

the oak tree produces leaves before the ash. In 1648 the winged seeds of the ash failed to appear at all, and a year later Charles I was executed. Consequently, it is a sign of the death of a prominent person if the winged seeds ever fail to appear.

Perfectly symmetrical ash leaves were worn as good luck charms. If a young woman slept with a sprig of ash under her pillow, she would have dreams of her future husband. Alternatively, she could place a sprig of ash in her left shoe, glove, or bosom. It was believed she would marry the first unattached man she met.

See *charms, oak, tree, wand, Wicca.*

Ashes: Ashes symbolize transformation, regeneration, and fertility. Ashes sprinkled over a field are believed to ensure a successful crop. Ashes also protected people from witchcraft. Ashes from May Day fires were often placed in shoes to protect the wearer from misfortune.

The ashes of the dead were believed to possess magical qualities, as they symbolize the person's rite of passage from one life to the next. Consequently, they have been used for protective and good luck purposes for thousands of years. In ancient Egypt, the ashes of a red-haired person were spread over fields to ensure a good crop. In Africa, the dead person's ashes were sometimes eaten with food

to ensure that the survivors received the deceased's good qualities.

Dreaming of ashes means that it is time to reconsider certain aspects of your life. You might need to let something go, or become aware of the transitory nature of life.

See *May Day.*

Astrology: Astrology is the study of the placement of the various planets at the time of a particular event, usually the time of someone's  birth. Astrology dates back some ten thousand years to the ancient civilizations of Sumer, Babylon, Egypt, and Assyria. Ptolemy (fl. 127–145 CE), the Greek astronomer who worked in the great library in Alexandria, wrote the first book on astrology. As Christianity became more and more influential, astrology became less popular, but it never vanished completely. In the past it was difficult to erect a horoscope chart, but today, thanks to computers, anyone with astrological software can erect a chart in a matter of seconds. This, combined with the popularity of Sun sign forecasts in newspapers and magazines, means that today more people than ever before are exploring and investigating astrology.

To erect a horoscope, or astrology chart, the correct time, date, and place of birth need to be known. The horoscope is a map that shows the position of the sun, moon, and planets at the time of birth. Once the chart has been erected, the astrologer can determine the person's character, including strengths, weaknesses, and aptitudes, as well as the trends of a person's life. The challenges and lessons that need to be learned in this incarnation are also shown in the chart. The chart reveals the astrological influences on the person's life, but he or she still retains freedom of choice. The chart can also be progressed to predict future trends.

People involved in magic use the positions of the various planets, particularly the sun and moon (which are considered planets in astrology), to determine the best times to prepare spells or perform rituals.

Sun sign astrology predictions as seen in magazines and newspapers are generalized, as they are based on the position of the sun. Although they are hugely popular, they should be regarded more as entertainment than serious astrology. The twelve sun signs are Aries, Taurus, Gemini, Cancer, Leo, Virgo, Libra, Scorpio, Sagittarius, Capricorn, Aquarius, and Pisces.

See *air, Aquarius, Aries, Cancer, Capricorn, divination, earth, fire, Gemini, Leo, Libra, magic, moon, Pisces, Sagittarius, Scorpio, sun, Taurus, twins, Virgo, water, zodiac.*

Athletes: Athletes are renowned for their superstitions, and many have particular habits, items of clothing they wear, or a mascot they carry to ensure luck in the game. They may refuse to wash their socks after a game, or walk onto the field at a specific number of minutes before the game starts. These rituals give them confidence, as they believe their superstitions will help their performance.

Baseball players consider it good luck to touch second base. A left-handed pitcher is often considered a good luck charm for the team. Ball players don't like to touch the foul line, or touch a base before running off the field.

Some athletic superstitions are complicated. Frank Viola, a three-time MLB all-star, would clean the mound before every inning. In the process of this, he would kick up dirt exactly four times. However, if something went wrong during the game, he would switch to either three or five kicks.

Former Red Sox and Yankees player Wade Boggs was highly superstitious. He was known as the "Chicken Man" because he ate poultry

before every game. Exactly sixteen minutes before the game, he'd start wind sprints. Before batting, he would write the Hebrew word *Chai*, which means life, in the dirt of the batter's box. If he was playing defense, between pitches he'd swipe the dirt with his left foot, adjust his cap, and tap his glove twice or thrice.

See *baseball, charms, horse racing, jasper.*

August: August was named after Emperor Augustus, the first Roman emperor. He considered it his lucky month, as he received his first consulship in August. He also celebrated three triumphs, reduced

the influence of Egypt, and ended the civil wars in August.

Farmers watch the weather in August with great interest:

> If a cold August follows a hot July,
> It foretells a winter hard and dry.

If thunderstorms occur in early August, they will continue for the rest of the month.

See *July, weather.*

Axe: Axes are potentially dangerous, as they possess a sharp edge and are made of iron. Axes are considered outdoor implements and should be kept in a tool shed or barn. It is bad luck to carry an axe into a house.

It is bad luck to dream about an axe, as this is a sign of imminent danger.

See *iron.*

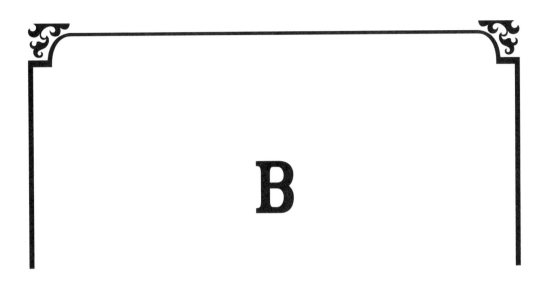

B

Baby: Few events are more exciting than the birth of a baby. Not surprisingly, thousands of superstitions have become attached to the event and the months preceding it. In most of Europe it was believed that a pregnant woman was in constant danger of attack from witches, demons, and evil spirits. Consequently, she had to wear a variety of amulets and charms to protect herself.

Immediately before the birth, the midwife had to untie all knots and unlock every door in the house. This was because witches might cause the baby to be stillborn by tying knots in the house. An additional precaution was to surround  the mother's bed with lucky charms. Even better was to arrange for church bells to be rung at the time of birth.

The day and time of birth were important to know for an astrology chart to be erected. Superstitions abound about the day of birth, and this well-known old rhyme is still frequently recited:

Monday's child is fair of face,
Tuesday's child is full of grace,
Wednesday's child is full of woe,
Thursday's child has far to go,
Friday's child is loving and giving,
Saturday's child works hard for a living,
But the child that is born
on the Sabbath day,
Is fair and wise, and good and gay!

The time of birth was also important. Children born on the "chimes hours" of three, six, nine, and twelve o'clock were believed to be naturally psychic and have the ability to see ghosts.

People were naturally interested in what sex the unborn baby would be. One ancient method for predicting the sex was to clean a mutton shoulder and hold it in a fire until it was scorched enough for the person's thumbs to pass through it. A loop of string was then passed through the two holes, and the shoulder was hung on a nail attached to the back door of the house immediately before the occupants went to bed. The first person to come into the house the following day would be of the same sex as the unborn child.

It was believed that a baby's hands should be inspected immediately after birth to see if they are open or clenched. If the hands were open, the child would have an optimistic and generous nature. If they were closed, the child would be secretive and mean-spirited. An associated superstition said that the child's right hand should be kept unwashed for at least one month after birth. Washing this hand would wash away the child's luck. The child's hands

should also be closely observed to determine his or her luck in life. If the baby

first used the right hand to pick something up, he or she would be lucky in life. Sadly, if the left hand was used, the child was thought to be doomed to disappointment and misfortune.

In Scotland it was believed that fairies held newborn babies under a spell until they sneezed. Consequently, snuff was sometimes used to encourage the child to sneeze. After this, the sign of the cross would be made over the baby's forehead to acknowledge the child's release.

It was said that the baby's fingernails should not be cut with scissors until he or she turned one year old. Cutting them before then would turn the child into a thief. The first nail clippings should be buried in the roots of an ash tree, because this would provide the child with a beautiful singing voice.

A child born with no hair was thought to be intelligent and quick to learn. A common superstition says that a child will die if his or her hair is cut before the age of one.

All visitors to the home of a newborn baby need to drink a toast to the child and have something to eat. This custom is sometimes kept right up to the baby's christening.

Traditionally, you were thought to gain good luck by kissing a newly born boy baby. Why similar luck did not accrue from kissing a girl baby is not known. Nowadays, kissing a baby of either sex provides good luck.

In some cultures, you are not allowed to comment on how beautiful the baby is. This is because the compliment might attract the evil eye. Likewise, you cannot call a baby an "angel," as this is seen as virtually asking for the baby to be transported to heaven.

Baby clothes are important, too. Baby boys should be dressed in blue. Blue is associated with the Virgin Mary, and is thought to provide protection for the child. Dressing girls in pink came much later. It is considered bad luck to put baby's clothes on over the child's head.

The baby should always be carried upstairs after birth. If the baby is born on the top floor, or in a single-storied house, standing on a chair or other furniture will symbolically carry the baby upwards. This custom reflects the belief that the child will find it extremely hard to progress in life if his or her first trip is downwards.

It is considered bad luck to bring a new pram into the house before a baby is born. The cradle of an unborn baby should not be rocked, as this apparently creates bad luck for the child in later life.

If you rock an empty cradle, you symbolically rock another baby into it. In the nineteenth century, "C. W. J.," a contributor to *The Book of Days*, described the look of alarm in a mother's face as she dashed across a room, her tenth baby in her arms, to stop one of her other children from rocking the cradle.[17]

Finally, if a baby smiles while sleeping, it is a sign that he or she is communicating with angels.

See *amulet, astrology, bells, Bible, cat, charms, child, christening, clothes, cradle, evil eye, fairy, fire, garlic, ghosts, Good Friday, hair, hand, knots, lizard, malachite, mirror, owl, parsley, pearl, pendulum, pixies, pregnancy, prenatal influences, sailors, toast, witches.*

Baby shoes: Many long distance truck drivers hang a pair of baby shoes inside the cabs of their trucks as an amulet to protect them from accidents. These shoes can be either real baby shoes or miniatures made of silver.

See *amulet, silver.*

Baldness: Sudden hair loss indicates a loss of health, possessions, or a child in the near future. If you cut your hair during the waning moon, you run the risk of permanent

hair loss. It is important to prevent birds from weaving strands of hair into their nests. If your hair is used in this way, you will initially suffer from headaches, and will then become bald.

One well-known remedy for baldness was to vigorously rub the bare patch with half a raw onion. Once the bald patch became red, the person smeared it with honey.

In New England, the prescribed remedy for baldness was to wash the scalp with sage tea.

See *hair, rosemary, rum, sage.*

Banana: A strange superstition says you'll get fat if you eat bananas. There is no scientific basis for this.

In the Ozarks, a method of ridding the chicken house of chicken lice was to hang a banana skin on a nail.

Banshee: The banshee is a wailing spirit that portends misfortune or death. According to Scottish and Irish folklore, the banshee usually appears in the form of a weeping ghost of a washerwoman who calls out your name. She then asks you to make three wishes. Unfortunately, these wishes are a mixed blessing, and people who get their wishes granted usually die soon afterwards.

See *ghost.*

Baseball: Professional sports people are a superstitious lot, and baseball players are more superstitious than most others. In fact, baseball has been called the most superstitious sport of all. Many ballplayers have a variety of rituals they need to do before playing. They might spit into their gloves to provide good luck. They sometimes place their gloves down so that the fingers point to their own dugout when it's their turn to bat. Many believe that only a certain number of hits can be made with a single bat. Consequently, they are reluctant to share a bat with their teammates. And it is important for everyone, ballplayers and spectators alike, to refuse to comment on the fact that a pitcher has not yet allowed an official hit.

Individual baseball players have their own idiosyncrasies, such as wearing a "lucky" cap or refusing to play on a certain day of the week. Almost all baseball players try to avoid stepping on the foul line, as they believe this creates bad luck.

Team mascots are common, and batboys sometimes also act as team mascots. One of the more unusual mascots was a man called Charles Victor Faust, who offered his services to the New York Giants in 1911. He told John McGraw, the team's manager, that he was destined to help the

Giants win the National League pennant. Mr. McGraw immediately put him to the test, and found that Charles Faust had no skill at the game. However, an idea formed in his mind. He told the players he was going to try Faust, and that they should ensure he got a home run. All the players cooperated. They deliberately fumbled the ball and allowed Faust his home run. The players dubbed him Charles "Victory" Faust, and made him part of the unofficial lineup. He warmed up for every game, but never pitched. He constantly reminded the players that he had been sent to help them win the pennant. Charles "Victory" Faust's enthusiasm and belief paid off. The Giants won the pennant that year and the following two years. Charles Faust died in 1914, and the Giants lost the pennant.[18]

Another interesting mascot was a black cat who happened to wander into the Denver Broncos practice area one Friday the 13th in 1987. Most people would consider this double combination a particularly bad omen, but the Broncos won their next game.

See *athletes, cat, Friday the 13th, mascot, pin.*

Basil: Basil is an Indian plant that is considered sacred to Vishnu and Krishna. Hindus believe that a sprig of basil placed on the dead body ensures that the person's soul will get to heaven. However, basil does not fare so well in other places. It is considered unlucky in Greece, although lucky in Italy. When it was first introduced to England, it was not eaten, but used to provide peace of mind and freedom from pain.

Bastard: Until recently, there was considerable stigma attached to being born out of wedlock. All the same, since at least Roman times, such people have been considered "lucky bastards." This possibly relates to the fact that under Roman law their fathers' authority did not restrict them.

Bat: It is easy to understand how superstitions developed around the bat. Its appearance, eerie cry, and nocturnal habits must have terrified primitive people. Some people associate bats with witches, who were

believed to rub a few drops of bat's blood on their bodies before flying on their broomsticks. The blood enabled the witches to fly the way bats do, without the risk of bumping into anything.

If a bat flies near you, it is a sign that someone is trying to use witchcraft on you. It has always been considered bad luck to kill one. A bat flying around a house three times is a sign that someone living inside will shortly die. Finding a bat inside a house has the same meaning. You are about to be deceived or taken advantage of if a bat flies close to you.

Not every superstition about bats is bad. It is considered a sign of good weather if bats fly early in the evening. Five bats are sometimes depicted on Chinese plates. They symbolize the five blessing of health, wealth, longevity, love of virtue, and a peaceful death. This came about because the Chinese character for "bat" sounds exactly the same as the one for "blessing."

See *jade, witches.*

Bay: The bay laurel was sacred to Apollo in ancient Greece, and was considered a symbol of victory and honor. Champions wore bay laurel wreaths to signify success. Bay was also considered impervious to lightning because Apollo defeated the Cyclops, who made thunderbolts. In Roman times, Pliny, Tiberius, and other emperors wore wreaths of bay leaves as protective amulets. In Greek mythology, the nymph Daphne was turned into a bay tree to protect her from being raped. Bay leaves are still called *daphne* in Greece today.

Bay trees are believed to protect the house from harm. Originally, this belief extended only to lightning, but gradually the bay became a more universal form of protection.

Bay leaves can be worn as an amulet, or placed under the pillow to induce prophetic dreams.

See *amulet, dreams, trees.*

Beans: Beans have been associated with death since the time of the ancient Egyptians. The Romans ate beans at funerals, and also made offerings of beans to the dead. Beans are also often associated with magic, as the fairy tale *Jack and the Beanstalk* shows.

The flowers produced by bean plants are believed to contain the souls of dead people. Consequently, care needs to be taken to avoid accidents while they are in

bloom. It is also un-
lucky to smell the blos-
som of broad beans.

It is a sign of an
imminent death in the
family if a white broad
bean is found. In some places, finding a
white bean plant also indicates a death.

The farmer's family usually ate only
one out of every four broad beans planted. An old rhyme says,

> One for the mouse,
> One for the crow,
> One for rot,
> And one to grow.

Despite all of this, beans themselves
are considered lucky, and a good crop of
beans brings prosperity and happiness.

See *elm, funeral, Good Friday, magic.*

Bear: Dancing bears were a popular entertainment in days gone by, and many
children were placed on the backs of
these bears to prevent them from catching whooping cough.

An old superstition says that bears mate
only once every seven years. Every time this
occurs, any preg-
nant cattle in the
neighbourhood
will produce still-
born calves.

Beard: Many people, including Jews, Turks,
and Persians, consider the beard a symbol of
manly dignity. Muslims swear by the beard
of the Prophet. Early Christians thought it
was ungodly, while Sikhs consider it an important symbol of their faith.

A common superstition says that men
with beards are not to be trusted. To touch
someone else's beard caused offense to the
bearded person and brought bad luck to
the person daring to make the affront.

See *bread, whistle.*

Bed: The bed is where some of the most
important human activities occur. Consequently, the number of superstitions associated with it is not surprising.

The most common of these is the notion that someone who is in a bad mood
got out of bed on the wrong side. This
originated with the belief that the left side
of the bed was always the wrong side. The
left side was the devil's side and was associated with evil and bad luck. If the placement of the bed meant you had to get out
on the left side, you could avert the bad
luck by putting your right sock and shoe
on before getting out of bed. If you forgot to do this, you
could still avert di-
saster by putting

your right sock and shoe on before your left ones.

Regardless of which side of bed you get out of, be sure to put your right foot on the ground before your left.

The placement of the bed is important, too. The rays of the moon should not fall across the bed. The bed should not be placed under overhead beams. The foot of the bed should not face the door directly, as this is known as the coffin position. (Coffins are carried out feet first.)

Sweeping under a sick person's bed is considered a sure way of hastening his or her death. It is dangerous to sit on the bed of a sick person, as you risk falling sick yourself.

To preserve your good luck, you should not make a bed that a guest has slept in for at least an hour after he or she has left.

Making a bed should be completed on one go. Sneezing while making a bed is unlucky, but can be remedied by making the sign of the cross. Three or more people making a bed together is considered highly dangerous, as it is believed that one of them will die in the next twelve months.

It is thought to be bad luck to turn the mattress of a bed on a Friday or Sunday.

It is a good idea to look under your bed before retiring, to make sure the devil is not hiding there. Single girls must not do this, though. If they do, they will never get married.

See *cross, death, devil, Friday, left side, moon, right side, umbrella, wedding cake.*

Bees: Children in France and Wales were taught not to swear or use bad language within hearing distance of a hive. If they  did, they were told, the bees would come out and sting them.

I used to keep bees, and at the funeral of a beekeeper friend witnessed a swarm of his bees come to say goodbye. His family had formally invited them to attend. Traditionally, if the swarm settled on a dead branch, it was a sign that their new master would not live for long. In the past, a black scarf or crepe was placed on beehives when their owner died. A wine-soaked funeral biscuit was sometimes placed at the entrance of the hive, also.

Many country people reported any death to the bees. Sometimes births and marriages were also told to the bees. In northern England, it was thought that bees were highly spiritual and hummed the Hundredth Psalm in their hives.

It is considered bad luck for a swarm of bees to land in your property and not be claimed by their owner. This is a sign that someone in the family will die within a year.

It is considered a good sign to dream of bees. It means that your hard work will be richly rewarded.

See *marigold, virginity, wassailing.*

Beetle: It is considered bad luck to see a black beetle inside a house. It is an indication of death if the black beetle crawls over someone's shoes or someone who is lying down. A beetle tapping inside a wall is another sign of an impending death in the family. As it is bad luck to kill one, you must pick up the beetle on a sheet of paper and carry it outdoors.

The clicking noise that some beetles make when seeking a mate was always a bad omen. This is why these insects came to be known as "deathwatch beetles."

See *death, ladybug, scarab.*

Beggar: It is bad luck to see a beggar shortly after leaving your home. To avert the bad luck, you need to return home and start the trip again.

Beginner's Luck: An old superstition says that a special sort of luck is reserved for beginners in any activity. Although this may be true, the law of averages ensures that beginner's luck is only temporary. Despite this, football teams in the United Kingdom always pass the ball from the oldest person on the team to the youngest as the final part of the warm-up before the game starts. This is to ensure that the beginner's luck will encompass the whole team.

Bell: Church bells protected people from evil spirits, and it was a good sign to live within earshot of the bells. If the church bells were rung during a storm, the weather would immediately improve. An old rhyme outlines some of the benefits church bells provide:

Men's death I tell, by doleful knell,
Lightning and thunder, I break asunder,
On Sabbath all, to church I call,
The sleepy head, I raise from bed,
The winds so fierce, I do disperse,
Men's cruel rage, I do assuage.

Church bells sometimes predicted death, as well. If the church clock chimed, either while the hymn before the sermon was being sung, or while the text of the sermon was being announced, one of the parishioners would die in the following week.

In many parts of the world, it is considered a sign of death to hear two bells ringing at the same time.

See *baby, death, lightning, New Year, Santa Claus, storm, thunder, weather.*

Bell, Book, and Candle: The bell, book, and candle are the three implements used by the Roman Catholic Church when excommunicating someone. The priest tells the unfortunate person that he is being excommunicated, and then closes his Bible, tosses the candle to the ground, and rings his bell. There is powerful symbolism in all of this. The book represents the "book of life," the extinguished candle symbolizes the soul that is lost for all eternity, and the bell is tolled as if the person was already dead.

In earlier times, excommunication was equivalent to death, and the psychological effect on the people who were treated this way must have been profound.

See *bell, candle, death.*

Belt: Wearing a belt is believed to protect the wearer from witches. Consequently, it is dangerous to throw away a belt, as a witch could use it to influence its former owner. It's a sign that you're in love if you accidentally twist a belt while putting it on.

See *witches.*

Bermuda Triangle: The Bermuda Triangle lies in the Atlantic Ocean between Bermuda, Puerto Rico, and Southern Florida. The area has become well known as a place where boats, planes, and people have mysteriously disappeared and are never found. Superstitions began about this area in 1945, shortly after six United States Navy planes disappeared in the Bermuda Triangle.

Some people believe that this area contains a vortex that "sucks" objects and people into another dimension. Another belief is that aliens might be based in this area and remove anyone or anything that ventures too close.

Bezoar Stone: The bezoar stone is a concretion that forms in the stomach or intestines of many animals, including goats, deer, horses, and cows. The stones were placed in drinks to determine if they had been poisoned. In addition, they were sometimes powdered and swallowed to protect people from poison.

Bible: The Bible used to be the one book that every home had. Births, marriages, and deaths were all recorded in the family Bible. However, the Bible has been used for many other purposes as well.

A Bible can be carried with you as a protective amulet. Many soldiers carry a Bible with them for this purpose.

An open Bible can be placed in a cot with a baby to protect it during the night. Adults can place a Bible under their pillow to provide protection while they sleep.

Placing a page from a Bible under the doormat is believed to cause thieves to stumble, alerting the household of the danger.

Divination with the Bible took a number of forms. A key, suspended from a chain or cord, acted as a pendulum when suspended over a Bible and asked questions. In Cornwall, it was a common practice to open a Bible at random on New Year's Eve and allow the forefinger of the right hand to indicate a line on the page.

This line would be studied to determine the prospects of the following year.

A Bible and key could also be used to determine the identity of a thief. A cord was placed through the key, which was placed on the page containing the Fiftieth Psalm. The Bible was then closed and tightly bound, to prevent the key from falling out, and suspended from a nail or hook. The Bible would then turn, to indicate the guilty person after his or her name was repeated three times.

The Bible can also be used to curse people. This is done by reciting any verse from the Bible three times in a row. The name of the person you are cursing has to be included each time. This is an extremely risky procedure that falls into the category of black magic.

See *amulet; baby; bell, book, and candle; bibliomancy; birthday; clover; key; magic.*

Bibliomancy: Bibliomancy is the art of predicting the future by randomly opening a book and reading the message that is revealed. Usually this is done using a Bible or other sacred book.

Bibliomancy was used extensively between the fourth and fourteenth centuries. Kings, church leaders, saints, and educated people all practised bibliomancy. It is less popular today, but is still practised by some religious sects and individuals who gain comfort and guidance from the practice.

See *Bible*.

Birch: The birch tree is sacred to the Norse god Thor. People used to wear a sprig of it to provide protection and keep themselves safe from harm. Sometimes livestock were adorned with birch too, to protect them from witches. Boughs of birch were also placed over doorways to prevent evil spirits from entering the home.

It is a good idea to plant a birch tree near your front door, as any witch wanting to enter your home has to count every leaf on the tree first. The tree must not touch or overhang the house, though, as this will bring misfortune to the occupants.

See *tree, witches*.

Birds: Early man believed birds possessed special magical qualities, as they had the power of flight. It was thought that birds were messengers from the gods, and consequently people watched their movements

with great interest to see if they predicted good or bad news. An eagle soaring high in the sky with wings outstretched, for instance,

was a sign of prosperity and good luck in the near future.

The ancient Romans were particularly fond of predicting the future by following the flight of birds. This was called auspicy. The augur, or diviner, stood in a sacred place facing east and divided the sky into four quarters. He then waited for a single bird to appear, and noted where it came from, what direction it took, and where it finally disappeared. All of this could be interpreted. Birds flying to the right indicated a positive result, while birds flying to the left exhorted caution and delays. Birds flying directly towards the augur indicated good times ahead. Birds flying away indicated a lack of opportunities in the near future.

The higher the birds flew, the better, as it indicated a positive outcome. A bird that sang as it flew indicated the time was right to proceed.

The Romans also practiced a form of divination using chickens. Circles were drawn on the ground and marked to indicate different outcomes. Corn was tossed into the circles and the chickens were observed to see which area they pecked at first. This form of divination is called alectromancy.

Even today, birds are used in a variety of folk divinations. Certain birds, such as crows and ravens, have always had a bad reputation. The owl is also looked at with suspicion, as it flies at night when decent animals are asleep. Magpies produce neither good nor bad luck, but are interpreted by the number of them that are seen.

Fortunately, some birds also brought good luck with them. The robin and the swallow are the main examples of these. The cuckoo also brings luck, especially in North America. The stork brings good luck, especially to young families. Because storks are so famously devoted to their own young, it is not surprising that they became associated with birth in humans.

It is good luck for any bird to deposit a dropping on you as it flies overhead.

See *crow, cuckoo, magpie, owl, raven, right side, robin, stork, swallow, wand.*

Birth: A child born during the summer was believed to be more intelligent than a child born in a different season. There is no scientific evidence for this old superstition.

It is bad luck to be born during an eclipse, as you will remain poor and have to struggle throughout life.

See *knot, stork.*

Birthday: Birthday greetings offered first thing in the morning provide the recipient with good luck. In the case of a child, these should be offered as soon as he or she is awake.

A Bible and the knowledge of a woman's birthday could be used to help a man choose a wife. After learning of the woman's birthday, he had to read the last chapter of the Book of Proverbs to gain insight into her character and nature. The verse that corresponded with her age was of most importance and had to be studied closely. This told him the woman's true nature, and enabled him to decide whether or not to propose.

See *Bible, days of the week.*

Birthmark: Birthmarks are usually blamed on evil influences the mother was exposed to during pregnancy. Divination by the shape and placement of birthmarks is known as maculomancy. Hippocrates (c.460–c.377 BCE), the Greek physician, believed birthmarks should be looked at closely when examining a patient. For divination purposes, birthmarks are read in the same way as moles.

An old superstition says birthmarks can be removed by touching them with the hand of a dead child. A more practical method is for the mother to lick the birthmark every morning for at least three weeks, starting as soon after giving birth as possible.

See *hand, moles, pregnancy.*

Birthstone: The tradition that each month of the year has a special stone dedicated 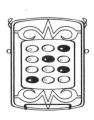 to it can be traced back to the first century Jewish historian, Josephus. Each stone was believed to contain a specific virtue that related to people born in the different months. Josephus connected these stones to the twelve stones in the high priest's breastplate (Exodus 28:17–30). According to Josephus, the stones in the breastplate were:

Sardonyx, Topazos, Smaragdos, Anthrax, Jaspis, Sappheiros, Liguros, Amethystos, Achates, Chrysolithos, Onyx, Beryllus.

Over the years, biblical scholars have been unable to agree on the actual stones that were in Aaron's breastplate. Different translations and interpretations of the ancient names of the stones have led to a number of changes. In the King James Version of the Bible (1611 CE), the list reads

Sardius, Topaz, Carbuncle, Emerald, Sapphire, Diamond, Ligure, Agate, Amethyst, Beryl, Onyx, Jasper.

In the 1963 New World Translation of the Bible, the list reads

Ruby, Topaz, Carbuncle, Emerald, Sapphire, Jasper or Diamond, Hyacinth or Leshem, Agate, Amethyst, Beryl, Onyx, Jade.

St. Jerome, one of the fathers of the Roman Catholic Church, also wrote on birthstones in the early fifth century. The tradition of wearing a birthstone came from the writings of Josephus and St. Jerome.

Despite this lengthy history, the Western tradition of wearing birthstones is comparatively recent. The Gemological Institute of America says the custom began in Germany in about 1562.[19] Other sources believe it began in eighteenth century Poland.[20]

In the sixteenth and seventeenth centuries, it seems people had a set of twelve stones, one for each month, and wore the correct stone for the month in order to receive the qualities and therapeutic benefits of that particular stone. Gradually, people started wearing the birthstone that related to their month of birth. The Foundation Stones listed in Revelation 21:19–20 replaced the earlier stones of the breastplate. This provided a new listing of stones, but one which has little resemblance to the stones of the month worn today:

March—Jasper
April—Sapphire
May—Chalcedony
June—Emerald
July—Sardonyx
August—Sardius
September—Chrysolyte
October—Beryl
November—Topaz
December—Chrysoprasus
January—Jacinth
February—Amethyst

The new list of birthstones started with March, following the Roman calendar (despite the Julian calendar in use during the sixteenth century). Over time, people in different parts of the world developed a variety of lists, often based on the gems that were available locally. To end the confusion, and no doubt also to capitalize on the interest in birth stones, the National Association of Jewelers created their own list in 1912:

January—Garnet
February—Amethyst
March—Bloodstone or Aquamarine
April—Diamond
May—Emerald
June—Pearl or Moonstone
July—Ruby
August—Sardonyx or Peridot
September—Sapphire
October—Opal or Tourmaline
November—Topaz
December—Turquoise or Lapis Lazuli

Not everyone agreed with this list, and various trade groups drew up their own lists. The National Association of Goldsmiths of Great Britain created a new list in 1937. The Jewelry Industry Council in the United States accepted this list in 1952. Consequently, the list that most people accept today is not much more than half a century old:

January—Garnet
February—Amethyst
March—Aquamarine or Bloodstone
April—Diamond or Rock Crystal
May—Emerald

June—Pearl, Moonstone
(also Alexandrite in U.S.A)
July—Ruby
August—Peridot or Sardonyx
September—Sapphire
(also Lapis Lazuli in U.K.)
October—Opal
(also Pink Tourmaline in U.S.A)
November—Topaz
(also Citrine in U.S.A)
December—Turquoise
(also Zircon in U.S.A)

Despite all the changes that have occurred since Josephus first wrote about them, wearing the birthstone of your month of birth is still believed to produce good luck for the wearer. One superstition says it's bad luck to wear a stone that is not connected with your month of birth. This is particularly the case with opal, which is believed to provide good luck for people born in October, but bad luck for everyone else.

See *gemstones, opal, pearl, ruby.*

Black: Despite the fact that black sheep are often considered lucky, black is usually considered a sinister color. Black is worn at funerals, and most people think this is to pay respect to the deceased. In fact, it is a continuation of a Roman custom that says that, in the presence of death, we humans are insignificant.

Actors and actresses do not like wearing black clothes on stage, as they feel it presages someone's death. They prefer to replace any black material with dark blue.

Witches are usually depicted in black clothes, and their familiars, often a cat or raven, are also black. Black cats are often seen at Halloween, as during the Middle Ages the devil was believed to transform himself into a black cat while socializing with witches.

If you find yourself in the presence of an evil spirit, the best thing you can do is offer the spirit a gift of something black. Obviously, you should then run away as fast as you can while the spirit is admiring your gift.

See *actors and actresses, blackberries, cat, crow, devil, familiar, green, Halloween, raven, thirteen, witches.*

Blackberries: It is considered bad luck to eat blackberries after September 30. This is because the devil gets inside them on that date. Apparently, the devil became tangled in a blackberry plant when he was cast out of heaven, and cursed the unfortunate plant. The poor blackberry

has often been associated with evil, as it is black in color.

See *black, devil.*

Blackbird: Blackbirds used to be considered messengers from the dead. Consequently, the sight of a blackbird near your home was a sign of an imminent death in the family. However, it is a sign of good luck when two blackbirds sit together. This is a rare occurrence, as blackbirds  usually drive off other blackbirds that dare invade their territory.

See *death, St. Valentine's Day.*

Blacksmith: Because blacksmiths work with fire and iron, they are often thought to possess supernatural and mystical powers. Sick children were often held over a blacksmith's anvil in the belief that this would cure them.

Blacksmiths are famously reluctant to work on Good Friday, as hammering nails on that day exposes them to the devil.

See *devil, fire, Good Friday, iron, nail.*

Blanket: It is bad luck to wash blankets in May, June, July, or August, as these months do not include an "r" in their names.

Bless You: When someone sneezes, we often say "bless you" to him or her. This custom dates back to the days when it was believed a sneeze had the power to blow the soul out of the body. In India, Africa, and North America, a sneeze was a sign of evil spirits. Obviously, a blessing had to be made to exorcise them.

Blister: A superstition that says breaking a blister can be fatal was given credence in 1924 when President Calvin Coolidge's son got a blister on his foot while playing tennis. The blister broke and he died.

Blood: Jewish people believe that "the blood is the life." They equate it with the soul. Consequently, they refuse to eat the blood of animals. Kosher dietary laws still preserve this belief today.

Gypsy couples sometimes mingle their blood on their wedding day. They sometimes also eat a cake that contains a few drops of their blood.

I had a couple of blood brothers when I was a child.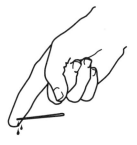

We pricked our fingers and exchanged the blood to symbolically become brothers. (This age-old custom is probably less popular today due to diseases such as AIDS.) Herodotus (c.485–425 BCE) reported a much earlier version of this ritual. The people becoming blood brothers dropped some of their blood into a goblet of wine. They then drank the blood-and-wine mixture.

Blood sacrifices are often associated with protecting new buildings. In Normandy, for instance, a cock had to be killed and its blood sprinkled over the threshold of a new house before it could be occupied. If this was not done, it was believed the occupant would die within twelve months.

Vampires were believed to suck blood from the living. Vampire bites were considered fatal unless the victim was able to eat earth taken from a vampire's grave and smear himself with his own blood.

Dragonsblood, a gum used in wood staining, can be burned at midnight to rekindle the passion of a lover who seems to be losing interest.

In Europe, it was believed that a murdered person would bleed if touched by

his murderer. Consequently, suspects were asked to place two fingers on the face of the dead person, then on the wound and the navel. If the dead person bled at this touch, the suspect was considered guilty of the crime. This probably derives from God's words to Cain after he killed Abel: "The voice of thy brother's blood crieth unto me from the ground" (Genesis 4:10).

See *coral, nose, salt, sapphire, sewing, vampires, witch.*

Bloodstone: Bloodstone is a dark-green chalcedony that contains inclusions of iron. These create brown and red spots inside the stone. Because these spots look like blood, bloodstone was often placed in ancient Egyptian tombs to protect the deceased. Bloodstone was known as the "Blood of Osiris." Roman and Greek soldiers wore bloodstone amulets into battle, believing they would protect them from a loss of blood if they were wounded. In Christianity, the "Blood of Osiris" became the "Blood of Christ." Bloodstone was said to originally have been a green stone at the foot of the cross of Jesus. Drops of blood fell onto the stone, creating the red spots it still bears.

Bloodstone was originally called a "touching stone," because people believed it would reveal tainted food or drink when placed in contact with it. Bloodstone was also reputed to boil water, prevent disagreements, promote courage, and provide mental clarity. It had medical uses as well, as it was believed to stop bleeding, internally and externally.

Bloodstone is still a popular stone for amulets today, and is worn to protect the person from stress and problems with circulation. It also instills confidence and a sense of self-worth.

See *cross, gemstones*.

Blossom: Trees and shrubs that bloom in season are welcome sights, but blossoms that occur at other times are considered a sign of bad luck. If a large number of fruit trees blossom at the wrong time, it is a sign of a long, hard winter ahead.

It is bad luck to take blossoms of blackthorn, broom, and hawthorn inside.

See *tree, wedding*.

Blue: The color blue has always been associated with purity and the soul. This is because the sky is pure and blue, and heaven lies beyond it.

All around the world, baby boys are dressed in blue. This originates in the belief that evil spirits congregate around newborn babies. Fortunately, these spirits detest the color blue, as it is deprives of them of their power. Consequently, dressing a baby boy in blue provides him with protection at a time when he is totally vulnerable. Blue was also considered an effective way of averting the evil eye. Back then, girl babies were not considered to be as important as boys, and weren't given any protection. Finally, when people realized how discriminatory this was, girls were given the color pink.

See *evil eye*.

Blushing: People blush when they are embarrassed or ashamed. However, an old superstition says that people blush only when telling a lie. This must have caused problems for people who blushed easily.

Boasting: An old superstition says you invite trouble when you boast about your good fortune. This applies in all areas of life. If you boast that your car never breaks down, you can virtually guarantee something will happen to it. The remedy for any form of boasting is to touch or knock on wood.

See *knock on wood*.

Bogeyman: The bogeyman was thought of as a form of goblin. Children were told to beware the bogeyman, as he would punish them if they did something wrong. In some areas, the bogeyman was believed to carry naughty children away.

See *goblin*.

Boils: A boil is a pus-filled, inflammatory sore caused by a microbic infection. There are many superstitious cures for this problem. A useful cure, if you lived in the country, was to make a poultice of fresh cow dung and apply it to the boil. This had to be replaced every time it cooled down, until the boil disappeared. A much easier method was to find a rooted arch of bramble and crawl through it three times in a westerly direction. You could also hang three nutmegs or a camphor bag around your neck to eliminate the boils.

Leaves of periwinkle could be placed over the boil to draw out the inflammation. Another method was to soak Madonna lily petals in brandy and place them, rough side down, on the boil.

You could also cure a friend's boils, as long as he or she was of the opposite sex from you. This remedy involved walking around a freshly dug grave six times, and then crawling across it three times on a night when the moon could not be seen.

See *moon*.

Bones: Because of their strength, bones are thought to possess magical properties. Eve

was created from one of Adam's ribs, and consequently bones were considered the seat of the soul. In the Middle Ages, bones of saints were considered precious relics by the Church, and were believed to be responsible for many miraculous healings.

Primitive cultures used bones for divination purposes. The children's game of knucklebones derives from this.

Boots: The expression "to die with your boots on" reflects the idea that men found it hard to die in bed. Consequently, throughout Europe and parts of Asia, terminally ill people were taken out of their beds and laid on the floor to help their souls leave the bodies.

Bottle: Bottles are made of glass, and it is considered bad luck to break one. Fortunately, the bad luck is minor compared to that created when a mirror is broken. The remedy is to break a match into three pieces. This will avert the bad luck and also prevent any further breakages.

See *glass, mirror*.

Bread: Bread is known as "the staff of life." Terms such as "bread line" and "bread winner" show the importance bread has always had in people's lives. Consequently, there are many superstitions relating to its preparation and eating.

It is good luck to carry a crust of bread in a pocket. Menstruating women are not allowed to handle dough, because they will prevent it from rising. There will be a death in the family if the loaf cracks during the baking. All the dough has to be used. Any scraps left over should be baked into small morsels for the children to eat (this is because all the baking will be ruined if anything is wasted). The cook should not sing while baking bread.

The loaf has to be placed on the table in an upright position. If it is laid on its side some grave misfortune will occur. If the loaf crumbles while being cut, it is a sign that an argument is about to occur.

If a slice of buttered bread falls to the ground and lands butter side up, it's a sign that you'll shortly have a visitor.

Marking bread with a cross is still common in many places. This protects the household from evil forces.

Witches don't place bread on their tables, as it is a mere spell away from becoming the body of Jesus Christ.

Boys who eat a lot of bread will grow into men with extremely hairy chests. Small boys should keep well away from women who are kneading dough, because they will never grow beards if a doughy hand strokes their faces.

It is generally considered bad luck to take the last piece of bread on a plate. However, there is one exception. A bachelor can improve his chances of marrying a wealthy woman by taking the last piece of bread. A single woman will never marry if she takes the last piece of bread. The exception to all this occurs if you are offered the last piece of bread. You should always accept this, as it will bring you love and good fortune.

Finally, here are two strange superstitions about bread. It is considered unlucky for anyone to place a loaf of bread on the table upside down. And it is thought to be extremely dangerous for a woman to put a round loaf on the table upside down. This is a sign that she spends a great deal of time lying on her back. Obviously, there are sexual connotations attached to this superstition.

See *beard, cross, housewarming, singing, spell, toast, waiter, well, witches.*

Bread and Butter: Bread that has been buttered can never be "unbuttered." Consequently, if two people are walking side by side and are temporarily separated by an object or another person, they can say "bread and butter" to repair the bad luck that the separation has caused.

Saying the words "bread and butter" also removes any difficulties caused by certain actions that might bring

bad luck, such as accidentally walking under a ladder. If two people are involved, both need to say the words.

See *ladder.*

Breakages: An old superstition says that if you break two things, you'll break a third. Sometimes a cheap object will be deliberately broken after two other breakages, in order to eliminate the possibility of breaking something valuable.

If someone frequently breaks objects, such as plates and glasses, he or she has to go and buy something, as this will change the person's luck.

If a mirror breaks, it was once said to be a sign of a death in the family within a

year. Nowadays, a broken mirror merely means seven years bad luck.

See *mirror.*

Breath: The breath has always been associated with the spirit, or life force. Many ancient words for "breath" also mean "spirit." Examples include the Hebrew *ruach,* Greek *pneuma,* and Latin *spiritus.* The concept of breathing on something for luck has been carried on for thousands of years. Gamblers still blow on their cards for luck. Recently, I saw someone blowing on a Lotto ticket.

See *gambling, nose, yawning.*

Bride: There are many superstitions connected with weddings, and the bride has received more than her fair share of these. Traditionally, the bride is dressed in white because this color symbolizes innocence and purity. It is considered extremely lucky for the bride to wear the same wedding dress as her mother. Silk is the preferred material, as it provides additional luck. Satin should not be used, as it creates bad luck.

The bridal bouquet symbolizes fertility, ensuring that a family will follow in due course after the wedding. The ribbons tied around the bouquet also provide good luck.

It is bad luck for the bridal party to pass a policeman, priest, doctor, lawyer, or blind man on the way to the wedding. The bride should enter and leave the church by the same door.

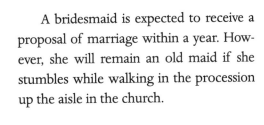

The groom should carry the bride over the threshold of their new home after the wedding. This custom dates back to the days when men would physically carry off their brides. By carrying her over the threshold, the groom is symbolically still carrying her off to her new life.

See *cat, door, flowers, garlic, mirror, orange, plate, rose, wedding, wedding cake, wedding dress, widow*.

Bridesmaid: The custom of bridesmaids (and the best man) dates back to the days when people opposed to the marriage would try to carry the bride away. The bridesmaids' task was to ensure that this didn't happen.

It is considered unlucky to be a bridesmaid three times, as this means you're destined to be an old maid. The remedy for this is to become a bridesmaid another four times (seven in total), and then the bad luck is lifted.

It is very lucky for the bride to have a matron of honor in her wedding party. This is because a happily married woman symbolizes the blessed union of two people.

A bridesmaid is expected to receive a proposal of marriage within a year. However, she will remain an old maid if she stumbles while walking in the procession up the aisle in the church.

Bridge: As bridges can symbolize the crossing from life to death, they need to be treated with respect. You should not say goodbye to someone on a bridge, as this means you will never meet again. An old belief says that the first person to cross a new bridge will have to give his or her soul to the devil.

It is bad luck to stop and talk to anyone under a bridge.

It is bad luck to walk under a railway bridge while a train is passing overhead. However, it is good luck to be on a bridge while a train is passing underneath.

See *devil*.

Broom: Brooms play important role in superstitions. Everyone knows that witches fly on them on their trips to see the devil, or to commit dastardly deeds. In fact, witches have never flown on brooms, or besoms,

as they are sometimes called. This belief came about because witches practiced a form of sympathetic magic by straddling their brooms and jumping up and down to show the crops how high they should grow.

According to superstition, the first time a new broom is used it should sweep something into the house, as this symbolically sweeps good luck in as well. Brooms should be stored with the bristles uppermost. If the bristles rest on the floor, a stranger will visit the house. It is a sign of misfortune if a resting broom falls over without cause. It is also bad luck to step over a broom that has fallen to the floor.

Since Roman times, it has been considered bad luck to buy a broom in May. This old superstition is even celebrated in rhyme:

> If you buy a broom or brush in May
> You'll sweep the head
> of the household away.

The Romans considered May the month of death, and gathering broom, a yellow-flowering shrub, in May risked death or calamity to any man who dared try it.

Broom was also considered an aphrodisiac. This probably led to the superstition that any single girl who walked over a broomstick would have a baby out of wedlock.

Brooms are still used to protect homes from evil. As negative energies are likely to come in through the front door, the threshold should be kept clean, and the broom hung up nearby for protection and accessibility.

The besom, or Wiccan broom, is used in pagan weddings. The couple jumps over the broom to announce their union and to attract fertility into their marriage.

If your house contains two or more stories, make sure to sweep upstairs before noon. Carrying dust downstairs after noon is a sign that a dead body will shortly be carried down, too.

It is generally considered bad luck to do any sweeping at night. This is because it could disturb the spirits of the dead, who might be out walking in the night air.

See *aphrodisiac, devil, Friday the 13th, housewarming, magic, Wicca, witches.*

Building: A common superstition in the building trade is to leave a tiny detail of every building unfinished, to avoid tempting fate. The toast that is drunk when the building is finished is not only a celebration of a job well done, but also a way of deterring evil spirits. Sometimes rituals are performed when the first sod is turned over at the start of the project. This is done to symbolically provide the project with protection.

See *toast*.

Burial: Although church graveyards are on consecrated ground, the north side of the graveyard has always been unpopular, as people believed it was inhabited by ghosts and evil spirits. Because of this, the north side was usually reserved for the graves of suicides, people who were unbaptized, and stillborn babies. William Wordsworth referred to this practice in his poem "'Tis Said, That Some have Died for Love":

'Tis said, that some have died for love:
And here and there
a churchyard grave is found
In the cold north's unhallowed ground,
Because the wretched man
himself had slain,
His love was such a grievous pain.

The north was believed to be the abode of Satan. Jesus came from the east, and is believed to return to the world from that direction on Judgment Day. He also apparently lay in the sepulchre with his feet toward the east. This placed the north

on his left. In the parable of the sheep and the goats, the sheep were on his right hand, and the goats on his left (Matthew 25:33). Consequently, no one wants to be included amongst the goats.

An old European superstition says that the first corpse buried in a newly consecrated graveyard would belong to the devil. The remedy for this was to bury a dog or pig in the graveyard. This removed the problem, and the ground became suitable for human burials.

See *ghost*.

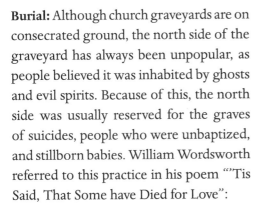

Business: Business people are often considered hardheaded and down-to-earth, but a large percentage of them are highly superstitious. These superstitions include general ones, such as avoiding making business decisions on Fridays or the thirteenth of any month.

Success in business can be helped with the aid of certain superstitions. Amulets and charms can be worn to provide protection and attract good fortune to the venture. A lucky horseshoe made of flowers is sometimes presented to the owner of a new business on the day it first opens.

It is a sign of a lucky week ahead if the first sale on Monday morning is made before 9 AM. It will be a good day if the first potential customer in the morning buys something, no matter how small.

Long-term leases need to be for an odd number of years to ensure that the business thrives. This is why leases are for ninety-nine years, rather than one hundred.

Shaking hands to cement a business deal is an old custom that symbolizes mutual progress and good luck.

See *amulet, charms, Friday, horseshoe, thirteen.*

Buttercup: Throughout the Western world, children are still told that if a buttercup held under the chin casts a yellow shadow, they love butter. There is no truth in this, but butter manufacturers must love this superstition.

Butterfly: Butterflies generally bring good luck. It is a sign that someone in the household will shortly be getting married if a butterfly flies indoors.

See *jade.*

Button: Most people know that it is bad luck to do up buttons incorrectly. Fortunately, the remedy is easy: all you need do is undo the buttons, take off the item of clothing, put it on again, and then do up the buttons correctly.

It is good luck to do up an odd number of buttons. If your garment has three buttons, for instance, you can do up either one or all three of them. However, if your garment has two buttons, you should do up the top button only, or leave the garment unbuttoned.

It is good luck to be given buttons as a gift. Finding a button while undertaking your daily tasks is a sign that you'll make a new friend.

A seventeenth-century rhyme used for counting cherry stones, daisy petals, and other small objects was sometimes also recited with buttons. Young women could count the buttons on their clothes to determine whom they would marry:

Tinker, tailor, soldier, sailor,
Rich man, poor man, beggar-man, thief.

See *dressing.*

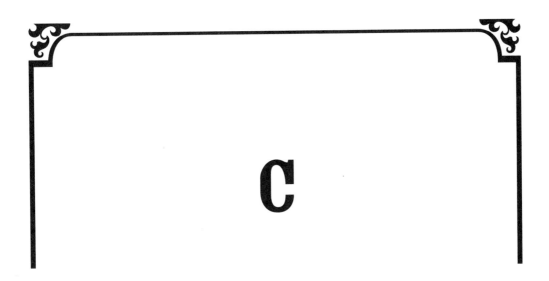

C

Cabbage: People used to believe that cabbage was hard to digest. Consequently, it was cooked for several hours in the belief that this made it easier to eat. Fortunately, this superstition has died out.

Apparently, according to a Pennsylvanian superstition, St. Patrick's Day (March 17) is the best day of the year on which to plant cabbages.

See *Good Friday.*

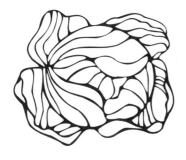

Cake: Cake charms, known as *Agnus Dei,* were made to protect people from the wiles of Satan. One side of the cake bore an imprint of a lamb holding a flag, and the head of Jesus was on the other side. Cooked inside the cake was a piece of paper containing texts from the Gospel of St. John. These cakes were not eaten, but kept as protective amulets. In the same way, hot cross buns were often kept from one Good Friday to the next to protect the family from sickness.

An interesting Bavarian superstition involved the making of corpse cakes. The dough was allowed to rise on the dead body. This enabled all the good qualities and virtues of the deceased to enter into the dough. The relatives of the deceased ate the cakes made  from it, to ensure that the person's special qualities remained inside the family.

Cakes should be baked in the morning while the sun is rising in the sky. The first cake (in a batch of small cakes) taken out of the oven should be broken open, and not cut. If it is cut, every other cake baked on that day will be soggy.

It is considered bad luck to dispose of the eggshells until after the cake has been baked.

It is bad luck if a slice of cake is placed on your plate and then tips onto its side. If this occurs, avert the bad luck by saying "bread and butter."

See *amulet, bread and butter, charms, eggs, food, Good Friday, sun, wedding cake.*

Calendar: It is unlucky to hang up a calendar before the New Year. Similarly, some people believe it's bad luck to turn to the next day, week, or month in a calendar until the actual date has arrived.

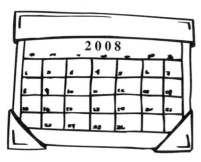

Some days are considered unlucky. In 1565, Richard Grafton, an astrologer and historian, constructed a list of sixty-one days that he believed were unlucky. There are three Mondays that are traditionally considered unlucky: the first Monday in April, as it was Cain's birthday and also the day on which he killed Abel; the second Monday in August, as it is the day on which Sodom and Gomorrah were destroyed; and surprisingly, the last Monday in December, as it is thought to be the day Judas betrayed Jesus. However, this one appears to be a few months early, unless Judas betrayed Jesus a number of times.

See *New Year.*

Cameo: A cameo is a small piece of onyx or other hard stone that is carved in relief against a background of a different color. It is usually worn as jewelry, but also works well as a lucky charm.

A cameo should be owned and loved for seven years for it to gain full effectiveness as a charm. After this time, it will continue to work as a lucky charm for successive generations of the same family.

See *charms.*

Canary: Pet canaries, like  other household pets, bring luck to a home. But a strange canary flying into the home is a sign of bad luck that could mean death to a family member.

You will have bad luck for two years if a strange cat kills your pet canary.

See *birds, cat*.

Cancer: Cancer is the fourth sign of the zodiac. Its symbol is the crab. Its element is water, and its gemstone is ruby. The keyword for Cancer is: I feel.

Cancer is ruled by the moon, which emphasizes the sensitive, emotional side of our natures. Cancers love the security of home and family, and enjoy the responsibility of parenthood. They enjoy buying things for their homes, and many of them build up collections of objects that appeal to them. Cancerians are loyal friends and are always willing to provide a shoulder to lean on when others need it. Cancerians are highly intuitive, and can sum people up at a glance.

See *astrology, element, gemstone, moon, ruby, water*.

Candle: Candles have had a magical, hypnotic influence on mankind since Stone Age times. Almost twenty-five hundred years ago, Egyptians used candles to help encourage precognitive dreams. The dreamer sat in a cave facing south and gazed into the candle flame until he saw an image of a god or goddess in it. He would then sleep, and the deity would answer his questions in the form of dreams.[21]

In medieval times, farmers protected their flocks from witches by surrounding them with candles that had been blessed by priests.

Today, at a birthday party, the birthday child makes a wish and tries to blow out all the candles in a single puff to ensure that the wish is granted. A rarer form of this is for each guest at the party to make his or her own silent wish, and then blow out a single candle. This is a form of candle magic, and it works extremely well as long as the people involved believe in magic.

It is a sign of a wedding if a candle is snuffed out accidentally.

It is a sign of a storm brewing if a candle is hard to light. Bad weather is on its way if a candle gutters in a room with no drafts.

An extinguished candle can sometimes symbolize death. At one time it was common for a candle to be buried with the corpse. This was to light the way to the next world. If a candle flame develops a bluish hue, it is a sign of a death in the family.

See *bell, book, and candle; Christmas Eve; dreams; storm; three; wedding; widdershins; witches*.

Candlemas: Originally, February 2 was the second of four fire festivals practiced by the Celts. The Christian Church took over this festival and dedicated the day to the Virgin Mary. According to tradition, she presented Jesus at the temple on February 2. Candles are blessed for the year on Candlemas Day. This day was traditionally a day for women, and candles were burned around young mothers and their children to symbolize spiritual protection.

In Wicca, February 2 is Imbolc, one of the eight sabbats, or seasonal festivals, of the Wiccan year. It celebrates the start of spring, with its promise of rebirth and renewal. "Imbolc" means "in milk," and cows usually start producing milk again about this time.

It is considered bad luck for any Christmas decorations to remain on display after this date. Christmas decorations on display in a church after February 2 are unlucky for the entire congregation. It is believed that this can lead to the death of one of the congregation.

Candlemas is also popularly known as Groundhog Day in the United States. According to tradition, the groundhog emerges from its nest on February 2 to assess the weather. If it sees its own shadow, it will hibernate a little longer, as this is a sign that the weather will remain bad for at least six weeks. If the day is cloudy, it will stay above ground, as it assumes that spring is about to start. Consequently, the weather on Groundhog Day predicts what the weather will be like for the next six weeks. Bears and wolves are also believed to come out of their lairs on February 2 to check on the weather.

Early settlers to the United States instituted Groundhog Day. In Europe they had used the hedgehog, but as they couldn't find these in the new world, they adopted the groundhog instead.

Sailors are reluctant to leave port on Candlemas Day, as they believe any voyage starting on February 2 is doomed and disaster will result.

See *February, Groundhog Day, sailors, Wicca.*

Capricorn: Capricorn is the tenth sign of the zodiac. Its symbol is the goat. Its element is earth, and its gemstone is onyx. The keyword for Capricorn is: I use.

Capricornians are solid, practical, hardworking people who slowly but surely reach their goals. They are determined and ambitious, but keep their feet firmly on the ground. They are cautious, conservative, logical, and fair. Capricornians find it hard to express their emotions, but with the right partner can be highly romantic.

See *astrology, earth, element, gemstone, goat, onyx.*

Car: Despite its short history, the car has already attracted a large number of superstitions. Many motorists refuse to drive cars that have number plates that add up to thirteen. Some cars are believed to be jinxed in some way, and are more likely to be involved in accidents as a result. Certain roads are also believed to be jinxed. Many people adorn their cars with lucky amulets, such as St. Christopher medals, to provide protection while they are driving.

Never discuss accidents or near misses before driving your car. It is also bad luck to discuss how fast you drive before setting off on a trip.

An interesting superstition held by many people who claim not to be superstitious is that cleaning your car is bound to cause rain.

See *amulet, charms, funeral, garlic, jinx, St. Christopher, thirteen.*

Cards, Playing: Gamblers frequently use playing cards, and many have become associated with either good or bad luck. People who are lucky at cards are believed to be unlucky in love, and vice versa. If someone is dealt a large number of black cards

(spades and clubs) in succession, it is a sign of an imminent death in the person's family. The four of clubs is considered unlucky, as it symbolizes the devil's four-poster bed. The ace of spades has always been considered the unluckiest card, as it signifies death. In 1692, the Earl of Stair used the nine of diamonds to signal the massacre of Glencoe. As a result, it became known as "the curse of Scotland."

You are thought to be unlikely to win the hand if you are holding a pair of aces and a pair of eights. This is known as the "dead man's hand." Apparently, a legendary hero of the American West was holding this hand when one of his enemies shot and killed him.

It is considered extremely bad luck to steal a deck of cards. Burglars who steal cards always get caught. It is also bad luck to play cards with a dog in the room. You should not cross your legs while playing cards, as this creates bad luck and you will lose money. You should pick up the cards with your right hand, as this is your lucky hand.

You can change your luck by blowing at the cards while shuffling them. You

can also walk around your chair, or the table, to change your luck. Alternatively, you can turn your chair 180 degrees and sit astride it. An even simpler method to change your luck is to sit on your handkerchief.

If you have a "lucky" card, touch it with the index finger of your right hand before starting to play. This will improve your luck.

It is bad luck to use the same deck of cards for both fortune telling and card games. The remedy is to have two decks of cards, each one dedicated to a specific purpose.

Card tables are usually covered with felt. This is because it is bad luck to play cards on a bare table.

Cartomancy is a form of divination using either playing cards or Tarot cards. Each card has a specific meaning that can be interpreted. In a deck of playing cards, the clubs represent business matters, the diamonds money and status, the hearts love and romance, and the spades obstacles and difficulties.

See *divination, right side, thief.*

Carnelian: Carnelian (formerly called cornelian) is a red form of chalcedony. It is easily recognizable because the stone is translucent.

Carnelian has been used as an amulet since the days of the ancient Egyptians, who created many amulets from it including the scarab. Napoleon acquired a carnelian in Egypt that he had attached to his watch chain as a protective amulet.

Arabs wear carnelian as an amulet to prevent envy. Mohammed wore a silver ring containing a cylinder seal of carnelian on his little finger. Muslims believe that people who own a cylinder seal of carnelian can never be separated from God. They also believe that those who wear carnelian will have all their needs met and will be treated with respect by everyone they encounter.

Carnelian is still worn as an amulet to help people speak boldly. Consequently, actors, public speakers, auctioneers, and other people who need to express themselves frequently use it as a lucky charm. It is also worn to relieve depression, anxiety, and stress.

See *actors and actresses, amulet, gemstones, scarab.*

Carrots: At one time carrots were prized as aphrodisiacs, and they have always been thought to possess magical properties. The best-known superstition about carrots is the myth that eating them will improve a person's

eyesight. During World War II, the Royal Air Force conducted some experiments to see if carrots could improve night vision. Carrots contain vitamin A, which helps produce visual purple, a pigment in the retina that is essential to effective vision in poor light. As the results were inconclusive, the experiments were dropped. However, stories began spreading that the British airmen were superior to the German ones because they ate large amounts of carrots, which enabled them to see in the dark.

See *aphrodisiac*.

Cat: Cats were sacred to the goddess Isis in ancient Egypt. Bast, daughter of Isis, was depicted with the face of a cat. Cats were so revered that anyone who killed one, even accidentally, was put to death. It was in ancient Egypt that the belief began that a black cat crossing your path brings good luck.

The opposite tradition began in the Middle Ages in Europe. Cats fared badly at this time, as people thought they were witches' familiars. Black cats were believed to be witches in disguise. An alternative belief was that after seven years of service to a witch, a black cat would turn into a witch. Consequently, a black cat cross-

ing your path was an indication of bad luck, as the devil was watching you.

When people moved from one house to another, it was considered bad luck for the new house to be too clean. This was because all the good luck was removed along with the dirt. The remedy was to throw a cat into the new house before moving in. Any bad luck or evil spirit would attach itself to the cat, which would quickly die.

It is good luck to walk somewhere and find a cat on your right side. However, it is bad luck to see a cat on your left. It is a good financial omen if the cat on the right side crosses your path and continues to the left. Naturally, it's bad for your finances if it does the opposite. It's a sign of a quarrel about to happen if you see a cat turn around two or three times.

It's a sign of good luck if your cat sneezes in the morning. One sneeze at any time of the day is a sign of rain coming. Three sneezes in a row is a sign of good luck. It is extremely good luck for a cat to sneeze near a bride on her wedding day.

The old superstition that cats crawl closer and closer to your face while you are asleep with the intention of sucking all the breath out of your body is related to the idea that cats are witches' familiars. Even today, mothers shut cats out of their

babies' rooms due to concerns for the baby's breathing.

A common belief is that cats can fall from great heights without injuring themselves, and always land on their feet. Cats possess a reflex that enables them to instantly twist themselves, so they usually do land on their feet. However, the myth that they do not hurt themselves is incorrect, and veterinarians regularly see cats with broken jaws and pelvises they've sustained in falls.

Another common misconception is that cats can't swim. Cats were first domesticated in the deserts of Egypt and don't have a natural affinity for water. However, cats that are introduced to water as kittens enjoy playing in it. The Bengali machbagral is found in India, Nepal, and China, and is known as the "swimming cat." It has extremely long claws that help it catch fish.

If your cat starts washing its face, it is a sign that a visitor will call.

Black cats bring good fortune to the home. It is also a positive sign if a black cat enters your home. Allow it to stay as long  as it wishes. If you chase it out of the house, it will take all your good luck with it.

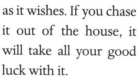

Cats can even be used to increase numbers when thirteen people are sitting down to dinner. If a cat is placed in the lap of one of the guests, numbers are increased to fourteen, and sufferers of triskaidekaphobia (fear of thirteen) can relax. If a black cat is used, good luck will come to everyone at the table.

See *baseball, black, bride, canary, devil, familiar, mascot, pregnancy, ships, sneezing, theater, thirteen, tongue, wedding, white, witch.*

Caul: The caul is the amniotic sac that surrounds the fetus and contains the fluid that protects the unborn baby. The sac bursts and releases the water shortly before the baby is born. The sac itself becomes part of the afterbirth.

Occasionally, a baby is born with the caul clinging to his or her head. This is considered a lucky omen. The child will lead a particularly fortunate and happy life, and will not die by drowning.

Because the caul protects the fetus in the womb, it is not surprising that people believed it could protect them later in life also. It was not uncommon for people to sell cauls, and these were highly sought after by sailors because they believed it would protected them from shipwrecks and drowning.

See *drowning, omen, sailors.*

Chain Letters: A chain letter is one of a series of letters that tells the recipient to send copies to a specific number of other people.

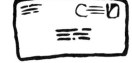

Most people ignore chain letters' exhortations to pass them on. However, because of the wording of these letters, some people still believe it is bad luck to break the chain, and good luck to pass it on.

Chair: It is a sign of bad luck for a chair to fall over. The person who caused it to fall should make the sign of the cross while righting it to avert any bad luck. If the chair is knocked over by a single girl, she will be delaying her future wedding by several months. If the chair falls over when someone is getting up from the table, it is a sign that he or she has been lying.

Gamblers can change their luck by either turning a chair around three times or walking around it three times. This should only be done when they are losing. Chairs should not be turned around on other occasions, as this can cause arguments.

It is bad luck to have an empty chair at a formal dinner. The chair, and the table service, of the person who failed to arrive has to be removed to avert this bad luck.

See *cross, gambling, table, walnut, wedding.*

Changeling: A changeling is a baby left by fairies to replace a human child that has been abducted by elves or fairies. The changeling seems identical in every way to the abducted child, but usually appears to be precocious or slightly different. Changelings can sometimes be identified because they cry frequently and are always hungry.

There were two main ways to get a changeling to reveal itself and break the enchantment. This process also returned the real child to the parents. The first was to make the changeling laugh. The second was to beat the child until his fairy mother appeared to take him or her away.

Parents sometimes explained children with birth defects or socially unacceptable behavior as changelings.

See *fairy.*

Charmers: Charmers are people who are able to charm away warts, shingles, and many other problems by reciting a charm or spell.

Charmers do a lot of good work, but they do not like to be thanked, as they believe this will reverse the charm.

See *warts, spell.*

Charms: Charms are worn or carried to provide good luck, health, and happiness. Originally, charms were words that were either spoken or sung. The word "charm" is derived from the French word *charme*, which means "song." Saying "white rabbits" on the first of the month is an example of a spoken charm. It was only when people began writing the words down, rather than saying them, that charms became associated with magical objects such as amulets and talismans.

St. Christopher is the patron saint of travelers, and a medallion containing his image is still widely worn by travelers. It has even gone into outer space. In 1968, contractors working on the Vanguard rocket project for the United States Navy blamed a series of failures on the absence of St. Christopher medals on the rockets. A medal was attached to the next rocket and it worked perfectly. Despite this success, the Roman Catholic Church deleted St. Christopher from the *Calendarium Romanum* in 1969. So far this has made no difference whatsoever to the appeal of

St. Christopher charms. When Edward White, the astronaut, went to the moon, he carried a St. Christopher medallion, a gold cross, and a Star of David in the

right-hand pocket of his space suit.[22]

In earlier times, the Christian church preached that all illnesses were a divine punishment. As a result, doctors were not given much in the way of encouragement, and people sought charms and amulets to protect and heal themselves.

Charms are probably more popular today than ever before. John D. Rockefeller always carried a lucky eagle stone with him to provide good luck. In 1839, Queen Victoria sent her friend Viscount Melbourne "a little *charm*" with a note saying that she hoped it would "keep [him] from *all evil*"; she also said it would make her "very happy" if he would put it with his keys.[23] Carole Lombard (1908–1942), the film star, was given a smooth pebble by Clark Gable and kept it as a lucky charm.

See *abracadabra, acorn, amulet, athletes, cameo, charmers, coin, copper, elephant, film stars, gemstones, hand, heart, horseshoe, hunchback, key, ladybug, Lee penny, lizard, luck, rabbit's foot, rain, St. Christopher, salespeople, shamrock, shell, spitting, talisman, words.*

Chastity: The sapphire was believed to encourage chastity. This belief was so strong that Pope Innocent III (1160–1217) ordered all his bishops to wear sapphire rings. Bishops still wear sapphire rings, although today this is more likely to be due to tradition rather than superstition or chastity concerns.

See *sapphire, unicorn*.

Cheese: Until comparatively recently, people thought the veins in blue vein cheese were caused by the copper needles that were used to pierce the cheese to allow air in to facilitate the bacterial growth. This was a logical belief, as copper develops a greenish-blue color as it oxidizes. Once stainless steel needles began to be used, people discovered that it was the introduction of bacteria to the cheese, rather than copper needles, that caused the blue veins to occur.

Children: It is good luck for a child to be born under a full moon. This luck will stay with him or her throughout life. It is also good luck to be born during the nighttime. This means the child will never see ghosts or spirits.

It is bad luck to step over a small child who is crawling on the floor. This is believed to stunt the child's growth. You can also stunt the child's growth by measuring him or her with a tape measure.

If you give away all your baby clothes or the cradle, you will soon be buying more, as another baby will be on the way.

See *cradle, ghosts, kiss, malachite, mistletoe, moon, numbers, orange, table, umbilical cord, wedding, wedding cake*.

Chimney: Witches were believed to travel through the air with the help of the devil. People also thought they left their homes via the chimney.

See *devil, pixies, Santa Claus, sickle, soot, witch*.

Chimney Sweep: Chimney sweeps are believed to pass on good luck to everyone they associate with. This tradition began in eighteenth century England when a sweep saved a king on a runaway horse. Before the king had time to thank him, the sweep had disappeared amongst the crowd. Another version of this story says that it was King George III who was saved by a chimney sweep.

Shaking hands with or kissing a chimney sweep is extremely lucky, and ensures a happy marriage.

See *marriage.*

Christening: It is considered good luck to call a child by its intended name before the christening. It is also good luck to christen a child on the same day of the week as its birthday, and if the child cries after being sprinkled with holy water.

It is bad luck for the child being christened if his or her godmother is pregnant. This also risks bad luck to the godmother's unborn child.

According to superstition, if a boy and girl are being christened at the same time, it is important to christen the boy first. If the girl is christened first, the boy will never be able to grow a beard but the girl will.

If a stranger visits a house containing an unchristened baby, especially a girl, it is important that he eat or drink something before leaving. If he fails to do this, he will take the child's beauty away with him when he leaves.

See *wedding cake.*

Christmas: It is good luck to be born on Christmas Day. This indicates a happy life, free of cares and worries.

In Shropshire, every member of the family traditionally had to take a turn at stirring the Christmas pudding. At Christmastime, any bread baked in the house had to be baked at night. Small Christmas cakes were not to be counted by the cook. All the same, there had to be enough of them so they could be named after every member of the family. If any of these named cakes broke while being baked, that person would supposedly die in the next twelve months.

Mince pies (sometimes known as mince tarts) are a popular part of Christmas. Most people think they will gain a month of good luck for every mince pie they eat during the Christmas season, as long as a different person makes each pie. One hundred years ago, the tradition was that each pie had to be eaten at a different person's house, and they had to be consumed between December 25 and January 6. This gave you twelve days in which to eat enough pies to guarantee a year of good luck.

It is an indication of good crops to come if the sun shines through the branches of the apple trees on Christmas Day.

A rhyme from New England illustrates one of the benefits of a white Christmas:

> When Christmas is white
> The graveyard is lean,
> But fat is the graveyard
> When Christmas is green.

Christmas decorations should be put away on January 6. It is bad luck to keep them up after this date.

See *ghosts, mince pies, mistletoe, thief, Twelfth Night, wishbone.*

Christmas Eve: In Ireland, people believed that Christmas Eve was the only day on which you could die and avoid purgatory. Consequently, some people met their maker earlier than expected as friends and relatives helped them to die on Christmas Eve.

During the Dark Ages, the French feared Christmas Eve, as it was considered the day when Satan and his helpers strode the earth. Consequently, people placed their animals in shelters and locked themselves in their homes. Only oxen and asses were allowed to remain outdoors, because they had witnessed Christ's Nativity. People also believed that oxen had the power of speech on Christmas Eve. However, nobody was keen to hear what the oxen had to say, as they never heard anything good about themselves, and feared hearing a prediction of a sudden or violent death.

Any candles lit on Christmas Eve should be left burning until Christmas morning, or until they burn out by themselves.

It is good luck to become engaged on Christmas Eve. This indicates a long and happy marriage.

See *candle, Santa Claus, shadow, sheep, wassailing, werewolf.*

Christmas Pudding: Good luck comes to everyone who stirs the Christmas pudding while it is being made. It has always been good luck to add coins to a Christmas pudding. Whoever finds one will enjoy good luck for the next twelve months. Traditionally, a silver coin, a ring, and a thimble are placed into the pudding. The person who finds the coin will have good luck. The person who finds the thimble will enjoy prosperity, and the person who finds the ring will get married in the near future. If the finder of the ring is already married, someone close to him or her will become engaged.

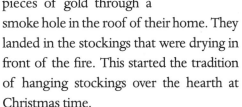

Christmas Stocking: An old legend says that St. Nicholas heard of three beautiful sisters who were so poor that they had to prostitute themselves. He tossed three pieces of gold through a smoke hole in the roof of their home. They landed in the stockings that were drying in front of the fire. This started the tradition of hanging stockings over the hearth at Christmas time.

See *fire, Santa Claus.*

Christmas Tree: Christmas trees are a comparatively recent development, al-though trees were used in winter festivals long before Christianity began. The origin of the Christmas tree was possibly the custom of decorating fir trees with apples to symbolize the Tree of Knowledge in the Garden of Eden. These trees were used to demonstrate good and evil in fifteenth-century German morality plays. They gained popularity in Germany during the time of Martin Luther, the sixteenth century Protestant reformer. He decorated a fir tree with candles for his family.

Hessian troops introduced the Christmas tree to the United States during the Revolutionary War. Apparently, they were homesick and recreated a custom that they enjoyed at home.

It was Prince Albert, husband of Queen Victoria, who introduced the Christmas tree to Britain. After that, the Christmas tree quickly gained popularity around the world.

The "General Grant" sequoia tree in Kings Canyon National Park, California, was made the official Christmas tree of the United States in April 1926.

See *tree.*

Church: There are many superstitions involving churches, but most of these are local. It is commonly believed that rainwater collected from the roof of a church contains numerous health benefits, and can even cure a variety of ailments. Butter made from the milk of cows that have grazed in a churchyard is also believed to possess medicinal properties.

If a church door rattles unexpectedly during a church service, it is a sign that a member of the con-gregation will soon die. A bird perching on a church weather vane indicates an even more imminent death, usually within a week.

If you sit in a church between 11:00 PM and midnight on Halloween, you will see the spectral forms of all the parishioners who will die in the following year.

See *clergyman, gargoyle, Halloween, Midsummer's Eve, rose, thief, twins, wedding, widdershins, witch.*

Circle: Throughout history, the circle has been considered a symbol of good fortune. It signifies completeness, wholeness, and perfection. The good luck aspect of the circle may have come from observation of the sun's apparent circle around the earth.

People also felt that as the circle was lucky, evil spirits would not be able to cross it. As a result of this, rings, wreaths, and other circular decorations and adornments were created. Even lipstick was invented because of the circle. Because people thought evil spirits could enter the body through the mouth, they started painting a red circle around the mouth.

See *rings, sun.*

Citrine: Citrine is a yellow variety of quartz. The name citrine comes from the French *citron*, which means "lemon." It is sometimes known as the "merchant's stone" or the "money stone" because it is believed to bring prosperity and abundance to anyone who owns or wears it. Frequently, crystals of citrine were kept in a safe or money box to increase the fortunes of their owner. Citrine is also known as the "cuddle quartz," as it creates feelings of warmth, hope, love, and positivity. It is also believed to purify the body of toxins and negativity. To do this, the crystal is placed in pure water for an hour or two. The water is then drunk.

See *gemstones.*

Claw: An amulet made from an animal's claw provides the wearer with protection according to the strength of the animal. A tiger's claw amulet will be more powerful than one made from a badger's claw, for instance. A bear-claw amulet is believed to help women during childbirth.

See *amulet.*

Clergyman: It is bad luck to encounter a priest or clergyman. This has nothing to do with the individual people, but the function they perform. Clergymen are frequently involved in sad occasions, such as funerals, and unconsciously carry the negative energy these occasions produce with them. This does not apply if you already know the clergyman, or see him in a church or churchyard.

The remedy is to cross your fingers or to touch something made of iron.

See *church, funeral, iron, nuns, ships.*

Clock: A comparatively modern superstition says that a clock will stop ticking when its owner dies. This might have come about because older clocks needed frequent attention. If the owner became unwell and stopped winding the clock, it is possible that it would stop ticking about the same time as the owner died. The American songwriter, Henry Clay Work (1832–1884), stayed at the George Inn in

 Piercebridge, Yorkshire in 1875 and was shown a longcase clock that had stopped when its owner died. A year later, he published his most enduring song, *Grandfather's Clock*:

> Ninety years without slumbering,
> Tick, tock, tick, tock,
> His life's seconds numbering,
> Tick, tock, tick, tock.
> It stopped short,
> Never to go again,
> When the old man died.

It is a sign of imminent death if a clock strikes more than twelve.

See *thirteen*.

Clothes: There are many superstitions concerning clothing. One of the oldest originated with William the Conqueror, who accidentally put his chain mail on backwards before the Battle of Hastings. His courtiers were upset about this, as they considered it a bad omen. William reassured them by saying it was a good sign because he was about to progress from duke to king. Ever since then it has been considered lucky to accidentally put an item of clothing on inside out. However, you must keep it on that way until the time you would normally take it off for the good luck to have maximum effect. Another possible origin for this superstition is that death recognizes us by our clothes. If your clothes are worn in a different way, death, and other evil spirits, will fail to recognize you.

Wives of fishermen sometimes deliberately wore their blouses inside out, believing this would help protect their husbands at sea.

You should always start putting on clothes using the right hand or foot. Using the left hand or foot is believed to attract the attention of the devil.

It is good luck to wear a holey sock for one day, but this changes to bad luck if the sock is worn again without being mended.

It is bad luck to button up any clothes wrongly. However, undoing the buttons and starting again can avert the bad luck.

It is also bad luck to repair any item of clothing while it is being worn. The wearer is likely to suffer a major loss of reputation, money, or family members.

You are allowed to make a wish when putting a new garment on for the first time. You should always wear new clothes on Easter morning. You will never run short of money if you place a coin in the right-hand pocket of your clothes when you wear them for the first time.

At one time it was considered good luck

for a bride to get married wearing nothing under her wedding gown. This custom began when a husband had to pay any debts his bride had incurred before the wedding. It was thought that any creditors would feel sorry for a bride getting married in nothing but a dress, and would not insist on payment.

When I was living in Scotland in the 1960s, a common superstition said it was bad luck to start making a garment unless it was completely finished before the end of the year.

See *baby, days of the week, death, devil, Easter, fishermen, left side, right side, salespeople, thread, washing, wish, women.*

Clouds: It is a sign of settled weather when clouds look like fluffy balls of wool. It is a sign of rain when clouds appear to increase in number. When they seem to decrease, it is a sign that the weather is improving.

Weather conditions were extremely important for our forbears, and they were always looking for signs of change. Clouds thickening and appearing closer to the ground indicated deteriorating weather. Other indications of this were clouds increasing in number and racing across the sky, clouds at different heights moving in a variety of directions, and an unseasonable change in the temperature. As a general

rule, the higher the clouds are, the better the weather will be.

See *rain, right side, sky, weather.*

Clover: Because a three-leaf clover is supposed to be lucky, the much rarer four-leaf clover must be exceptionally lucky.

An old legend says that when Adam and Eve were expelled from the Garden of Eden, Eve took a four-leaf clover with her to remind her of the happiness she had enjoyed there. Consequently, finding a four-leaf clover became a sign of good luck and happiness.

Christians like the four-leaf clover, as the cross of Jesus had four parts. The four leaves symbolize faith, hope, love, and luck. As a child, I was taught a simple rhyme that had different meanings:

> One leaf for fame,
> One leaf for wealth,
> And one for a faithful lover,
> And one leaf to bring you glorious health,
> Are all in the four-leaf clover.

In the seventeenth century, four-leaf clovers were sometimes strewn in the path of a bride to provide her with extra protection from evil spirits on her special day.

Some people claim that when you find a four-leaf clover you should place it in a shoe. A more popular hiding place is the family Bible.

If a single woman finds a four-leaf clover and places it in a shoe, the first single man she meets will become her future husband. Another method is to pin the four-leaf clover above the front door of her home. Again, the first unmarried man who walks through the door will become her husband.

If someone has done well in life, he or she is said to be living "in clover." This probably originates from the fact that cattle grow best when grazing in fields of clover.

The luckiest four-leaf clover is one you find when you are not looking for one.

See *amulet, Bible, cross, luck, shoe, travel.*

Coal: Coal is considered lucky, as it's associated with fire. Even today, many people carry a small piece of coal around with them as a lucky charm. In the nineteenth century, burglars carried coal in the belief it would prevent them from being caught. Sailors believed that carrying a piece of coal would protect them from drowning. They considered a lump of coal found on a beach to be the most effective form of protection.

Young women placed a piece of coal under their pillow, believing it would enable them to dream of their future husband. John Aubrey mentioned this superstition in his *Miscellanies* (1696):

The last summer, on the even of St. John the Baptist, 1694, I accidentally was walking in the pasture behind Montague house, it was 12 o'clock. I saw there about two or three and twenty young women, most of them well habited, on their knees very busy, as if they had been weeding. I could not presently learn what the matter was; at last a young man told me, that they were looking for a coal under the root of the plantain, to put under their head that night, and they should dream who would be their husbands: It was to be sought for that day and hour.

If you find a piece of coal while out walking, you should make a wish, and then pick it up and carry it home with you.

See *drowning, fire, marriage, pumpkin, sailors, thief, virginity.*

Cock: The cock is considered a lucky animal, as one is said to have announced Christ's birth. Another Christian superstition is that every cock, living or dead, even weather-vane cocks, will start crowing on Judgment Day. Their crowing will wake every soul that has ever lived.

In the Bible, Peter denied knowing Jesus three times before the cock crowed twice (Matthew 26:34, Mark 14:30, Luke 22:34).

It is said that you will enjoy a good day if you hear a cock crowing while on your way to work. A cock crowing at nightfall is predicting bad weather on the following day. Hearing a cock crow late at night is an indication of a death in the neighborhood.

It is good luck to keep a cock, as it will ward off ghosts. A white cock is luckier than a black one.

See *death, ghost, pancake, wishbone.*

Coffee: Bubbles appearing in a cup of coffee are a sign of good luck, especially if they are caught with a spoon and eaten. This is hard to do, as the bubbles disappear quickly. However, anyone who achieves it will receive a surprise windfall.

The movement of any bubbles on the surface of a cup of coffee can be interpreted. It is a sign of money ahead if they move toward the drinker. Unfortunately, it means the opposite if they float away from the drinker.

It is bad luck to stir coffee with a fork.

The sediment of brewed coffee can be read in the same way as tea leaves. This form of fortune telling began in Italy about two hundred years ago, and quickly spread around Europe and ultimately most  of the world. The cup of coffee is drunk, leaving about two teaspoons of liquid in the bottom of the cup. The cup is quickly swirled and turned over. When it is turned upright again, the patterns the grounds have created are interpreted.

Muslims believe the archangel Gabriel invented coffee. One day when Mohammed was extremely tired, Gabriel brought him a cup of coffee. This invigorated Mohammed so much that after drinking it he defeated forty horsemen and satisfied forty women.

See *tea leaves.*

Coffin: It is considered highly dangerous for anyone to lie in a coffin while they are still alive. This is believed to hurry their demise. The corpse should not be buried wearing the clothes of anyone who is still alive. As the clothes in the coffin deteriorate, so will the health of the owner of the clothes.

It is bad luck to keep miniature coffins in the house. A surprising number of supposedly humorous ornaments are made

in the shape of a coffin. You should toss them out if you possess any, as they produce negative energy and bad luck.

It is also thought to be bad luck for the deceased person's family if the coffin is carried along a newly made road on the way to the graveyard.

See *corpse, cramp, death, funeral, grave-yard, iron, rosemary, shadow, storm, wedding, will.*

Coin: Coins have always been considered lucky. A popular one-liner says, "Any coin that happens to be in my possession is a lucky one." Giving a coin to a beggar always brings good luck, as does tossing a coin into a fountain.

The custom of throwing coins into a well or fountain originated when people believed spirits lived inside them. You risked receiving bad luck if you did not honor them when you went past. But tossing money into the well is more than simply honoring the spirits. You are also paying the spirits to protect you.

Millions of people a year toss coins into the magnificent Trevi Fountain in Rome. This is because they believe that by doing this, they will one day return to the Eternal City. Iranians do the same thing when they toss money into the beautiful

pool at the mausoleum erected to honor Saadi, their national poet.

The custom of placing a coin under the mainmast of a ship originates in Greek mythology. When people died they had to cross the River Styx to reach the Elysian Fields, the abode of the blessed. Charon owned the only ferry that crossed the river. He charged one obulus for the one-way trip. He refused to carry anyone who did not have the money to pay him. Because of this, the Greeks started burying their dead with a coin, which was placed in the deceased's hand or mouth. In time, the concept of placing a coin under the main mast began as a form of protection money that was offered to the spirits of the sea.

Paying to receive a present may seem like a strange idea, but is sometimes still done. It is considered bad luck to give someone a gift of a knife or scissors. This is because the sharp implement could cut the friendship. To avert this possibility, the recipient has to give a small coin to "pay" for the gift. This superstition has its roots in black magic. If a sharp object, such as a needle or pin, was imbued with negative magic and then given to someone, it would cause him or her harm. However, the evil effects would be averted if the recipient paid a small amount for the object.

It is considered bad luck not to pick up a coin found lying on the ground. This superstition is not as well known nowadays as it used to be. Many years ago, I conducted an experiment using coins of different denominations. Few people bothered bending down to pick up one or five cents, but almost everyone picked up coins of greater value.

The custom of placing coins over the eyes of the dead is common in many countries. It originates in the belief that dead people could open their eyes and look around for people to join them in the other world.

Sailors used coins with a hole punched through the middle as amulets and charms. This superstition dates back to when early man first found stones with holes in them at the seashore. He believed these were worn by sea gods, and by wearing them himself he would gain protection.

Coins that had been bent were also favored as lucky coins. John Foxe (1516–1587) wrote in his *Book of Martyrs* that before Alice Bendon was burned at the stake in 1557, her father sent her a shilling, which he had "bowed."

The best coin to keep as a lucky charm is one that was minted in the year you were born. Keep it in a small bag that you can carry with you, or have it mounted on a pendant you can wear.

See *charms, death, frog, golf, heads or tails, knife, Lee penny, money, needle, penny, pin, purse, rain, sailors, salespeople, scissors, ship, teeth, wind, wish, wishing well.*

Colds: One well-known way to avoid catching a cold is to carry an onion around with you at all times. A good cure if you happen to catch a cold is to go to bed with a drink containing one spoonful of honey, two shots of Scotch whisky, and boiling water. After drinking it, you'll be happy to have the cold.

One interesting North American cure for colds was to drive a hickory peg into the ground. It was important to tell no one you were doing this. You had to pull the peg out again every day for twelve days, blow into the hole seven times, and then replace the peg. By doing this you transferred the cold into the ground.

A less appetizing method was to eat cooked mice. Mice were believed to possess healing properties, and eating them transferred this quality to you. If this does not appeal, you could try tying a dirty woollen sock around your neck.

Naturally, it's much better not to catch cold in the first place. One method of achieving this is to stand under an oak tree in autumn and wait for the leaves to fall. If you manage to catch one as it falls, you will be free of colds for the next twelve months.

Folk magic says you cannot catch a cold in a church.

See *garlic, leaf, oak, onion, rosemary, sage, topaz, wine.*

Comb: It is rumored to be bad luck to pick up a comb that has accidentally been dropped. To avert the bad luck, tread lightly on the comb before picking it up.

It is also bad luck to drop a comb. The remedy for this is to walk around the comb three times in a clockwise direction, and then pick it up.

If a young woman is interested in a man, she must never let him carry her comb in his pocket. If she does, he will quickly lose interest in her.

You must never count the number of teeth in a comb. If you do, you will lose some of your own teeth.

See *teeth.*

Cooking: The kitchen is one of the most important rooms of the house, and is often considered the heart of the home. It is important that the cook stirs food in a clockwise direction. The cook should also leave a cooking utensil in the oven when it is not being used. This old Jewish superstition says that a completely empty oven is tempting fate, and you may ultimately end up with nothing to eat.

See *bread, eggs, meat, salt, tea.*

Copper: Many arthritis sufferers wear a copper bracelet to ease the pain of this crippling affliction. There is no scientific evidence that this charm works. However, people have been wearing copper bracelets since the Middle Ages, and today they seem to be more popular than ever.

See *wedding anniversaries.*

Coral: Coral works well as a protective amulet. It works best when worn as a necklace, ring, or bracelet. It will protect you from skin disorders and diseases of the blood.

See *amulet, blood, gemstones.*

Corn: It is considered good luck to find an ear of red corn. If you are fortunate enough to find one, you should keep it in your pocket until the next harvest.

Corn Dolly: The corn dolly is a small image made by plaiting dried and twisted straw. Sometimes they depict female figures, but they can also be fashioned into bells, crosses, fans, hearts, and lanterns. Corn dollies were traditionally made from the last sheaf of corn and were hung on the chimney to ensure the success of the next harvest.

The tradition began with the belief that the corn spirit was preserved in the final sheaf of corn. This had to be preserved, as otherwise the corn spirit would die and there would be no crops in the following year. Consequently, the last sheaf was fashioned into a doll and kept safely indoors until the following spring. During the winter, this figure protected the family and served as a fertility emblem. In the spring she was taken back into the fields so her spirit could enter the newly sown seeds, and the cycle could start again.

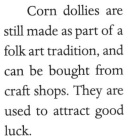

Corn dollies are still made as part of a folk art tradition, and can be bought from craft shops. They are used to attract good luck.

Corns: A corn is a small area of horny, usually tender, skin on the toes or feet. It is caused by pressure or friction. Corns used to be a big problem for our ancestors, as many of them could not afford to buy well-fitting shoes and had to wear other people's old shoes.

One popular remedy was to apply the juice of a leek onto the corn. Ivy leaves that had been soaked in vinegar could also be applied. A more radical method was to bury some stolen beef in the ground. The corns would disappear as the meat rotted.

See *ivy*.

Corpse: The eyes of a corpse should be closed as soon as possible after death. This is because they are said to have the power to will anyone they see to accompany them to the grave. Placing coins over the corpse's eyes prevents them from accidentally opening again. Tears should not be allowed to fall on the corpse, as this will upset the deceased person's soul. However, it is considered good luck to touch the corpse, and this also prevents the deceased from appearing in nightmares that might disturb the living.

It is important that the corpse be carried away feet first. This ensures that his or her ghost doesn't come back to haunt the living. If the corpse is being carried from a house, the front door step should be thoroughly cleaned right away to remove any traces of bad luck that may have been left behind.

See *coin, death, eye, pregnancy, rain, suicide, toothache, werewolf, zombie.*

Coven: A coven is the term given to a group of witches who work together to perform magical rituals and ceremonies. There are usually thirteen witches in a coven, as there are thirteen full moons in a year.

See *Friday, moon, thirteen, witch.*

Cow: At one time it was thought that cows knew the way to heaven. Consequently, cows used to be included in funeral processions in Scandinavia and Germany.

If a cow licks the forehead of another cow, it is a sign that their owner is about to die. It is also a sign of imminent death if a cow enters your property. Three cows means three deaths. Yet another reason for keeping your gates closed, especially if you live in the country!

It is important to wash your hands thoroughly after milking a cow. If you don't, you will receive no milk on the following day.

A cow's breath is believed to have health-giving properties, and people suffering from tuberculosis were at one time encouraged to sleep with the cattle.

An old English superstition says that cows kneel down on Christmas Eve and pay homage to Jesus. They speak in human voices, but anyone who hears them will die before being able to tell anyone about it.

You should take a calf out of the barn backwards to prevent its mother mourning the loss of her child.

See *funeral, milk, music, wasp.*

Cradle: A well-known superstition says that if you rock an empty cradle you will find it occupied again within a year. However, in some parts of Europe, rocking an empty cradle risks the life of the child who last slept in it.

See *baby, children, iron, malachite, rabbit's foot.*

Cramp: A cramp is a sudden, painful, involuntary contraction of a muscle or group of muscles, often caused by cold or exertion. The cure for cramps in your legs is to place your shoes upside down, and side by side, under your bed. Tying a red string or cord around the body can cure cramps in the stomach. Part of the thread needs to go over the affected part. Tying cotton string around an ankle is also said to cure cramps.

Another remedy is to wear a "cramp ring." These rings are made from metal stolen from an old grave. This symbolic connection with the dead was believed to give strength to the living. The best metal was silver, although any metal that had been used in a coffin would do.

Corks were also thought to help, and many people wore garters made of corks to alleviate or eliminate cramps. Corks could also be placed under the mattress to help people who suffered from cramps during the night.

See *coffin, grave, ivy, ring, shoes, silver.*

Crickets: It is a sign of good luck for crickets to enter a house. It is bad luck to kill a cricket on a Sunday.

The chirping of crickets predicts changes in the weather, the arrival of friends, and changes in luck.

See *weather.*

Cross: The cross predates Christianity by many years. The Scandinavians used runic crosses to mark boundaries, and also placed them over the graves of kings and heroes. The Egyptians considered the cross a sacred symbol. Two mummified, cross-marked baked buns were discovered at Herculaneum.

Today, the cross symbolizes Christianity, but is also a source of fascination for superstitious people. It is believed to ward off evil and provide protection whenever

necessary. A physical cross is not always necessary. Crossing the legs or fingers works just as well if you suddenly need protection. Many gamblers cross their legs to provide them with luck.

Illiterate people signed their names with a cross. In effect, they were placing their protective symbol on the paper to prevent any evil happening to the document.

It is considered bad luck to place knives and forks or shoes is the form of a cross, as this is believed to be insulting God. To avert any bad luck that might come as a result of doing this, someone else has to uncross the crossed items.

Any food that is marked with a cross, such as hot cross buns, is protected from evil spirits.

See *ankh, bed, bloodstone, chair, clover, friends, gambling, hot cross buns, knife, knock on wood, magpie, mandrake, nightmares, palmistry, rowan, shoes, sparrow, tattoo, water, wood.*

Cross-eyed: Actors and actresses believe bad luck will come to any production that includes a cross-eyed person. This applies to stagehands and anyone else working in the theater.

It is dangerous for small children to deliberately cross their eyes, as they might become permanently cross-eyed.

See *actors and actresses, miners, rabbit's foot, sailors, women.*

Crossed Fingers: The usual way to cross your fingers is to place the second finger over your forefinger. This is known as St. Andrew's cross, and is done to attract luck and provide protection. There is another, lesser known, version called the Greek cross. This is made by placing the knuckle of the first finger of one hand over the first knuckle of the other hand at right angles.

You can increase your luck by crossing your fingers after making a bet. You should also cross your fingers to avert bad luck of any kind. A good example of this is if you sense someone looking at you with an evil eye.

Everybody lies from time to time. Sometimes it is necessary to avoid hurting someone else's feelings. You can prevent harm by crossing your fingers while telling a small lie.

If two people happen to say the exact same words at the same time, they should both cross their fingers and make a wish.

See *dice, evil eye.*

Crossroads: Until recently, suicides and executed criminals could not be buried in consecrated ground. This was because their actions were considered so offensive that God would not want them buried in land that had been blessed with his name. As a result of this, these unfortunate people were buried at crossroads, the traditional preserve of the devil.

Witches were also believed to gather at crossroads. This belief goes back thousands of years. In mythology, Artemis, the Greek goddess, was associated with the moon, as was Diana in Roman mythology. They were often mistaken for Hecate, goddess of the night and protector of witches and magicians, and Hades, who was associated with sorcery, witchcraft, and crossroads. Because Hecate was associated with witchcraft, she was regularly invoked in magical rites, and statues of her and Artemis were placed at crossroads. Some of these statues showed the goddess with three faces (Artemis, Demeter, Hecate), depicting the three stages (maiden, mother, crone) of the Triple Goddess. (Another possible reason Hecate appeared at crossroads was so that her three heads could look in three directions simultaneously.) Because of all this, witches and the dead gathered at crossroads. Naturally, Christians considered crossroads to be

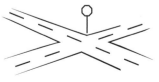

evil places, and avoided them as much as possible.

However, the original reasons for this belief were gradually forgotten, and another explanation was suggested. People felt that crossroads would confuse the soul of anyone buried there, making it impossible for the soul to find its way back to the home he or she had lived in when alive. Obviously, if it arrived back home, it would haunt the people living there. To further prevent this from occurring, many people buried at crossroads also had a stake driven through their hearts to ensure that no part of them could ever leave.

See *devil, ghost, suicide, witch.*

Crow: The crow has almost always been regarded with fear, as it usually foretells illness and death. The origin of this is told in Greek legend. Apollo, the god of prophecy, had a white crow as his companion. Apollo fell in love with a young nymph named Coronis. The crow told Apollo that she was unfaithful. In his rage, Apollo killed the nymph and turned the crow black. However, the crow still had its second sight and ability to predict the future. Consequently, it became the bearer of bad tidings. Unfortunately for the poor crow, this bad reputation still survives.

There are many superstitions concerning crows. A typical one says that when a crow starts cawing near a house, it is a sign that some disaster is about to befall the occupants. This can be averted by bowing to the crow, or taking off your hat if you are wearing one.

Crows are attracted to bright objects and steal buttons, jewelry, and other small things. This, plus their annoying habit of damaging crops and attacking smaller birds, has done nothing to help their reputation. Crows are often depicted as witches' familiars.

If you happen to see a solitary crow flying, you should quickly make a wish. If it vanishes from sight before flapping its wings, your wish will come true. However, if it flaps its wings you should turn away for ten seconds. If the crow has vanished from sight during that time, your wish will probably be granted.

An old rhyme says that seeing one crow is bad luck, but your luck will change if you see more of them:

> One crow sorrow,
> Two crows mirth.
> Three crows a wedding,
> Four crows a birth.
> Five crows silver,
> Six crows gold.
> Seven crows a secret
> Which must never be told.

See *birds, black, death, familiar, ornitho-mancy, witch.*

Cuckoo: Most superstitions concerning the cuckoo are European in origin, but they have traveled all around the world. American cuckoos, for example, are different than European cuckoos, but  the superstitions attach to them nonetheless.

The cuckoo's name is derived from its call, which people wait to hear as it portends the start of spring. If the sound comes from your right, you can expect a good year ahead. You will experience bad luck if you hear it from your left. If you want a happy year, it is also important to see a swallow before seeing a cuckoo.

What you are doing when you hear the first cuckoo of spring predicts your progress in the following twelve months. If you are doing something active, you will have a progressive and successful year. If you are lying in bed, you are likely to experience poverty and lack of progress.

See *birds, swallow.*

Curse: A curse is an oath intended to draw supernatural misfortune, destruction, or evil on a person or object. In the past a curse had enormous power. A curse could be extremely damaging, and even fatal, if the person who received the curse believed in it. Even today, most people would be disturbed if someone curses them.

In Russia, the remedy for a gypsy's curse was to throw salt at the gypsy.

See *salt.*

Cutlery: Because cutlery is made of iron, there are many superstitions attached to it.

Two teaspoons accidentally appearing in the same cup is believed to be an indication of a forthcoming marriage. Two crossed knives is a sign of an argument or disagreement, and some people consider it an omen of death. To avert this, the bottom knife has to be removed before the top one.

Unexpected visitors are indicated by accidentally dropped cutlery. A knife indicates a man, a fork a woman, and a spoon a baby.

See *death, iron, knife, marriage, omen, rust, spoon.*

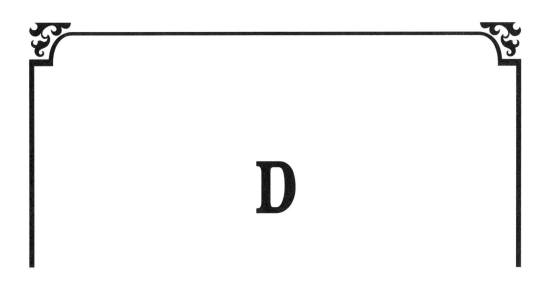

D

Daffodil: The daffodil is a popular flower that welcomes the first signs of spring each year. It is believed that the first person in the household to see a daffodil at the start of spring will receive good luck and financial rewards over the next twelve months. It is good luck to bring bunches of daffodils indoors, but a single daffodil should not be brought indoors on its own, as this brings bad luck.

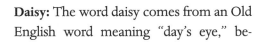

See *flower.*

Daisy: The word daisy comes from an Old English word meaning "day's eye," because the daisy closes its petals when the sun sets and does not open them again until morning. An ancient legend says that daisies sprouted from the tears of Mary Magdalene.

Young children delight in plucking off a daisy's petals one by one while chanting that the beloved "loves me" or "loves me not." Teenagers sometimes take this childish game more seriously, and have a specific person in mind when they perform it as a ritual at midday. A similar superstition involves young women on a daisy-laden lawn closing their eyes and grabbing a handful of grass. The number of daisies

found in the bunch indicates the number of months until they meet their future lovers.

See *flowers*.

Dandelion: Young girls enjoy blowing the seed heads off dandelions to see how many years it will be before they get married. The number of years is indicated by the number of blows required to completely disperse the seed heads. They can also use the process to determine how many children they will have.

Dandelions apparently close their petals when it is about to rain. An old tradition says that if you pick a dandelion, you'll wet your bed that evening.

An old New England superstition says that if you fail to dislodge all the dandelion seeds after blowing three times, it is a sign your mother wants you back home.

See *flowers, marriage*.

Days of the Week: Each day of the week has its own character, and specific superstitions connected to it. Ancient astrologers related each day to a planet, which determined its basic nature.

Different cultures have, at different times, considered different days to be either lucky or unlucky. Medieval astrologers considered Monday, Wednesday, Thursday, and Sunday lucky days. This meant Tuesday, Friday, and Saturday were unlucky.

In folk tradition, the day of the week someone is born on will determine his or her destiny:

Monday's child is fair of face,
Tuesday's child is full of grace,
Wednesday's child is full of woe,
Thursday's child has far to go,
Friday's child is loving and giving,
Saturday's child works hard for a living,
But the child that is born
on the Sabbath Day,
Is blithe and bonny, good and gay.

There are various versions of this rhyme, providing different fates for the various days. However, all of them agree that the best day to be born on is Sunday.

There are also rhymes about the workdays of the week. Here is one from Maine:

Monday for health,
Tuesday for wealth,
And Wednesday the best day of all.
Thursday for crosses,
Friday for losses,
And Saturday no luck at all.

Monday is ruled by the moon ($\math231$). Even though many people suffer from Monday morning blues, it is considered a day of peace and happiness. In Ireland, many people consider Monday to be the luckiest day of the week. However, there are three unlucky Mondays each year. The first Monday in April is considered Cain's birthday. Sodom and Gomorrah were destroyed on the second Monday in August. Judas Iscariot's birthday was on the last Monday in December. (Some people say Judas betrayed Jesus on this day.)

Tuesday is ruled by Mars ($\mars$). Mars is a warrior god, and Tuesday is the day on which you are most likely to argue and quarrel. It is considered unlucky if the first person you meet on a Tuesday is left-handed. Tuesday is considered a good day for business dealings.

Wednesday is ruled by Mercury ($\mercury$). It is a good day for any business dealings. Mercury governs communication, making this a good day for writing letters or having important conversations. It is also a good day for any medical procedures.

Thursday is ruled by Jupiter ($\jupiter$). It's a day of courage, expansion, and progressive ideas. Thursday is considered a lucky day by most people. It is a good day for a wedding. However, in the seventeenth century, some people considered Thursday unlucky, as King Henry VIII and his children Edward VI, Mary, and Elizabeth I all died on a Thursday. Thursday is also considered unlucky in Germany.

Friday is ruled by Venus ($\venus$). Friday symbolizes the passion of Christ, making it a difficult, unlucky day. However, if you dream on Friday night and tell other people about it on Saturday, your dream will eventually come true. It is considered bad luck to start a journey on a Friday. Because Adam and Eve were expelled from the Garden of Eden on a Friday, people who get married on this day will experience many ups and downs in the marriage. An old proverb says that if you laugh on Friday, you'll cry on Sunday. Children born on a Friday make natural healers, and are highly intuitive.

Saturday is ruled by Saturn ($\saturn$). It is a day of danger, restrictions, and ill health. Saturday is the Sabbath for Jews, making it a sacred day. People born on Saturday are able to see ghosts. It is unlucky to leave the hospital on a Saturday. If the new moon occurs on a Saturday, it indicates bad luck and wet weather. In Cornwall, this moon was known as "the sailor's curse."

Sunday is ruled by the sun ($\odot$). It is the Lord's Day, making it the holiest and luckiest day of all. New clothes are believed to last twice as long if worn for the first time on a Sunday. It is bad luck to cut your fingernails on a Sunday, but it's good luck to get out of bed after an illness on a Sunday. It's also a good day to start on a vacation or voyage of any sort.

Despite the above, ancient superstition says the day of the week you were born on is the luckiest day of the week for you.

See *clothes, engagement, fingernail, Friday, ghost, moon, Saturday, thunder, wedding, Wednesday.*

Death: Death is the ultimate mystery, and every culture has a variety of superstitions concerning it. Anything untoward, such as plants blooming out of season, or a cock crowing late at night, is said to predict a death in the family. Apples and pear trees producing buds out of season are particularly bad omens in this regard.

Dogs are believed to be able to see, or at least sense, death. A dog howling outside in the middle of the night is a sign of death. If the dog howls at any time while someone in the house is sick, it's a sign that the patient will die. A horse neighing during the night is another omen of death.

Ravens, crows, and owls indicate death if they fly close to the house. Julius Caesar is an example of someone who heard an owl hooting just one day before he was killed. William Shakespeare wrote:

Yesterday the bird of night did sit,
Even at noon-day, upon the market-place,

Hooting and shrieking.
(*Julius Caesar,* Act 1, scene 3)

The deathwatch beetle gained its name because people though it indicated a death when it scratched wood. In actuality, the scratching sound is how it communicates with other deathwatch beetles.

People turn to superstition while waiting for death, also. Often doors, windows, drawers, and cupboards are opened to enable the soul to leave the house as easily as possible. Mirrors are turned to face the wall, as they might confuse the soul. Knots in the house are untied, too. It is bad luck to stand at the foot of the dying person's bed, as this could hinder the soul's departure.

Church bells used to be rung after someone died. This was done for two reasons. It symbolized good Christian people praying for the soul of the deceased, and also drove away any evil spirits who might have been attracted to the dying person.

The dead person's eyes had to be closed. It was believed that if they stayed open, they were looking for someone else to accompany them on their last journey. Coins used to be placed over the eyes of dead people to enable them to pay the ferryman who transported them across the river of death.

Often, a vigil was kept over the dead person until the funeral. This was to en-

sure that he or she was never alone, and to prevent any evil spirits from interfering with the body. It was lucky for the survivors if the corpse was laid in the coffin with his or her feet pointing towards the rising sun. Sometimes candles were lit, so the soul would not be frightened by the dark. Gradually, the watch turned into a celebration, and many places still conduct a wake for the deceased.

The south side of the graveyard was considered the holiest place to be buried. The evil north side was reserved for murderers, suicides, and people who had not been baptized.

The custom of not speaking ill of the dead has been practiced since Roman times. Many people believe this is because the dead can no longer stand up for themselves. In fact, it began as a fear that the ghost of the dead person might return.

See *apple; bed; beetle; bell, book, and candle; blackbird; candle; clothes; cock; coffin; coin; corpse; crow; cutlery; dog; door; dove; eagle; eggs; eye; fate; feather; funeral; ghost; graveyard; green; Halloween; horse; key; knot; mirror; noises; opal; owl; parsley; peacock; rat; raven; robin; sewing; shoelaces; shoes; storm; suicide; teeth; thirteen; trees; violet; vulture; yellow; yew; zombie.*

December: It is considered a sign of snow if squirrels are seen searching for nuts in December.

If the breastbone of the Thanksgiving goose contains many spots, it is a sign of a severe winter. However, winter will be mild if only a few spots can be seen.

If it rains before Mass on the first Sunday in December, it will continue raining for a week.

See *rain, squirrel, weather.*

Devil: People have always been aware of evil and bad luck. Obviously, misfortune could not come from a benevolent god, so people personified evil in the form of the devil. He is sometimes known as Asmodeus, Belial, Lucifer, Satan, Beelzebub, or the Prince of Darkness, but many people preferred not to say his name out loud and called him "Old Nick" instead. Nick was a popular man's name in the seventeenth century when this custom began. At that time, old people were respected and highly regarded, so calling the devil Old Nick made him think you were being friendly and affectionate to him. Hopefully, as a result of this, he would not harm you. "Old Harry" was sometimes said as an alternative to Old Nick.

The devil was able to manifest himself in different forms, such as a cat, dog, monkey, or cloven-footed goat. In the Christian tradition, the devil was originally an angel named Lucifer. He was good and perfect, but fell from grace and was cast out of heaven. He now spends all his time trying to spread corruption around the world. Life itself becomes a battle between good and evil.

"Satan" is a Hebrew word. Satan describes someone who objects, argues, or is cynical about something that is occurring. In the Hebrew Bible, Satan is a person, rather than a fallen angel or force for evil (see Job 1:6–12). However, Zoroaster, founder of Zoroastrianism, taught that forces of good and evil ruled the world. As this became accepted by other religions, Satan became more and more associated with evil and the powers of darkness. He became the embodiment of evil in Christianity, and millions of people around the world accepted this as part of their faith.

Satan was believed to identify all of his followers with a secret mark, such as a birthmark, mole, wart, or skin blemish. This would be located on a secret or private part of the person, such as in the armpit or concealed under pubic hair. Consequently, when someone was believed to be a witch, the entire body would be shaved to see if he or she possessed the devil's mark. As almost everyone has a skin blemish somewhere, the witch-hunters found witches everywhere. In the few cases where the suspected person had no blemishes, a bodkin was used to prick the person on different parts of his or her body. If the victim did not bleed, or did not appear to suffer pain, he or she was deemed guilty.

A New England superstition says you can see the devil if you recite the Lord's Prayer backwards.

Although belief in the devil has declined enormously over the last three hundred years, he still plays a leading role in fundamentalist Christianity.

See *blackberries, cat, chimney, crossroads, dog, fingernail, goat, horseshoe, iron, jaybird, jet, knife, ladder, mole, owl, prayer, salt, shadow, ships, shoes, spitting, storm, two-dollar bill, unicorn, wart, witch.*

Diamond: Diamond is the hardest substance known to man. Not surprisingly, it is called the "king of gems." Until the eighteenth century, when diamonds were discovered in Brazil, India was the only known source. The Indians regarded it as an amulet that would protect them from almost everything, including serpents and evil spirits. The Romans considered the diamond to be invincible, and to have power over all illnesses.

Marco Polo wrote in *The Book of Marvels* that the diamond averted all dangers and prevented bad luck from occurring. In the Middle Ages, men wore diamonds as a symbol of courage and virility. According to St. Louis (1214–1270), the Virgin Mary was the only woman worthy of wearing a diamond. Almost two hundred years later, Agnes Sorel, Mistress of Charles VI of France (1368–1422), became the first woman to wear diamonds.

However, diamonds have not always been lucky for people who owned them. The 44.5 carat, dark blue Hope Diamond is the perfect example, as it is linked to a dozen violent deaths, including suicide, murder, drowning, and decapitation. It is also linked to the financial ruin of two royal families. New York gem merchant Harry Winston presented the Hope Diamond to the Smithsonian Institution in 1957. The curse that some people feel is attached to this stone has not yet had any adverse effect on the Smithsonian.

Diamonds were also considered healing gems, and people rented and borrowed them to try to cure themselves of their afflictions.

Diamonds are popular in engagement rings, as they are believed to increase the love between two people. Diamonds are also believed to increase one's faith, concentration, and stamina. They protect peo-

ple against cowardice and insanity, and provide magical protection in battle.

See *Aries, drowning, engagement, gemstones, murder, ring, suicide, wedding anniversaries.*

Dice: Ivory, metal, wood, and glass dice have been found in excavations in Egypt, Greece, and Rome, which shows how long they have been used by mankind. According to Robert Graves, the Roman emperor Claudius decided to invade Britain because a roll of the dice told him it would be successful.

Dice are still cast in Tibet to help interpret oracles. A recent example occurred in 1995, when dice were cast to determine which one of twenty boys was the reincarnation of the Panchen Lama.

It's considered good luck to carry dice in your pocket. If you happen to find a die somewhere, take note of the number of spots on the side facing up. One spot means you'll shortly receive important news, probably in the form of a letter. Two spots indicate enjoyable travel in the near future. Three spots indicate a pleasant surprise. Four spots indicate bad luck;

be alert for problems in the near future. Five spots show that your partner will be untrue. Six spots are extremely fortunate, and indicate unexpected money.

Dice should not be cast on a Monday, a Wednesday, or during stormy weather.

Dice players regularly blow or spit on the dice to attract good luck. Many talk to them as well. Some gamblers like to rub the dice on a friend before tossing them. It is common for dice players to cross the fingers of one hand while shooting dice with the other.

If you snap your fingers, you can prevent tossing a pair of ones, known as "snake eyes." This is the lowest possible number on the dice.

Chanting "come seven, come eleven" will help you win at dice.

See *crossed fingers, gambling.*

Dimple: A dimple is a small dent or hollow in the skin of the cheek or chin. An old folk belief says people with a dimple cannot commit murder.

See *murder.*

Disappearing Pattern: A disappearing pattern is used to cure certain ailments by making them disappear one letter at a time. The most common example of this is the word "abracadabra." The first line contains the entire word. The second line shows the words with the first, last, or sometimes both letters removed. This pattern is repeated line after line until only the last one or two letters remain. The ailment is believed to vanish in the same way the word does.

See *abracadabra.*

Divination: Divination is the art of predicting the future. Since caveman times, people have wanted to see into the future. The concept that fate is predetermined by forces we cannot control is an extremely old one, and many people still believe it. Of course, everybody possesses free will, and makes many choices each and every day. Because of this, divination cannot tell exactly what is going to happen. However, it can disclose a variety of possibilities that may not otherwise have been considered.

Some people, generally known as "psychics," seem to be better attuned to the omens, signs, and symbols around them. They listen to their hunches and feelings and are able to interpret them without judgment or prejudice. Naturally, they are not always right. They can only predict the outcome if the person continues life in the same way he or she has in the past. Any significant changes the person makes will obviously affect his or her future.

Divination can be performed in a variety of ways. Examining part of the client's body, such as the face, palms, or feet, is one preferred method. The person's birth details are used in both astrology and numerology. The person's handwriting can also be interpreted. Reading random objects, such as tea leaves, rune stones, and Tarot cards, is another popular method. All of these methods use a system. The other method of predicting the future is to somehow communicate with an external agency, such as ghosts or spirits. Gazing into a crystal ball, mirror, or flames from a candle or fire is called scrying.

See *amethyst; astrology; cards, playing; fire; ghost; moles; numerology; oneiromancy; ornithomancy; palmistry; scrying; well.*

Dog: Dogs have been considered "man's best friend" for thousands of years. An old superstition says that when dogs howl near a door it is a sign of a major calamity, possibly even a death. It is a sure sign of death if a dog howls at the moon. If a dog whines  when a baby is being born, the child will ultimately become a criminal. People believed that dogs possessed special supernatural powers that enabled them to see,

or at least sense, ghosts. This enabled them to know when the household was in danger. Dogs are also credited with being able to sense people's characters instantly, and will growl and back away from anyone they don't trust.

It is good luck to be followed by a yellow or golden colored dog. It is also good luck for a strange dog to follow you home.

Seven years bad luck is promised to anyone who deliberately kills a dog. The only exception to this is a veterinarian who is putting the dog down to prevent the animal from further suffering.

See *death, devil, door, familiar, gambling, ghost, hair, ladder, lightning, marriage, moon, wedding, white, wine.*

Door: The door is the main entrance to the home, providing access for people, luck, and evil spirits. Not surprisingly, superstition demands that this entrance be well protected. Hanging a horseshoe above the door provides good luck and protection. Ornaments, such as statues, are sometimes used also. A cross might be placed on the door to repel witches. The front and back doors should not be open at the same time, as this allows evil spirits easy entrance and exit.

A new bride should not walk into her new home. It is her husband's duty to carry her over the threshold. For the maximum amount of good luck, it is important that he carries her through the front door rather than through another entrance.

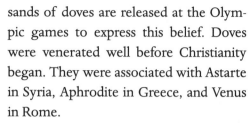

Visitors should enter the house with their right foot first. If their first step into the house is with the left foot, they can bring bad luck inside. Visitors to the house must leave by the same door they entered. If they leave by another door they will take all the occupants' good luck away with them.

A door that opens by itself is a sign that someone is about to visit. This is not likely to be a friend. A door that slams is bad luck, as it risks harming the spirit of the house. Someone who slams a door deliberately will experience bad luck for the rest of the day.

Doors and windows should be kept open when a child is born, or when someone is dying. This enables the souls to move freely.

See *bride, cross, death, dog, horseshoe, witch.*

Dove: Because they are closely associated with the Holy Ghost in Christianity, doves, especially white doves, have become a popular symbol of purity, devotion, and the Holy Spirit. Every four years, thou-

sands of doves are released at the Olympic games to express this belief. Doves were venerated well before Christianity began. They were associated with Astarte in Syria, Aphrodite in Greece, and Venus in Rome.

An ancient legend says that the devil can change himself into many different forms, but cannot transform himself into either a dove or a lamb.

Another superstition says that no one can die while lying on a mattress stuffed with dove feathers. This is because doves symbolize the Holy Spirit, and death is unable to visit anyplace where the Holy Spirit abides.

Doves are closely associated with love and romance, and it is considered good luck for lovers to see a dove in the air.

See *death, devil, lamb, miners, ornithomancy, St. Valentine's Day, turtledove.*

Dragonfly: Dragonflies were believed to be able to sew up people's ears, eyes, lips, and noses. In Iowa, people believed dragonflies could also sew up any exposed appendages, such as fingers and toes.

Dreams: People have always been fascinated with their dreams, and believed they provided a direct link with the supernatural. Thousands of years before psychoanalysts became interested, people were studying and evaluating their dreams to determine their significance and meaning. Naturally, a large number of superstitions developed about dreams and dreaming.

One popular belief was that dreaming the same dream for three nights in a row meant it would eventually come true.

Many books have been written on dream interpretation, but it is usually better to evaluate your own dreams. This is because interpretations in dream books often contradict each other. For instance, dreaming of a white horse can indicate future wealth or a death, depending on which book you consult.

It is good luck to wake up knowing you have been dreaming, but unable to remember what it was. If you remember your dreams, you should not tell them to anyone else until after breakfast.

See *bay, jade, leaf, moon, nightmare, oneiromancy, onion, St. John's wort, sleepwalking, teeth, walnut.*

Dressing: It is believed to be good luck to put your right arm into an item of clothing before your left. However, you should put on your left sock before putting on your right.

It is bad luck to replace a button, or make any other repair to your clothing, while wearing it.

If you accidentally do up your buttons the wrong way, you need to undo them and take off the item of clothing to avert bad luck. Wait a few seconds, and then put the item of clothing back on again.

It is good luck to accidentally put on a garment inside out. It is better to leave it this way all day, if possible, to preserve the luck.

See *button.*

Drowning: The best-known superstition about drowning is the widely held belief that someone who is drowning surfaces twice before going down for the third and final time. The body of a drowned person is believed to float to the surface on the seventh, eighth, or ninth day. The exact number of days varies from place to place. It is said that drowned men float face upward, but drowned women float face downward.

An old weather superstition says that a drowned person's voice can be heard shortly before a storm.

A Native American superstition says that a rooster can find the body of someone who has drowned. If you take a rooster out in a boat, he will crow when you are directly above the body.

See *caul, diamond, petrified wood, pig, sailors, storm, sweater, weather.*

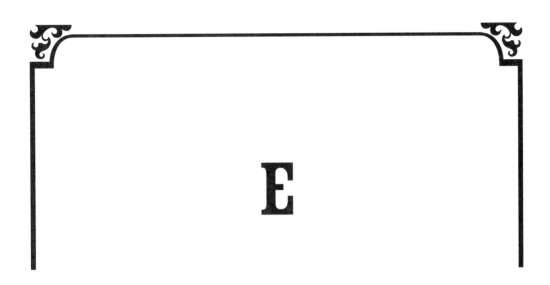

E

Eagle: The eagle has always been associated with strength, courage, and immortality. In mythology it frequently represents the sun. The Romans used an eagle on their military standards. They also released an eagle from the funeral pyre of their emperors to symbolize his soul soaring up to join the gods.

It is bad luck to see an eagle hovering over a particular spot for any length of time. This is a sign that someone is about to die. Some people consider an eagle's cry to be a sign of death, too.

In the past, eagles were killed for their body parts. The heart could be used to make an aphrodi-siac, the gallbladder could be mixed with honey for problems with the eyes, and the marrow could be used as a contraceptive. Eating the brain of a freshly killed eagle was supposed to produce hallucinogenic dreams.

See *aphrodisiac, death, eye, mascot, right side, sun.*

Earache: One old remedy for earache was to blow tobacco smoke into the sufferer's ear. If your ears tingle, rather than ache, it is a sign that someone is talking about you.

Ears: If your ears tingle or itch, it is a sign that someone is talking about you. Hopefully your right ear will tingle or itch, as this means the person is saying good things about you. If your left ear is tingling, the person is saying harmful things about you. Fortunately, you can stop the person from saying bad things by biting your tongue or by tying a knot in your handkerchief. This will cause the person to immediately bite his or her own tongue.

In ancient Rome, people with large ears and fleshy earlobes were considered generous and easy to get along with. People with small ears and pale earlobes were considered mean and dangerous. Julius Caesar refused to deal with people who had small ears.

Ringing ears is thought to be a sign of the imminent death of a close friend or family member.

Pierced ears are popular nowadays for both sexes. A popular, but untrue, superstition says that piercing the ears will improve the person's vision.

See *handkerchief, itching, ring, shell, tinnitus, tongue, wine.*

Earth: People used to consider the earth magical, as it nurtured and sustained the crops and trees. People sometimes buried themselves in the earth temporarily in the hope of being cured of their ills.

An old English superstition says that a single woman can learn the occupation of her future husband by digging a hole in the earth at noon on Midsummer's Day. She has to put her ear to the hole and listen carefully to what it has to say.

Earth is one of the four elements of Western philosophy. The others are air, fire, and water. The three signs of the zodiac that symbolize the earth element are Taurus, Virgo, and Capricorn. Earth is considering nurturing, fertile, feminine, and practical, as it nurtures material affairs also. In Wicca, the earth elemental helps energize spells to bring them into fruition.

See *air, Capricorn, elemental, elements, fire, Taurus, tree, Virgo, water, weeds, Wicca, zodiac.*

Easter: Easter is the most important event in the Christian calendar. It celebrates the resurrection of Jesus Christ on the third day after his crucifixion. Because of this religious significance, the customs involving decorated eggs, hot cross buns, rabbits, and new clothes may seem out of place. In fact, each one has a lengthy history, some even predating Christianity.

Easter is celebrated on the first Sunday after the first full moon on or after the spring equinox. Consequently, Easter can fall anywhere between March 22 and April 25. This date was set by Emperor Constantine at the Council of Nicea in 325 CE.

No one knows the origin of the name "Easter," although the Venerable Bede (c.673–735 CE), the English theologian and historian, thought it was named after a pre-Christian Germanic goddess of springtime called Eostre or Eastre. Her name relates to the east. Eastre's symbol was the hare, and her festival was held at the time of Easter.

People believed that the sun danced on Easter Day. Sir John Suckling refers to this in his poem "Ballad Upon a Wedding" (1646):

> But oh, she dances such a way,
> No sun upon an Easter day
> Is half so fine a sight.

The concept of eggs symbolizing fertility and renewal of life is an ancient one, as is the custom of painting eggs and eating them at the spring festival. In Christianity, the egg came to symbolize the Resurrection.

You will have good luck for an entire year if you wear three new items on Easter Sunday. Easter parades celebrate this tradition. Incidentally, it is bad luck to refuse the gift of an Easter egg. You also risk losing the friendship of the person who offered it to you.

An old tradition says that if it rains on Easter Sunday, it will also rain on the next seven Sundays.

See *clothes, east, eggs, food, hare, hot cross buns, rabbit, sun.*

Eating: It is bad luck to accidentally miss your mouth and drop the food while eating. This superstition applies no matter what implement you happen to be using.

If you're single, you'll remain that way unless you eat the last mouthful of food on your plate.

You can prevent indigestion by cutting up onions and placing the pieces in a bowl of water.

See *food, onions.*

Eclipse: For thousands of years, any unusual or abnormal changes in the heavens were looked at with suspicion and sometimes dread. An eclipse, which is the obscuring of the light from one celestial body by the presence of another, is a good example.

Superstition says that you need to be cautious and take extra care for three days before and after any eclipse has taken place. An eclipse of the sun delays progress for a seven-day period. An eclipse of the moon is a sign of bad luck, making it a bad time for investments and important decisions.

See *moon, sun*.

Eggs: Most ancient civilizations believed that the egg symbolized the universe. A charming Greek myth tells how the world was created. Apparently, night was seduced by the wind and laid the primordial egg. The egg hatched, giving birth to Eros, the god of love. The two halves of the egg's shell became heaven and earth. As well as providing an explanation for the world, this myth also demonstrates that love is required for heaven and earth to exist.

The ancient Japanese believed that the world was created from a cock's egg. The Indians also believed the world was created from a golden egg that contained the essence of the gods Brahma, Vishnu, and Shiva. The Hawaiians believed the

island of Hawaii was hatched from a large egg laid by an enormous bird.

Double-yolked eggs are believed to be a sign of good luck. (However, in some parts of Britain, a double-yolked egg is a warning of a death.) Approximately one egg in every thousand is double-yolked. These are produced by hens who have just started laying eggs (as their reproductive cycle is still working out how to perform the task correctly), or by hens who ovulate too quickly. It is a sign of good luck to eat a double-yolked egg at Easter.

People frequently crush the shell after eating a boiled egg. Alternatively, they might push their spoon through the bottom. This is done to avoid bad luck, and derives from the old belief that witches collected egg shells to create spells to harm sailors. Some people believed witches rode on eggshells.

Dreaming of an egg indicates the creation or birth of something new in your life.

See *cake, cooking, death, Easter, food, robin, sailors, ships, swan, warts, wishbone, witch*.

Eight: There tend to be fewer associations with the number eight than with other numbers. Eight symbolizes man's resurrection. After the six days of creation and the seventh day of rest, the eighth day promises a new and better life in the world to come. Eight also symbolizes survival, as, according to the Bible, eight people were saved in Noah's Ark (Genesis 7:7).

Eight is sometimes considered a negative number. "Behind the eight ball" reflects this belief, as it indicates an uncomfortable, difficult situation. In a game of pool, fourteen of the fifteen balls are divided between the two players. One player has to pocket the balls numbered one through seven, and the other player pockets nine through fifteen. The eight ball has to be pocketed last. However, the eight ball has a habit of getting in the way of the other balls. A player loses the game if he or she accidentally pockets the eight ball before the other balls are played.

See *numbers*.

Elbow: An old superstition says that if you kiss your elbow, you'll immediately change sex.

An itching elbow means that you will soon be sleeping with someone other than your current partner.

It is always painful to hit or bump your "funny bone." This is thought to be a warning that bad luck is on its way. The remedy, painful though it may be, is to immediately bump your other funny bone.

See *itching*.

Elemental: Elementals are nature spirits who represent the four elements of fire, earth, air, and water. They play an important part in many magic traditions. In Wicca they are called "Lords of the Watchtower." Witches create magic circles that are divided into four quarters, representing the four elements. During ritual work, elementals are summoned to the relevant quadrants to help activate the spell and charge it with their particular qualities.

See *magic, spell*.

Elements: The four elements of ancient philosophy are fire, earth, air, and water. The entire universe is symbolically made up of these four elements. The first person to write about them was Empedocles of Acragas (fl. fifth century BCE), and the concept was firmly supported and promoted by Plato (c.428–347 BCE) and Aristotle (384–322 BCE). Aristotle described fire as a mixture of warm and dry qualities, earth was cold and dry, air was warm and moist, and water was cold and moist.

A large number of associations have been attached to each element. Fire, for instance, is active, spiritual, and creative, earth is solid, physical, and material, air is mental, intellectual, and mediating, and water is receptive, responsive, and emotional.

See *air, earth, fire, water.*

Elephant: The elephant has always symbolized wisdom, strength, and longevity. Consequently, small figures of elephants are popular as lucky charms. Larger depictions of elephants are sometimes placed at the entrances of houses to provide protection for the household. All elephant ornaments inside the house should face the front door to attract luck into the home.

A common superstition is that elephants go to an "elephants' graveyard" to die. In fact, elephants die wherever they happen to be, but because their remains are seldom seen, the belief began that they had a special place they went to, to die.

A hair from an elephant's tail is believed to be lucky, and it is possible to buy rings made from elephant hairs. An old story, dating back some three thousand years, tells of a maharajah who gave an elephant's hair charm to a worthy peasant. The charm worked all too well, as twelve months later the peasant returned at the head of an army and ousted his former ruler.

See *charms, ring.*

Elevator: It is a sign of delays in your career if you become stuck in an elevator. If someone releases you from this predicament by raising the elevator a floor or two, the delays will be temporary. However, if the elevator has to be lowered to the ground floor before you are let out, you will experience delays and frustrations for the rest of your career.

It is a good omen for retired people to be stuck in an elevator. This means they will live to a ripe old age.

Elm: An interesting agricultural superstition from the west of England relates the size of an elm tree's leaves to the success of the harvest. If seeds are planted when the elm leaves are the size of a mouse's ear, an abundant crop of barley will re-sult. A good crop of kidney beans will occur if they are planted when the elm leaves are as big as an English shilling, but no larger than an English penny.

See *beans*.

Emerald: Emerald is a bright green form of beryl. The green symbolizes new life and the promise of spring, which is why it was ultimately chosen as the birthstone for May. People have cherished emeralds for some eight thousand years, and there are records of the stone being sold in Babylonian markets as far back as 4000 BCE.

The ancient Egyptians used the emerald as a symbol of love and fertility. A wife who wore an emerald would remain chaste while her husband was away. However, the emerald would also increase passion when the couple was reunited.

Aristotle wrote that emeralds increased people's self-esteem, produced victories in litigation, increased eloquence, and soothed tired eyes. He also believed that an emerald ring, hung on a string around the neck to create a necklace, would prevent epilepsy.

In medieval times, magicians and alchemists wore emeralds for protection while performing their magic. Emeralds were also believed to help them see into the future.

Emeralds are still used today to protect people from ill health and danger while travelling. The emerald also enhances love, the imagination, memory, and prosperity.

See *gemstones, wedding anniversaries*.

Engagement: An engagement, or the announcement of plans to marry, is more fraught with superstition than one might expect. Certain stones in the engagement ring, for instance, are luckier than others. Diamonds, emeralds, rubies, and sapphires are believed to be the luckiest. Pearls are extremely unlucky in an engagement ring, as they symbolize tears. Opal is another unlucky choice, though it becomes lucky if the wearer was born in October.

It is considered bad luck if the ring does not fit and has to be adjusted in size. Unluckiest of all is if the engagement ring is lost or damaged before the wedding. Friends of the future bride can place the engagement ring on the tip of a finger and make a wish, which will always be granted. However, it is extremely bad luck if they put the ring fully onto their own ring finger.

It is no longer necessary for the man to drop on one knee to propose. However, he should not propose to his girlfriend in a public place or while traveling on public transportation.

Consideration should be given to the day of the week on which the proposal is made. The couple will lead eventful lives if the man proposes on a Monday. They will lead harmonious lives together if he proposes on a Tuesday. They will never quarrel if the proposal is made on a Wednesday. They will both achieve their goals if he proposes on a Thursday. They will need to work hard to achieve success if he proposes on a Friday. They will enjoy a mutually compatible, pleasurable life together if he proposes on a Saturday. A proposal should not be made on a Sunday, as that is the Lord's Day.

See *days of the week, diamond, opal, pearl, ring, spooning, wedding.*

Evil Eye: The evil eye is an extremely old belief that people can cause bad luck, illness, or death simply by looking at someone with resentment, malice, or envy. The concept of the evil eye is known all around the world. There are five thousand year old Sumerian and Babylonian cuneiform tab-

lets in existence that describe the damage the evil eye can do. The Sumerian god Ea waged a constant battle against the evil eye. The ancient Egyptians used the Eye of Horus as an amulet to protect themselves from the evil eye. Egyptian women also used eye shadow made from lapis lazuli, and painted their lips, to prevent the evil eye from entering their eyes and mouths. The ancient Hebrews used the Star of David as protection from it. The Hebrew Talmud says, "For every one that dies of natural causes, ninety-nine will die of the evil eye." In Greek mythology, the sorcerer Medusa destroyed the giant Talos with a malicious stare. The Romans legislated against the evil eye and punished people who deliber-

ately used it. Even today, many people in southern Italy carry horn amulets to protect themselves from the evil eye.

Christians used a cross to ward off the evil eye. This was usually a cross amulet, but making the sign of the cross while praying worked just as well. The evil eye is mentioned a number of times in the Bible. In Deuteronomy 15:9 we find,

> Beware that there be not a thought
> in thy wicked heart, saying, The

seventh year, the year of release, is at hand; and thine eye be evil against thy poor brother, and thou givest him nought; and he cry unto the Lord against thee, and it be sin unto thee.

And this, from Proverbs 23:6: "Eat thou not the bread of him that hath an evil eye, neither desire thou his dainty meats."

Jesus mentioned the evil eye on at least two occasions. In Mark 7:22 we read, "Thefts, covetousness, wickedness, deceit, lasciviousness, an evil eye, blasphemy, pride, foolishness: All these evil things come from within, and defile the man." In the Sermon on the Mount (Matthew 6:22–23), Jesus said, "The light of the body is the eye: if therefore thine eye be single, thy whole body shall be full of light. But if thine eye be evil, thy whole body shall be full of darkness."

Eight verses are devoted to the evil eye in the Koran, and these provide advice on how to protect yourself and others from its negative effects.

Most of the time, the evil eye is given unconsciously. You can accidentally put the evil eye on someone if you gaze at him or her for too long, especially if you are gazing with admiration or envy. You can also do it deliberately, by staring at someone while thinking negative thoughts about the person. This is sometimes known as

"putting the evils" on someone.

People have always had a fearful fascination with eyes. The iris was a mystery to primitive people. Different people had different colored irises, and they grew and contracted in size. It was also possible to see your reflection in someone else's eyes. The word "pupil" comes from the Latin word *pupilla*, which means "small doll." Eyes are extremely expressive, and a baleful, hate-filled, cold, or jealous stare can be extremely intimidating.

The evil eye can also be passed on, accidentally, by praise. Small children were considered especially vulnerable, and it was not uncommon for children to become ill after someone made a favorable comment about them. In some cultures, the person giving the compliment would then spit three times to eliminate any possibility of passing on the evil eye. In Italy, another way of averting the evil eye was to say *Benedica* or *Dio Benedica*, which means "God bless you," after making the compliment.

Even food can be affected by the evil eye. If a hungry visitor to your home glances at your food, he or she could accidentally poison it. Consequently, it is essential not to eat in front of someone else without offering him or her some food.

It is even possible to give yourself the evil eye. If you feel proud of something you have achieved and then feel suddenly exhausted, the chances are you've put the evil eye on yourself. In Azerbaijan they have a saying, *Ozumun ozume gozum deydi*, which means "I brought the evil eye on myself."[24]

People with slightly unusual eyes suffered enormously from accusations that they possessed the evil eye. Life was difficult for someone who happened to be cross-eyed or had a squint, but even people with inflamed or reddened eyes were suspect. In some cultures, people who were different in any way were accused of having the evil eye. Someone who was born with a clubfoot, for instance, would immediately be looked at with suspicion, as would someone who came from a different race.

There are many ways to avert the evil eye. In Syria, Palestine, and Turkey, women wear blue beads. Eye bead ornaments are also popular. In Italy, making the "devil's horns" is a popular method for averting

the evil eye. This gesture is created by holding the two center fingers down on your palm with your thumb. This leaves the index and little fingers raised to create the horns. There is no need to raise the horns. You can make this gesture with your hands

under a table, or in a pocket, if desired. This gesture also averts impotency in men, one of the most feared effects of the evil eye.

Another method that uses the hands is called the "fig," "figga," or "fico" in various cultures. You make this by turning your hand into a fist and placing your thumb between the first and second fingers. The fig symbolizes the male and female genitals, which gives it considerable potency and power. Pointing the fig at the person you suspect of giving you the evil eye will avert the danger.

The Jewish people use their entire bodies to avert the evil eye. The thumb of the right hand touches the palm of the left hand, while the left hand thumb touches the right palm. The fingers are then closed around this arrangement to create a circle of protection using the chest, arms and interlocked hands.

Benito Mussolini (1883–1945), dictator of Italy, had a strong fear of the evil eye and would move seats rather than sit next to someone he thought possessed it. On one occasion, he even changed planes to avoid spending time with someone who had the evil eye.

At least two popes possessed evil eyes. Pope Pius IX (1792–1878) was believed to inadvertently cast misfortune on anyone he looked at. It was even suggested that receiving a blessing from him was almost the same as receiving a death sentence.

His successor, Pope Leo XIII (1810–1903), was also thought to have the evil eye, and this was believed to be the reason why so many cardinals died while he led the Catholic Church.

King Alphonso XII of Spain was believed to possess the evil eye also. His visit to Italy in 1923 caused a series of disasters, including the death of several sailors while he was reviewing the Italian fleet. The final straw occurred when a dam collapsed shortly after the royal train had passed by. After that, Italians rattled their keys at all of his public appearance to avert the evil eye.

A number of things we take for granted today began as protection against the evil eye. Eye shadow is a good example. Originally, it had nothing to do with beauty, but was worn to protect the wearer from the evil eye. Nowadays we dress small girls in pink and boys in blue. Boys were dressed in blue because it averted the evil eye. In the East, small children and livestock wore blue beads. When the cord eventually broke, the child was considered old enough to withstand any future attacks of the evil eye.

Garlic cloves were another form of protection. They could be carried in a pocket or hung in the car, home, and workplace.

The eyes of dead people should be closed before they "see" another person, whom they can take with them.

See *amber, amulet, blue, cross, crossed fingers, fig, garlic, horn, key, lapis lazuli, nightmares, sage, topaz, urine, willow.*

Examinations: People frequently worry about upcoming examinations and other tests. A superstition I wouldn't want to totally rely on says that if you sleep with your books under the pillow on the night before the examination, you will pass the exam.

Exorcism: An exorcism is performed to expel evil spirits. It uses prayers and holy names to appeal to a supernatural power. Exorcisms are also sometimes practiced as a form of charm to cure different health problems, such as worms. The Church was opposed to these, as they invoke the Father, Son, and Holy Ghost just to effect a cure. Exorcisms were also performed to eliminate rats, flies, and other animals.

Robert Herrick (1591–1674) captured the spirit of an exorcism in his poem "The Spell":

Holy water come and bring;
Cast in salt, for seasoning:

Set the brush for sprinkling:
Sacred spittle bring ye hither;
Meal and it now mix together,
   And a little oil to either.
Give the tapers here their light;
Ring the saints' bell, to affright
Far from hence the evil sprite.[25]

See *charms, rat.*

Eye: An itching eye can give some indication of future trends. An itching right eye is a sign of good luck. An itching left eye means bad luck is on its way.

Cross-eyed people have suffered a great deal throughout history. Even today, some people believe that it is good luck to pass a cross-eyed person in the street only if that person is the opposite sex from them. If the cross-eyed person is the same sex, it is bad luck. The remedy is to spit as the person walks past, to avert any danger.

Eye problems can often be cured by rubbing the affected eye nine times with a gold wedding ring.

Boats, especially in the Mediterranean, are frequently adorned with eye symbols to provide protection for the boat and crew.

See *death, evil eye, illness, itching, lizard, meat, menstruation, moon, pumpkin, rain, sapphire, ships, swallow, topaz, wedding ring.*

Eyebrow: Almost everyone knows they shouldn't trust someone whose eyebrows are joined together. However, not many people know the meanings of other eyebrow variations. Someone with bushy eyebrows is supposed to be obstinate, bossy, and argumentative. Someone with thin, almost nonexistent eyebrows is believed to be indecisive,  sensitive, and weak. Someone with long, thick eyebrows is believed to be passionate, enthusiastic, and energetic. People with eyebrows that are widely separated from each other are believed to be good listeners. Someone with arched eyebrows is believed to be decisive and assertive.

See *werewolf.*

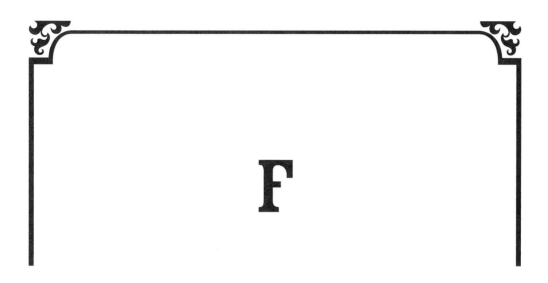

F

Fairy: Today, fairies belong largely to children's stories. However, these little people—elves, goblins, gnomes, and pixies—were traditionally the cause of many misfortunes, such as cows becoming dry of milk or someone breaking an arm or leg. They also stole babies from their cradles, substituting them with changelings.

So great was the fear of fairies that in the seventeenth century they were called "the good neighbors" or "good people," because no one wanted to mention them by name. Many people also crossed themselves and said "God save us" whenever the subject of fairies was raised. Even today, some people think it is unlucky to speak of fairies.

However, fairies were believed to perform good deeds as well as bad. Consequently, it made sense to thank them for any good fortune that came your way. The concept of knocking on wood is related to this. People believed that talking too much about their good fortune might attract the attention of evil spirits who would try to take it away. Consequently, they knocked on wood to ward off any evil effects their remarks might have caused. In Druidic times, people believed gods lived in trees. People would knock on the tree and ask for help. Once the request had been granted, they would knock again

and thank the gods. Gradually, the gods became woodland fairies. Knocking three times scared away any evil spirits who might be lurking nearby.

Fairies usually live in small communities, though some, such as leprechauns, choose to live alone. Fairies dance at midnight, and the fairy rings they danced in were frequently found in the grass. People avoided these rings when possible, and dire stories were told of people who accidentally slept in the fairy rings. People reversed their hats while walking past fairy rings. This was to confuse any fairies that might try to coax the person into dancing.

Many people still believe in fairies. When I lived in Cornwall, my landlady told me that fairies were the ghosts of ancient Druids. Most modern day believers in fairies consider them to be nature spirits who look after flowers and plants.

The term "away with the fairies" came about as a way of describing someone who was temporarily in another world.

In magic, fairies are the soul beings of the air element. Gnomes are earth beings, sylphs are air beings, undines are water beings, and salamanders are fire beings.

See *air, changeling, earth, element, fairy ring, fire, flowers, goblin, green, housewarming, knock on wood, pixies, pregnancy, teeth, tree, wand, water.*

Fairy Ring: A fairy ring is a circle of mushrooms or grass. People believed these were magical places where fairies had danced and socialized with each other. It was said that if you ran clockwise around the circle nine times, you would be able to see the fairies inside the ring. If you sat in the middle of the circle on the night of the full moon and made a wish, it would come true. However, you must not dance with the fairies, as they would enchant you.

Fairy rings are actually caused by a fungus. Fairy ring fungi live on dead organic matter, and the rings expand outward until the food supply is used up or the soil becomes too damp. Fairy rings vary in size, from a few inches to more than fifty feet in diameter. A seven-hundred-year-old fairy ring in France is said to be almost half a mile in diameter.

See *fairy, moon, wish.*

Familiar: Familiars are animal spirits that help and protect witches. They usually appear as cats, crows, dogs, goats, hares, owls, ravens, snakes, or frogs.

The Christian Church denounced familiars as demons and agents of the devil. In the witchcraft trials, virtually any animal could be suspected of being a familiar, even a fly buzzing at a window. The Bible says, "Regard not them that have familiar spirits, neither seek after wizards, to be defiled by them" (Leviticus 19:31). Unfortunately, this belief led to the death of many people who possessed a deep love for their animals but may have had difficulties in establishing close relationships with people. A lone woman with a black cat, for instance, would immediately have been suspected of being a witch. Sometimes even the animals were put on trial. In 1692, during the Salem trials, a dog was hanged after being found guilty of being a witch.

Even William Shakespeare mentioned familiars, in *Henry VI, Part II*: "Away with him! He has a familiar under his tongue" (Act 4, scene 7).

An eighteenth-century English witch called Moll White had an amazing familiar. Her cat spoke English with a strong regional accent.[26]

Modern day followers of Wicca sometimes have animals that help them in their magic. But they do not consider these animals to be demons or spirits in animal form. It is because of the psychic connection between the animal and human that they are partners in the magic.

See *cat, crow, devil, dog, frog, goat, hare, magic, owl, raven, snake, Wicca, witch.*

Fan: In Korea, it's considered life threatening to sleep in a room with the door and windows closed and a fan turned on. An American friend of mine who lived in Korea offered to do this to prove that the experience would not kill him, but his well-meaning Korean friends refused to allow the experiment to take place, so great was their fear for his life.

Fatal Twenty: By an amazing coincidence, every American president elected at twenty-year intervals between 1840 and 1960 died in office. These presidents are William Henry Harrison (elected 1840), Abraham Lincoln (1860), James A. Garfield (1880), William McKinley (1900), Warren G. Harding (1920), Franklin Delano Roosevelt (1940), and John F. Kennedy (1960). This caused many people to believe in the "fatal twenty" superstition. Ronald Reagan, who defeated Jimmy Carter in 1980, finally ended this superstition.

Fate: Fate is a future that is predetermined and cannot be altered or avoided. The ancient Greeks and Romans believed in three fates, named Clotho, Lachesis, and Atropos. They were sometimes referred to as the "cruel fates," as they controlled the mysteries of birth, life, and death in an apparently random, uncaring manner. Even the gods were not able to alter their decrees.

There are many superstitions concerned with fate. It was believed that if people boasted or became overly proud of their achievements, they tempted fate, which could easily pull them back down again. If you told someone personal details about yourself, you again risked fate, as this information could be used against you.

See *death.*

Feather: It is considered bad luck to walk past a feather. However, it is good luck to pick up the feather and stick it into the ground. The luck is doubled if it is a black feather.

Feathers in the room of someone who is dying are believed to postpone the death. This allows visitors from far away sufficient time to visit the patient's bedside.

See *death, owl, peacock, thunderstorm.*

February: William Shakespeare captured the spirit of February in *Much Ado about Nothing*, when he had Don Pedro, Prince of Arragon, say,

Good morrow, Benedick.
    Why, what's the matter
That you have such a February face,
    So full of frost, of storm,
        and cloudiness?
        (Act 5, scene 4)

February was the Roman month of purification. Candlemas Day, on February 2, is the Feast of the Purification of the Blessed Virgin Mary. It is also Groundhog Day.

If the weather is fine and frosty at the end of January and the start of February, it is a sign there is more winter ahead than behind.

See *Candlemas, Groundhog Day, January, weather.*

February 29th : An old tradition says people born on February 29th will always be lucky. Although this luck does not usually include money, these leap year babies will always have enough to get by, and will be lucky in many small ways.

Feet: According to superstition, you will be lucky if you always put your right shoe on before the left.

People used to believe that you could make someone lame by placing a sharp object in his or her footprints.

Fences: Fences between neighbors need to be kept in good repair. If they are poorly kept, problems will develop between the two families.

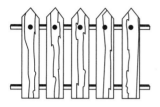

Fig: The fig sign is created when you make a fist of your hand, and then push your thumb between the first and second fingers. As this sign is considered an extremely rude gesture in many European countries, it needs to be used with caution. The fig sign is used to ward off the evil eye. It can

also be used when you've performed a good deed and don't want the devil to become aware of it.

See *devil, evil eye, jet, ladder.*

Figurehead: A figurehead is a carved figure on the bow of a sailing ship. Today, a figurehead is considered ornamental, and often serves as a mascot. In the past, it was considered the soul of a ship. Most figureheads depicted naked women, and this probably goes back to the days when ships were dedicated to specific goddesses. Sailors usually consider it unlucky to have women on board their ships, but are proud of the figureheads that adorn them.

See *mascot, sailors, ship.*

Film Stars: Film stars, like other actors and actresses, are highly superstitious. This is not surprising, as they live in an insecure world where they can be famous one day and forgotten the next. Many film stars have specific actions they perform to create good luck.

Arnold Schwarzenegger deliberately breaks a pair of sunglasses whenever he makes a movie. Many stars have lucky charms. Robin Williams has a carved ivory trinket that was owned by his father. Bob Hope always had a pair of gold cuff links that had been given to him by Paramount Studios. For more than thirty years he never went on stage without them. Sophia Loren always wore something red, as she believed this brought her luck.[27]

See *actors and actresses, charms.*

Finger: Crossing the first and second fingers is a universal sign to ward off bad luck. Almost as common is crossing the fingers behind the back while telling a lie. This is believed to protect the person from the bad luck that follows the telling of an untruth.

People with long fingers are patient and good with details. People with short fingers are impatient and restless. A crooked little finger is often considered a sign that the person will die rich, but this wealth is likely to have been made in a dubious way.

The forefinger of the right hand is sometimes known as the "poison finger." Because of this, it should never be used to rub ointment into a wound. The best fingers to rub ointment on with are the ring and middle fingers. The ring finger is also considered the best finger to scratch with.

The Greeks and Romans believed a nerve ran from the ring finger to the heart. They called it the "medical finger" and used it for stirring food, as they believed it would warn the heart if it contacted anything noxious. Wedding rings are worn on this finger because of people's belief in the nerve connecting this finger with the heart.

See *crossed fingers, palmistry, pointing, snapping fingers, thread, V-sign, wedding ring, wine, words.*

Fingernail: Witches were believed to hold power over anyone whose fingernail clippings they possessed, as nail clippings were an important ingredient when enchanting someone with a spell. Consequently, nail clippings could not be discarded carelessly. Cut-

ting each clipping into three pieces, or spitting on them, made them useless for witchcraft purposes.

Fingernails should be cut on a Monday or a Tuesday. Cutting them on a Friday or a Sunday is bad luck, as this rhyme attests:

Cut them on Monday,
cut them for wealth,
Cut them on Tuesday,
cut them for health,
Cut them on Wednesday,
cut them for news,
Cut them on Thursday,
a new pair of shoes,
Cut them on Friday,
cut them for woe,
Cut them on Saturday,
a journey to go,
Cut them on Sunday,
cut them for evil,
And be all week
as cross as the devil.

Babies' fingernails should not be cut until they are at least one year old. If you cut them sooner, the child will grow up to be a thief. Sailors do not cut their nails (or cut their hair) while at sea, as it risks causing a storm.

Burning your own fingernail clippings is considered an effective way of curing yourself of a variety of health problems.

If you cut the nails of someone who is unwell, he or she will never recover.

White specks on the nails also have meanings. A speck on the thumbnail means you will shortly receive a gift. A speck on the first finger means you'll receive a visit from a friend. However, a speck on the second finger indicates a visit from an enemy. A white speck on the fourth finger indicates a journey in the near future.

See *Friday the 13th, hair, sailors, spitting, storm, werewolf, witch.*

Fire: Fire has played a pivotal role in human evolution. It used to be considered a special gift of the gods, and sometimes even symbolized life itself. The fireplace is sometimes considered the soul of the household. Fire is one of the four elements (fire, earth, air,  and water) that the ancient Greeks believed made up the world. In astrology, the three fire signs are Aries, Leo, and Sagittarius.

Bonfires used to be lit at certain times of the year to preserve the good luck of the crops and livestock. In the British Commonwealth, Bonfire Night is celebrated on November 5. This is also called Guy Fawkes' Night, after one of the leaders of a small group who tried to blow up the Houses of Parliament in 1605.

Pyromancy is the art of divination by gazing into the flames of a fire. This art goes well back into pre-history, and it's not hard to imagine cavemen studying the flickering flames and the shadows they created on the walls of their caves. Pythagoras (fl. sixth century BCE) used pyromancy to answer questions. It was a popular method of divining the future in Roman times. Nowadays, people who practice pyromancy usually use candles, rather than roaring fires, to make their predictions.

See *candle, fire, St. Elmo's fire, shadow, three, umbilical cord.*

Firefly: If a firefly enters a home, it is a sign that an unexpected visitor will call on the following day. Two fireflies indicate an upcoming marriage of a single person living in the house. If no eligible single people live in the house, two fireflies promise good luck for the people living there. Several fireflies in the house indicate a party in the near future.

Fireplace: If a hot cinder of coal or wood falls out of a fire, it is a sign that a visitor will shortly arrive.

It is bad luck to poke someone else's fire, unless he or she has specifically asked you to.

See *fire.*

Fish: The superstition that fish is "brain food" began in the nineteenth century. At that time, scientists discovered that fish was rich in phosphorus. Because the human brain also contains phosphorus, people immediately started believing that  eating fish somehow fed the brain. This meant that the more fish you ate, the smarter you would become. Unfortunately, there is no truth in this. Fish is nutritious and good for you, but eating it will not make you more intelligent.

An old superstition says that fish should be eaten from the tail upwards. This ensures good catches in the future.

See *aphrodisiac*.

Fishbone: A quaint New England superstition says that you can dislodge a fishbone that has gotten stuck in your throat by pulling on your big toe.

Fishermen: Most of the superstitions ascribed to sailors also apply to fishermen. They also have a number of superstitions of their own.

It is good luck to have an argument with your wife before heading out to sea, as this means the catch will be good. But this argument has to happen by chance.

It is bad luck for a fisherman to come across a woman wearing a white apron, a cross-eyed man, a member of the clergy, a nun, or a dog while on his way to the boat.

It is bad luck to count the fish as they are caught. That task has to wait until the fishermen are back on shore again.

It is also bad luck to fish every day of the week. This sends out a message that you are greedy, and you will suffer as a result.

It is considered bad luck to ask a fisherman if he had a good catch. If you do, you are subliminally suggesting he has done something wrong and has lost the favor of the gods.

See *dog, nuns, red, sailors, spitting*.

Fishing: Superstition provides several methods for improving your luck when you go fishing. Avoid wearing white, as it is bad luck to wear white clothing when fishing. You are unlikely to catch anything if you pass a pig or a bare-footed woman while on your way to your boat  or fishing spot. Don't fish while sitting on an upturned bucket. It's also bad luck to change rods while you are fishing, unless the first one has become damaged. Keep your landing

net out of the water until you have hooked a fish. Don't answer if someone asks how many fish you've caught. If you do, you'll catch no more fish that day.

Good luck will come your way if you spit on your fishhook before lowering it into the water. It is also good luck to return the first fish you catch.

See *Friday the 13th, Good Friday, seagull, taboo, white.*

Five: Five is a magical number for many reasons. We have five fingers and five toes. Many people, denying the existence of a sixth sense, believe humans possess just five senses: sight, touch, taste, smell, and hearing. Jesus Christ suffered five wounds.

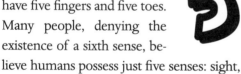

Five was inscribed on the portals of doors in ancient Egypt and Greece to ward off evil spirits. The pentagram, a five-pointed star, is used as an amulet to protect the wearer from evil influences. A magic square, which uses all the numbers from 1 to 9, places 5 in the central position:

$$4\ 9\ 2$$
$$3\ 5\ 7$$
$$8\ 1\ 6$$

This is the magic square, or *kamea*, of Saturn.

See *numbers.*

Fleas: If you find a flea on your head it is a sign that an important letter is about to arrive.

You can eliminate fleas from your home by tossing walnut leaves on the floor of every room.

See *walnut.*

Flowers: Wildflowers have always seemed mysterious and magical. Consequently, they're associated with fairies, elves, and witchcraft. In German mythology, roses were protected by dwarves and fairies, and people had to ask permission to pick them. Because they were so closely connected to magic, flowers were used as charms and amulets. Some were used to ward off evil. The Greeks, for instance, believed the peony protected people from storms and other violent weather conditions. Some flowers were considered aphrodisiacs. Hawthorn, primroses, roses, and violets are examples. These were candied and eaten.

Other flowers, such as the marigold, orchid, and rose, were popular love charms.

Flowers have always been given as gestures of love and friendship since Egyptian times, and it's believed they provide good luck to the recipient. The good luck is increased if there are an odd number of flowers in the bunch.

Yellow flowers provide good luck to the home. Purple flowers provide opportunities for financial advancement.

Lilies symbolize virginity, and it is important that a man does not damage one. This risks the reputation and purity of the women in his immediate family.

Brides carry flowers as a symbol of good luck and fruitfulness.

Actors and actresses believe that live flowers on stage are unlucky. It is also unlucky to display flowers that are out of season indoors.

Each sign of the zodiac has flowers associated with it. They bring good luck to people born under each sign:

Aries: anemone, daffodil, hawthorn, honeysuckle, and nasturtium.

Taurus: cherry, forget-me-not (shared with Scorpio), and red rose.

Gemini: hazel, iris, lavender, and London pride.

Cancer: clover, daisy, honesty (moonwort), and white poppy.

Leo: marigold, peony, and sunflower.

Virgo: lavender and lily-of-the-valley.

Libra: love-in-a-mist, white rose, and violet.

Scorpio: chrysanthemum, forget-me-not (shared with Taurus), and orchid.

Sagittarius: clove carnation, ivy (shared with Capricorn), and lilac.

Capricorn: ivy (shared with Sagittarius), jasmine, Christmas rose, and snowdrop (shared with Aquarius).

Aquarius: amaranth, mimosa, spring crocus, and snowdrop (shared with Capricorn).

Pisces: clove carnation, pink gardenia, goat's beard, love-in-a-mist, and sweet violet.

An old superstition requires nurses to remove flowers from patients' rooms overnight. The standard reason for this is that they will prevent the patient from receiving all the oxygen required. The real reason for this custom is the old belief that fairy spirits hid inside flowers and would attack the patient as soon as it was dark. Nowadays, flowers are not removed from the room at night unless their smell is over-

powering or they create a possibility of infection. This can come from the earth of potted plants or bacteria in the water that cut flowers sit in. Some people still believe that any flowers they are given in hospital should remain there after they leave. If they take them home, they run the risk of returning to the hospital as a patient before many months have passed.

It is also bad luck to give white flowers to someone who is unwell. This is because they signify death. Bunches of red and white flowers are considered even more dangerous, and just the sight of them might cause someone to die. This superstition dates back to Roman times, when people strewed red and white flowers on the graves of their dead lovers. It provides good luck to give a patient a bunch of red flowers only, as red symbolizes life. Purple flowers symbolize goodwill and orange flowers vitality, making them good choices too.

Flowers have always had hidden meanings that express joy, love, admiration, thanks, and sadness. *The Dream Book of Artemidorus* is an ancient Greek work that describes the meanings of all the flowers that were used as decoration or adornment.

Christianity gradually changed the meanings of some flowers. Ivy is a good example. It was originally a bacchanalian favorite that could be used to prevent drunkenness. However, under the Christian influence, it became a symbol of faithfulness in marriage. The white lily was believed to have come from the Greek goddess Eostre's breast milk. In Christian times it meant purity. Archangel Gabriel is regularly depicted holding a lily to signify the miraculous conception of Mary.

The code of chivalry in the Middle Ages created a whole new interest in the meaning and symbolism of flowers. Many stories from the time involve a knight receiving flowers from a maiden, or collecting certain flowers to present to his lady.

William Shakespeare revealed an extensive knowledge of flower meanings in his plays. In *Hamlet*, Ophelia wears a crown of flowers: crow-flowers, nettles, daisies, and long-purples. His audience would have been able to interpret this as: A fair maid (crow-flower), stung to the quick (nettles), her youthful bloom (daisies) under the cold hand of death (long-purples).

Flower interpretation was taken even further in the eighteenth and nineteenth centuries, and an entire language of flowers was created. This was extremely useful for chaperoned couples, as they could exchange messages in secret. Flower language was recorded in more than one hundred popular books. Here are a few interpretations:

White rose: chaste or innocent love
Red rose: passionate love
Yellow rose: jealousy
Red tulip: devotion and constant love
Hibiscus: delicacy and beauty
White lily: purity
Blue violet: faithfulness.
Forget-me-not: true love
Heliotrope: devotion.
Pansy: I think only of you
Anemone: I am forsaken
Yellow chrysanthemum: rejection
Snowdrop: hope
Geranium: melancholy
Purple hyacinth: sorrow
Lily-of-the-valley: happiness restored
Marigold: despair
Lavender: distrust

Two or more flowers could be displayed together to create more complex  thoughts. Lavender means "distrust" and lettuce means "cold-hearted." Consequently, when a bowl of lavender is placed next to a lettuce, the message is, "I don't trust you because you are cold-hearted."

See *actors and actresses, airplane, amulet, bride, charms, daf-fodil, daisy, dandelion, fairy, grave, hawthorn, ivy, lavender, lilac, lily, love, marigold, orchid, periwinkle, primrose, rose, St. John's wort, tattoo, violet, wedding, witchcraft.*

Fly: It is a sign of good luck if a fly falls into a glass you have been drinking from. This good luck extends to flies that land in cups of tea or bowls of soup, also. It is also considered lucky to see a solitary fly at Christmas (in the Northern Hemisphere). This 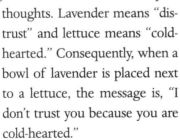 symbolizes a stranger who has come to offer help and support. Consequently, it's considered bad luck to kill it.

If a fly continues to buzz around someone, it is a sign that someone wants to meet him or her. You can ensure the meeting takes place by killing the fly.

If a fly lands on your nose, it's a sign that someone has something important to tell you.

See *Christmas, nose, spider, tea.*

Food: Food is essential for our survival. At one time it was considered magical, and offerings were made to the various fertility goddesses to ensure the continuity of food. Food was a blessing from the gods, and nourished the soul as well as the body.

Food symbolized life itself, and people rejoiced and feasted whenever possible.

Food rituals are still popular today. We eat roast goose and turkey at Christmas, eggs at Easter, and cakes at birthday parties, not realizing that by doing so, we're carrying on an ancient tradition.

Not surprisingly, superstitions grew around the subject of food. Not long ago, I counseled a man who had been in prison. He told me that the inmates always ate everything put on their plates. If they didn't, they believed they would have to return to the prison at a later date to finish the meal.

It is bad luck to leave the remains of a meal on the table overnight, as this acts as an offering to the devil and other evil spirits.

Some fishermen refuse to give away any fish, as this destroys their luck in the future.

It is considered unlucky to drop any food while eating. This is a sign of impending illness.

See *cake, devil, Easter, eating, eggs, fish.*

Foot: An itchy foot is a sign of travel in your future. It usually means visiting an exotic place for the first time.

See *toes.*

Four: Ancient people considered four a divine number, and most of their deities had four-letter names. The Hebrew IHVH is a good example. Other examples include the Assyrians with Adad, the Egyptians with Amun, the Persians with Syre, and the Turks with Esar. More recent examples include the Latin *Deus*, the French *Dieu*, and the German *Gott*.

Four is also considered the luckiest even number, as so many important things occur in fours. There are four elements, four seasons, four cardinal directions, four gospels, four evangelists, and also four suits (each containing four court cards) in the Tarot deck.

See *clover, elements, numbers.*

Fox: All around the world, foxes are considered cunning animals. They are not trusted, and in the past people believed witches could turn themselves into foxes.

Some people still believe that when it rains while the sun is shining, two foxes are getting married.

It is good luck to see a single fox when you are away from home. Some years ago, I was surprised to see a fox in central London. The people I was with, all London residents, considered it an extremely good omen. Although seeing one fox is good,

it is bad luck to see several. This is a sign that something extremely bad is about to happen. It is also bad luck to see a fox lurking near your home.

See *rain, sun, witch.*

Freckles: Freckles are light brown spots that are usually found on the face, but can also appear on other parts of the body. Not everyone is happy to have them. Fortunately, there is a remedy. All you need do is find a frog and rub him over all your freckles. Release the frog where you found him, and allow him to take all your freckles with him.

See *frog.*

Friday: Friday is considered an unlucky day, and Friday the 13th is the unluckiest of all. Friday is believed to be the day that Eve offered the apple to Adam. Jesus was crucified on a Friday, and some people believe Friday was the day that Noah set sail in his ark.

Witches hold coven meetings on Fridays. Accidents and mishaps of all sorts are allegedly more common on Fridays. Many people will not start a new project or travel on a Friday.

An old saying warns that people who laugh on Friday will cry on Sunday. Children born on a Friday are unlucky, but possess psychic and healing gifts.

Lord Byron (1788–1824), the English poet, considered Friday an unlucky day, yet he sailed for Italy on a Friday. He died of malaria shortly afterwards, also on a Friday.

However, not everyone considers Friday an unlucky day, and there are several reasons why Americans should consider it a lucky day. Christopher Columbus left Spain on Friday, August 3, 1492 and sighted the New World on Friday, October 12. The *Mayflower* arrived in Provincetown on Friday, November 10, 1620, and on Friday, December 22, 1620 the Pilgrim Fathers reached Plymouth Rock.

See *actors and actresses, bed, business, coven, Friday the 13th, jaybird, thirteen, travel, witch.*

Friday the 13th: As Friday the 13th combines two superstitions, it is an extremely difficult day for many people. In Ohio, there are thirteen activities you must never do on Friday the 13th:

You must not cut your fingernails. If you do, you'll suffer from toothache.

You must not sneeze. If you do, you'll create sorrow for yourself in the near future.

You must not use a broom

to clean your house, as this will create bad luck.

You must not do any sewing. You will die before wearing the item sewn.

You must not start a trip. You will suffer misfortune if you start to travel on this day.

It is bad luck to pay any debts on Friday the 13th.

If you laugh on this day, you'll cry on Sunday.

If you spill salt on this day, you'll have an argument with someone.

You must not learn anything new. If you do, you'll receive another wrinkle on your face.

You'll have toothache if you wash your hands and face, unless you dry your hands before your face.

You must not cut anyone's hair. You'll become involved in other people's problems if you do.

You must not plant anything in your garden. Anything you plant on Friday the 13th will die.

It's a waste of time to go fishing on this day, as you'll catch nothing.

This fourteenth tip is offered to avoid triskaidekaphobia (fear of the number thirteen): It is bad luck to roll over in bed on this day.

See *baseball, broom, fingernail, fishing, hair, hand, laugh, salt, sewing, sneeze, thirteen, toothache, travel.*

Friends: Wear an ornament of topaz if you want to have more friends.

If you want to keep your friends, do not wash your hands in the same basin together and then share the same towel to dry them. This is a sign that the friendship will soon be over. If you accidentally do this, you can preserve the friendship by making the sign of the cross using both thumbs.

See *cross, topaz.*

Frog: Frog amulets were used in Roman times to protect homes and their occupants. Romans also wore frog amulets to sustain romance and love.

In the Middle Ages, people wore the dried bodies of frogs, in small silk bags, around their necks to provide protection against fits.

The Chinese were fascinated with the frog, as, like the moon, it changed its form during different stages of its life. Today, the Chinese Moon Frog amulet is still

worn around the neck to attract longevity and wealth. Sometimes this frog has a coin placed in its mouth. This attracts wealth and wards off evil spirits.

An American tradition says to take note of what you are doing when you hear the first frog in any year. This is because you will spend much of the rest of the year performing the same task.

See *amulet, coin, familiar, freckles, nose.*

Funeral: It is considered lucky for the dead person's soul if rain falls during a funeral. An old rhyme says,

> Happy is the bride
> that the sun shines on
> Happy is the corpse
> that the rain rains on.

Funerals should not be delayed unnecessarily. The longer the delay, the more likelihood that someone else in the family will die. This is especially the case if the delay includes a weekend. It is bad luck to hold a funeral on a Sunday or on New Year's Day.

The funeral procession should return home from the cemetery by a different route than the one taken to get there. This makes it harder for a ghost to return home. You might also rearrange the furniture in the dead person's bedroom. If the ghost manages to find its way home, it won't recognize the place, and will leave again.

It is bad luck to count the number of vehicles in a funeral procession. The number of cars counted reveals the number of years you have left to live. (Another version of this superstition says that each car you count takes a year off your life.)

It is also considered bad luck to chance upon a funeral procession. If you do, you should immediately doff your hat to avert the bad luck. If you are not wearing a hat, bow your head and make the sign of the cross on your chest.

It is bad luck for an odd number of mourners to attend the funeral. This is a sign that one of them will soon die.

See *airplane, bean, car, clergyman, coffin, corpse, cow, ghost, hat, hearse, January, peacock, rain, rosemary, salt, thirteen, warts, weather, white.*

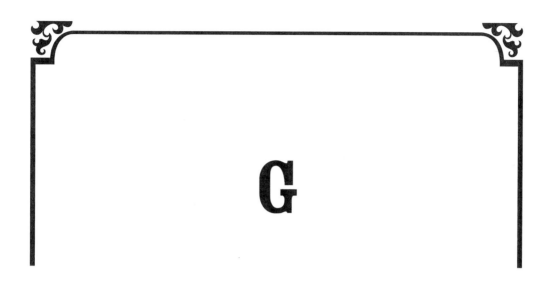

G

Gambling: Gamblers are highly superstitious, and employ a variety of charms and amulets to help provide good luck.

It is considered bad luck to gamble with your legs crossed. It is also bad luck to drop a card while playing. Women and dogs should not be allowed into any room where gambling is taking place. You should stack your chips neatly, and blow on your cards or dice to enjoy good luck.

It is important to keep your emotions concealed while gambling. You will always lose if you gamble while in a bad mood.

See *amulet, chair, charms, cross, dog, jade, kiss, two-dollar bill.*

Gargoyle: Gargoyles are hideous creatures, carved from stone or wood, that are attached to churches and other buildings to provide protection from evil spirits. Gargoyles have large mouths and throats to suck in any evil energy that may be lurking around the building.

See *church.*

Garlic: Garlic has been used as a form of protection for more than two thousand years. The ancient Egyptians believed it was a gift from God. Christian tradition says that the first garlic appeared on the spot where Satan's left foot trod when leaving the Garden of Eden.

Whatever its origin, garlic has always been a powerful form of protection. Roman soldiers believed it gave them courage. Sailors believed it protected them from shipwreck. German miners believed it protected them from evil spirits when they went underground. Brides often carried garlic in their clothes to protect them at their weddings. Garlic was placed under the pillows of babies to protect them during the night. Cloves of garlic were also hung around the house to provide protection from envy, illness, robbers, witches, vampires, and evil spirits.

Garlic has also been used to protect people from a wide range of illnesses and ailments, including sunstroke, toothache, bed-wetting, rabies, and leprosy. Garlic was added to food to provide protection for those who ate it.

Garlic can be carried in a pocket to ward off the evil eye. Cloves of garlic hung in a car, workplace, or house also provide protection.

Necklaces of garlic can be made by threading an odd number of cloves together using string and a needle. These can be worn around the neck whenever additional protection is required, or hung up in the house, preferably close to your bed. The garlic necklace needs to be replaced as soon as it shows signs of deterioration.

Modern day science has found that the oil in garlic, allicin, possesses antibacterial, antifungal, and antiviral properties. It is also a highly effective antibiotic and can help cure coughs, colds, and digestive problems. Garlic has also been shown to lower blood cholesterol and blood sugar levels. Our forebears chose wisely when they picked garlic for its protective qualities.

See *aphrodisiac, baby, bride, car, colds, evil eye, sailors, toothache, wedding, vampires, witch.*

Garnet: Garnet is an intense red stone that appears to glow with its own light. Not surprisingly, the Romans used the garnet to represent Mars, the god of war. They believed that garnet had the power to make people angry, passionate, and violent.

Christians noticed the blood-red color of the garnet and adopted it to symbolize Jesus' suffering on the cross.

Crystal healers today use the garnet to remove negative energies from their patients. It is also worn by people lacking in energy, and people who want to increase their compassion or attract a partner.

See *gemstones, wedding anniversaries.*

Gematria: Gematria is a Kabbalistic method of word correspondences. It is based on the letters of the Hebrew alphabet, turned into numbers using numerology. Words with the same numerological value are believed to have a special relationship or connection with each other. This enables Kabbalists to analyze a message and identify hidden meanings. Holy Scriptures can be read in a totally different way when using gematria.

A famous example of this is in the Book of Revelation, where St. John mentions 666 as the number of the Beast (Revelation 13:18). Early Christians thought this referred to Emperor Nero, who persecuted the Christians. His name in Greek adds up to 666.

See *numerology.*

Gemini: Gemini is the third sign of the zodiac. Its symbol is the twins. Its element is air, and its gemstone is opal. The keyword for Gemini is: I think.

The Gemini symbol comes from the twin stars Castor and Pollux, who were known to astrologers 8,000 years ago. The twins symbolize the dual nature of Gemini. Geminians are quick-witted, skilful, ingenious, and versatile people who are interested in almost everything. They are extremely versatile. They enjoy learning, but learn best in short bursts of activity rather than in lengthy periods of concentration. Geminians have a way with words, and are usually excellent conversationalists.

See *air, astrology, elements, gemstones, opal, zodiac.*

Gemstones: A gemstone is a mineral that has been cut and polished to reveal its natural beauty. Because they are both rare and beautiful, gemstones have always been prized as amulets and charms. The precious stones in a king's crown were not simply decorations or indications of wealth; they were amulets intended to protect him from the forces of darkness.

Because gemstones are beautiful, they gradually became appreciated more for their aesthetic qualities than for their magical powers. However, in the mid-twentieth century, people once again became fascinated with the protective and healing qualities of crystals, and more people than ever before are wearing them as amulets rather than as items of jewelry. The most popular gemstones for lucky charms are amethyst, citrine, hematite, malachite, clear quartz, rose quartz, tiger's eye, and turquoise.

See *agate, alexandrite, amethyst, amulet, aquamarine, Aquarius, Aries, bloodstone, Cancer, Capricorn, carnelian, charms, citrine, diamond, emerald, garnet, Gemini, hematite, jade, jasper, jet, lapis lazuli, Leo, Libra, lodestone, malachite, moonstone, obsidian, onyx, opal, Pisces, quartz, ruby, Sagittarius, sapphire, Scorpio, serpentine, Taurus, tiger's eye, topaz, turquoise, Virgo.*

Ghost: A ghost is a spirit or apparition, usually of someone who has died. Ghosts frequently haunt places that they were associated with when alive. They are also frequently found at crossroads. Criminals and

suicides were buried at crossroads to make it harder for their ghosts to find their way back home to haunt their relatives.

People who wore born in the hour after midnight are believed to be better at seeing ghosts than others. In Europe, it was believed that people born on a Sunday were able to see ghosts. In Scotland, it was commonly believed that people born on Good Friday or Christmas Day had this ability.

Not everyone believes in ghosts. In 1762, a ghost was haunting Cock Lane in London. Someone submitted a short poem to the *Public Advertiser*, which they printed on February 5, 1762:

Should Latin, Greek and Hebrew fail,
I know a charm which *must* prevail:
Take but an ounce of Common Sense,
'Twil scare the ghosts,
and drive 'em hence.

The best thing to do if you happen to meet a ghost is to speak to it. Say, "What in God's name do you want?" The ghost will either reply or disappear. If ghosts bother you, you can avoid seeing them by wearing a ring of chalcedony or basalt. Alternatively, you can repel Christian ghosts by holding up a crucifix.

See *baby, banshee, burial, children, Christmas, cock, crossroads, days of the week, death, dog, funeral, Good Friday, Macbeth, ring, widdershins.*

Glass: A curious superstition can be found at the end of Jewish weddings, when the bridegroom breaks an expensive glass. At this moment, all the guests call out *"Mazzal tov,"* which means "good luck." This is because the sound of breaking glass and shouting, coupled with the expense of the glass, diverts the attention of any evil spirits who might be at the reception away from the happy couple. If this isn't done, the evil spirits might be overcome with jealousy at the happiness of the bride and groom and send them bad luck. Today, a variety of alternative meanings have been proposed to explain the breaking glass ceremony. The glass might symbolize temporal joys, for instance, which can be destroyed, as opposed to eternal love, which cannot. Another suggestion is that as the husband and wife use the glass to consecrate the marriage, it has to be broken, as it cannot be used for anything else afterwards.

Many bartenders believe that glasses should be reserved for one liquid only. A beer glass, for instance, should never be used to hold any other liquid. This is because the glass is believed to hold the spirit of the original liquid.

See *bottle, picture, toast, wedding, wedding anniversaries.*

Glove: Gloves used to have huge significance. Knights wore a lady's glove in their helmets, and would defend it with their lives. In medieval times a folded glove acted as a pledge that a court judgment would be met. A glove might be thrown to the ground as a challenge. Clergy wore gloves to symbolically show that their hands were clean, and that they could not accept bribes.

If you drop a glove, it is considered bad luck to pick it up yourself. This is derived from the custom of a lady deliberately dropping a glove in the hope that a prospective lover will pick it up.

If you accidentally leave your gloves at a friend's house, you can not simply return to get them. If you do, you'll never be invited back. Instead, you must visit again, sit down for a while before picking up the gloves, and then stand before putting them on.

It is bad luck to lose a glove, and even worse to lose both. If a witch found your gloves she'd have power over you. It is good luck to find a pair of gloves, especially on a Sunday. This is a sign that the following week will be a successful and happy one.

If you give someone gloves as a present, you must receive something back in return. If this does not occur, bad luck will occur to both parties.

See *wedding dress, witch.*

Goat: The goat has been associated with debauchery, lust, and the devil for thousands of years. An old legend says that the devil created the goat. The devil is also often depicted as a goat, with cloven hooves and a goat's head. My father-in-law always kept a goat on his sheep farm. This was because he believed the goat would absorb any illnesses or problems that might harm his other stock.

"Old Father Time" is usually depicted wearing a goat's beard. This is because the goat was sacred to Saturn, the father of time. Consequently, the goat symbolizes the astrological sign of Capricorn, which is ruled by Saturn.

It is considered good luck to encounter a goat while traveling to an important meeting.

See *devil, familiar.*

Goblin: Goblins belong to the fairy family, and live deep underground or in dark forests where they can avoid daylight. They travel in large groups and delight in harassing and annoying travellers. Other fairies are afraid of goblins, as they try to kidnap and enslave them.

See *bogeyman, fairy.*

Gold: In alchemy, gold represents the sun and silver represents the moon. Gold is prized because of its value and rarity. Sailors believed they would not drown as long as they were wearing a gold earring.

It is also lucky to rub your eyelids with gold. Gold has always been considered helpful for any problems involving the eyes. The traditional remedy is to rub the sore eye with a gold ring

See *moon, sailors, silver, sun, rainbow, ring, wedding anniversaries, wedding ring.*

Golf: There are superstitions attached to almost all sports, and golf is no exception. The usual superstitions, such as wearing a favorite shirt or underwear, apply. There are also superstitions unique to golf, such as the belief that it is bad luck to take a club out of the bag to make a shot and then change your mind. Another example is never to clean a ball when you are playing well.

Jack Nicklaus always carries three coins in his pocket. Spencer Levin only plays with golf balls that have the numbers one and three on them. He also carries three pennies in his pocket, and the dates on them have to be 2002 or 2004. This is because he played well in those years. Many golfers carry dimes dating from the mid-1960s, as all golfers would love to shoot sixty-five or sixty-six.

See *coin*.

Goodbye: The word "goodbye" is a contraction of "God be with ye." The change occurred over many centuries. "God" gradually became "good" because of commonly used expressions such as "good morning" or "good night."

Good Friday: Good Friday is one of the most sacred days in the Christian calendar. The ground should not be disturbed on this day, making it a bad day for planting most crops. Cabbage, lettuce, parsley, radishes, and tomatoes are exceptions to this rule, as are any "hanging" crops such as beans and grapes. However, the opposite belief applies in the western United States. Good Friday is considered the perfect day on which to plant potatoes. It is even better to plant them under the light of the moon on this day.

Good Friday is an unlucky day to be born on. It is also unlucky for blacksmiths to work with nails on Good Friday. Children should not climb trees, either, as the cross of Jesus was made from wood. However, any wishes made at 3:00 PM, the time of Christ's death, will be granted.

Good Friday is the best day of the year for weaning babies. It is also a good day for fishing and for curing warts.

The wart cure involves getting up in the morning and cutting a potato in half. Rub the potato over the wart, and then feed it to a cow. As long as you do not speak to anyone from the time you get out of bed until the time the cow finishes eating the potato, the warts will disappear.

A hot cross bun kept from one Good Friday to the next is believed to protect the house and the occupants from injury or damage caused by fire.

See *cabbage, cake, cross, baby, beans, fire, fishing, ghosts, grape, hot cross buns, moon, nail, parsley, potato, pumpkin, ring, tomato, warts, washing.*

Grapes: Grapes grow in clusters and are considered a sign of good luck and abundance.

Wine, the blood of the grape, is also considered special, as it brings people together and helps make happy occasions even happier.

In many Spanish-speaking countries, people eat twelve grapes at midnight on New Year's Eve. This ensures twelve months of happiness and prosperity in the year ahead.

A superstition that is still believed by many people says that eating grape seeds will cause appendicitis. This is not the case. Appendicitis is an infection caused by germs.

See *Good Friday, New Year, wine.*

Grass: An old weather superstition says that if you see a cat or dog eating grass, you can be sure that rain is coming. In actuality, cats and dogs eat grass to help their digestion.

See *rain, weather.*

Grave: Graves were usually dug so that the dead person's feet faced east and head faced west. This meant that on Judgment Day, the occupant would be facing in the right direction to climb out of the grave and walk eastwards.

An old Russian superstition suggests placing a ladder in the grave so that the soul can more easily climb up to heaven. The ladder should have seven rungs, which relate to the "seven heavens."[28]

It is unlucky to walk on a grave, particularly one containing someone who has not been baptized, as you could contract a fatal illness called "gravemerelles." Samuel Taylor Coleridge referred to walking on graves in his ballad "The Three Graves":

> To see a man tread over graves,
>   I hold it no good mark;
> 'Tis wicked in the sun and moon,
>   And bad luck in the dark!

Wreaths of flowers are commonly placed on graves. They create a magic circle that prevents the dead person's ghost from leaving the coffin. The flowers also appease any evil spirits.

It is unlucky to pick any flowers growing on a grave.

Gypsies believe you should be buried in the same town or village you were born in. The closer your grave is to your birthplace, the better.

See *cramp, flowers, ladder, parsley, St. Swithin's Day, shadow, storm, stumbling, suicide, vampire, walking, yew.*

Graveyard: It is believed to be bad luck to plough up land that has previously been used as a graveyard. It is also a waste of time, as any crops grown on the site will be stunted.

Everything inside a graveyard is sacred, and it is bad luck to interfere or meddle with anything found there. It is particularly bad luck to use pieces of broken tombstones for paths or roads. Frequent accidents will occur as a result.

See *coffin, death, headache, rowan, shoelaces, yew.*

Green: Because green is the color of nature, it has always symbolized fertility and abundance. Surprisingly, it is also considered the unluckiest of all colors. This is because fairies, elves, pixies, and other spirits are believed to wear green. They live underground and give their color to all growing things every spring. They take this responsibility seriously, and cause bad luck to occur to anyone else who dares wear their color.

The Irish used to believe this, too. It took St. Patrick to change their beliefs. He taught them that God had created the shamrock, a three-leaved or trifoliate plant, to illustrate the  trinity. Green suddenly became favored again, and is now the national color of Ireland.

A more logical explanation for the dislike of green is the very fact that green is the color of nature. Green plants flourish in spring and summer, but lose their leaves and become black, the color of death, in winter. You can avoid the ultimate death by not having any green in your home or on your person.

Actors and actresses dislike green, especially on stage.

During World War II, Winston Churchill, at that time prime minister of Great Britain, gave someone ten pounds to get rid of a green sweater.[29]

See *actors and actresses, black, death, fairy, pixies.*

Gris-gris: Gris-gris are specialized amulets that are worn as protection against voodoo curses and spells. They are most frequently worn in Africa and the Caribbean.

See *amulet, spell, voodoo.*

Groundhog Day: Groundhog Day celebrates the belief that groundhogs emerge from hibernation on February 2 of each year. If they see their shadows at noon, they will return to their burrows and hibernate, as they expect another six weeks of winter.

Groundhog Day has been practised in the United States since at least 1898. That

year, seven men from Punxsutawney, 100 miles northeast of Pittsburgh, climbed a hill called Gobbler's Knob to drink beer and eat groundhog. They enjoyed themselves so much that they decided to repeat the exercise every year. They called themselves the "ground hog club."[30]

See *Candlemas, weather.*

Growing Pains: Superstition tells us that most children experience "growing pains." Many people would be surprised to learn that these pains have nothing to do with growing up. They are neuralgic pains in the legs caused by tiredness.

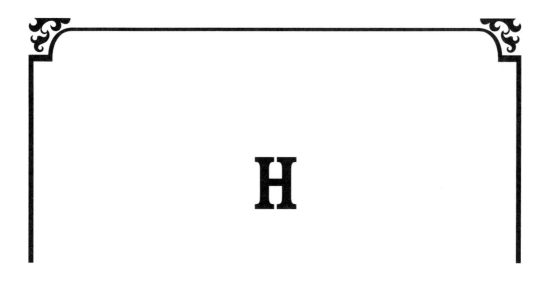

H

Hair: Giving someone you cherish a lock of your hair is an ancient custom. It is based on the superstition that hair contains a person's essential essence, or spirit. Consequently, anyone who has a strand of your hair has the power to bewitch or dominate you. It was considered a sign of unconditional trust and love to give such a valuable part of yourself to someone else. However, parents should not keep locks of their children's hair if they wish them to grow to adulthood. Parents who decide to keep a lock of their baby's hair need to guard it carefully.

Hair has always been associated with strength, which comes from the person's life force or spirit. In the Bible, Samson lost his strength when Delilah had his hair shaved off while he slept (Judges 16:19).

Young men with hairy arms are supposed to become wealthy.

Red-haired people have suffered because of superstition about their hair color. Scarlet was the color of sin, which is why Judas Iscariot is always depicted with reddish hair. Red-haired people are believed to have fiery tempers. Queen Elizabeth I is a good example of a fiery redhead. People with black or brown hair are believed to be reliable and brave, while people with fair hair are supposed to be timid.

If a woman's hair grows to a point in the middle of her forehead, creating a widow's peak, she will supposedly outlive her husband. If her hair suddenly becomes curly, it is a sign her husband has not long to live. It is bad luck to pull out any gray hairs. If you do, they will be replaced with ten more.

It is a sign of longevity if strands of a person's hair burn brightly when tossed into a fire. However, it is a portent of early death if it smolders slowly. In Ireland people believed that you should never burn hair, because at the Resurrection the owner would come back and look for his or her hair. As a result, hair was buried and not burned. The opposite notion was practiced in Europe, and hair was always burned. An important reason for this was to prevent the hair from getting into the hands of a witch who could use it to create black magic.

Another reason for disposing of hair carefully is the old belief that you will suffer headaches if a bird uses any strands of your hair to build a nest. The headaches will last until the nest is destroyed.

Even today, many people believe that cutting hair stimulates growth. In fact, it grows at the rate of about half an inch a month whether it is cut or not.

Another superstition says hair can turn white overnight if the person receives a sudden fright or undue stress.

The old saying "a hair of the dog" is used when suggesting that people suffering from hangovers have another drink. This idea that "like cures like" comes from the belief that possessing some hairs from a dog that had bitten you would cure the dog-bite.

See *baby, baldness, dog, fire, Friday the 13th, headache, illness, nest, potato, red, rum, sex, storm, thirteen, tooth fairy, walnut, white, wine, witch.*

Halloween: More than two thousand years ago, the Celtic Druids celebrated the end of the year on October 31. They called their festival *Samhain,* which means "summer's end." These festivities praised and honoured Baal, the sun god who had helped provide the harvest. They also asked Baal for help and support during the coming winter.

The Celts believed that on this day the souls of the dead could return to visit their loved ones who were still alive. Naturally, some of these ghosts or spirits made the most of their day back

in the world and amused themselves by playing tricks on people.

When the Romans conquered the Celts, they added two autumn festivals to Samhain. One of these honoured Pomona, the goddess of fruits and trees. This is the most likely explanation for the inclusion of apples in our present-day Halloween.

The Christian church tried to abolish the old pagan celebrations, and in many cases did this by superimposing their own festivals on the days used for pagan festivities. Consequently, in the eighth century, Pope Gregory III moved All Saints' Day from May to the beginning of November. One hundred years later, Pope Gregory IV decided that All Hallows' Eve would be held on October 31, All Saints' Day on November 1, and All Souls' Day on November 2. The word "Halloween" comes from "All Hallows' Evening." This was gradually contracted to "All Hallows' Even'," followed by "All Hallowe'en," and finally "Halloween."

Nineteenth century immigrants from Scotland and Ireland brought Halloween to the United States as a secular, enjoyable celebration incorporating bats, broomsticks, cats, demons, ghosts, jack-o'-lanterns, witches, fortune telling, and bobbing for apples.

Trick-or-treating is a twentieth-century idea that began in the United States. However, it does have historic antecedents. On the eve of All Saints' Day, poor people in England went from door to door begging for soul cakes. They carried jack-o'-lanterns made from a variety of beet called mangel-wurzel.

There are many superstitions attached to Halloween. It is, for instance, important not to turn around if you hear someone walking behind you on Halloween. This is because it is likely to be death, and it is fatal to look him in the face.

You can also part the veil of the future on Halloween. If you stop at a crossroads and listen to the wind, you will discover what the following year has in store for you. If a girl stands in front of a mirror and eats an apple while combing her hair at midnight on Halloween, she will see a reflection of her future husband in the mirror. She might prefer to peel the apple in one long piece and toss it over her left shoulder. The shape the peel creates will indicate the first letter of her future partner's name. Another variation is to hang the length of peel beside the front door. The first man to come into the house through that

door will have the same first initial as her future partner.

Ducking apples is a game in which apples are floated in a container of water and children try to take a bite from them. An old superstition says that you will eventually marry the person who provided the apple you took a bite from.

In Mexico, people celebrate El Dia de los Muertos, the day of the dead, on November 1. Families put out special food for their deceased relatives to enjoy when they return for this one day of the year.

See *apple, church, crossroads, death, ghost, mirror, wind.*

Hand: The hand symbolizes power, and many good luck charms are in the shape of a hand. Hand charms allow you to receive what is rightfully yours. The palm of the  hand should be clearly visible for maximum effect. The palm pushes away any evil that might affect you. The right hand has always been considered lucky, and is considered the hand of God. The left hand belongs to the devil, and is considered unlucky.

The "hand of glory" was the hand of an executed criminal that was cut off while the body was still on the gallows. This hand was believed to enable its new owners to commit crimes without being caught. The left hand was preferred, but either hand could be used.

The right hand of Father Edmund Arrowsmith, a Catholic priest who was executed in 1628, can still be seen in the church of St. Oswald in Ashton, England. Pilgrims touch it, believing that it can cure a variety of diseases and afflictions.[31]

If your right palm starts itching you will shortly receive some money or hear important news. Conversely, if your left hand starts itching, you will shortly lose money, probably from an unexpected expense. The remedy for an itchy left hand is to immediately touch or knock on wood.

People with damp hands are believed to be passionate. People with cold hands are believed to have warm hearts.

See *baby, birthmark, charms, devil, finger, Friday the 13th, knock on wood, right side, thread, washing, wedding ring, white, wine.*

Handkerchief: If you accidentally drop a handkerchief, it is bad luck to pick it up yourself. If someone picks it up for you, the dropped handkerchief provides good luck both for you and for the person who picked it up.

However, if you find a handkerchief, it is bad luck to pick it up if the owner is not present. This is because people cry into their handkerchiefs. As tears mean sadness and sorrow, you will receive bad news if you touch the found handkerchief.

People still tie knots in handkerchiefs to prevent them from forgetting something. The original belief was that the knot prevented the devil from making you forget whatever it was.

Tying a knot in a handkerchief also can protect you. If your left ear itches or burns, it means someone is talking badly about you. If you tie a knot in your handkerchief, the person will bite his or her tongue.

Single men should not fold a handkerchief before putting it in a pocket. If they do, they will never marry.

See *devil, ear, knot, tongue.*

Handshaking: It is usual for people to shake hands with their right hands. This creates good luck for both people. It is thought to be bad luck to shake hands with the left hand. Many years ago, I knew a man who had lost his right arm in an accident. He refused to shake hands with his left hand,

as he believed it would cause bad luck for anyone whose hand he shook.

It is also considered bad luck if four people shake hands across each other at the same time. If this occurs accidentally, all four people should cross themselves to avert any bad luck that might otherwise be created. However, another superstition says a wedding is promised if four people shake hands with the pairs crossing each other.

See *left side.*

Hangover: A popular cure for a hangover is to have another drink, following the adage that "like cures like." This hangover cure is called "a hair of the dog that bit you." This dates back to an old belief that if a rabid dog bit you, you should immediately eat a burnt hair from the same dog to avoid rabies.

Hare: Until Christianity replaced earlier religions, the hare was considered a sacred animal. As the early church disapproved of pagan beliefs, people  had to continue their earlier practices in a manner that would not offend the church. They started carrying a hare's foot with them to provide luck and protection, in case the new god proved ineffectual.[32]

Hares and rabbits have always been associated with witchcraft. Many people believed witches could disguise themselves as hares and rabbits. Consequently, they are considered a bad luck omen, and sailors would return home if a hare crossed their path while they were heading to their ships. Brides postponed their weddings if a hare crossed their path in the weeks leading up to the day.

It is unlucky for a pregnant woman to see a hare, as this means she is likely to give birth to a child with a harelip. The remedy is for her to make three small tears in her clothing immediately after seeing the hare.

At one time it was believed that hares changed sex every year, and that they did not need sleep.

The milk of a hare is believed to cure whooping cough. Carrying a hare's foot will cure rheumatism, and rubbing hare's blood on your skin will remove freckles.

See *Easter, rabbit, rabbit's foot, sailors, wedding, white, witch, witchcraft.*

Hat: Hats should never be worn indoors as this will cause a headache. Men should always remove their hats when a funeral passes by. They risk becoming the next person to die if they don't. It is bad luck to place a hat on a bed or a table. It is even worse luck to store a hat under a bed. If a hat is accidentally placed on the head backwards,

the person will have bad luck for the rest of the day. However, buying a new hat will avert the bad luck.

See *bed, fairies, funeral, sneezing, table.*

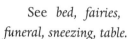

Hawthorn: The hawthorn tree has always had supernatural connotations because people believed that the crown of thorns that Jesus wore was made from hawthorn. Consequently, it was considered bad luck to bring hawthorn blossoms into the house. Witches were believed to use the thorns in their rituals to bring pain to unwitting victims. Some people believed that witches could turn themselves into hawthorn trees.

It is considered dangerous to sit under a hawthorn tree at Halloween, as you might be captured by the fairy folk who spend a great deal of time around hawthorn trees. This is why you need to ask permission from the fairies before cutting down a hawthorn tree. A branch of hawthorn hung over a doorway protects the occupants from evil spirits.

Legend says that when Joseph of Arimathea arrived at Glastonbury, he struck

the ground with his staff. The very first hawthorn tree appeared on the spot.

The hawthorn fared better in Greek and Roman culture. Greek women used to wear crowns of hawthorn flowers at weddings. The marriage torch was also hawthorn. The Romans placed leaves of hawthorn on the cradles of babies to protect them while they slept.

As the hawthorn doesn't flower until after the last frost, country folk use it to help predict the weather.

See *fairy, flowers, Halloween, lightning, tree, Wicca, witch.*

Headache: An old English remedy for headaches was to tie a piece of hangman's rope around the head so that it covered the temples. Another remedy, which was still in common use when I was growing up, was to push your thumb firmly against the roof of your mouth.

An interesting American remedy was to tie the head of a dead buzzard around your neck.

If you have a headache that continues for days on end, you could visit a graveyard, dig up a skull, and drive a nail through it.

Alternatively, you could drink some chamomile tea and go to bed.

To avoid having a headache for a whole year, you should allow your head to get wet the first time it rains in May.

See *amethyst, graveyard, hair, marigold, nest, St. Stephen.*

Heads or Tails: Since the times of the ancient Greeks and Romans, coins have been minted with the head of an emperor or other important leader on the front. The back of the coin has always been called the "tail."

The saying "heads you win, tails you lose" comes from the belief that the importance of the person depicted on one side of the coin makes that the more desirable side.

See *coin.*

Hearse: Some people believe it is bad luck to see a hearse. For most people, seeing or overtaking a hearse is neither good nor bad luck. However, it is considered bad luck to unexpectedly meet a hearse coming toward you. This omen is several times worse if the hearse is empty.

See *coffin, funeral.*

Heart: The heart is the traditional seat of the soul. The ancient Egyptians believed it was the home of the mind, also.

Heart-shaped charms and amulets are popular gifts that express one person's love for another. As well as providing protection, these charms attract good luck to everyone who wears them. Heart-shaped amulets, inscribed with a phrase from the holy Koran, are still worn in the Middle East today to ward off the evil eye.

See *alexandrite, amulet, charms, evil eye, scarab, serpentine, tattoo, thief, vampires, wedding ring.*

Heather: Heather is considered a lucky plant, and sometimes gypsies sell sprigs of it for luck. White heather is the luckiest variety, but in Scotland people have doubts about this. This is because a sprig of it was given to Bonnie Prince Charlie (1720–1788) in 1745 and it did him no good at all.

Hematite: Hematite is a form of iron oxide. It is known as the "stone that bleeds," as it gains a reddish streak when rubbed against a touchstone. Because of this, and also because it is iron ore, the ancient Greeks associated hematite with Mars, the god of war.

Hematite is believed to provide courage and motivation. Wearing hematite will eliminate procrastination, self-doubt, and fear.

Crystal healers use hematite to increase creativity, clear thinking, and memory enhancement.

See *gemstones.*

Hiccups: Hiccups are caused when the diaphragm and the muscles between the ribs contract. This creates an inhalation of air that can't reach the lungs, as the windpipe has been closed by the muscle spasm.

Until people realized this, hiccups seemed to occur for no reason at all. Consequently, they were blamed on the devil, and victims were said to be possessed. Some unfortunate people were "possessed" for days—or even years—on end. The world champion at hiccups was Charles Osborne of Indiana. From 1922 to 1990, he suffered seven million hiccups a year. He died one year later, in 1991.[33]

An old European superstition says that when you suffer from hiccups someone is talking about you, probably unkindly. If you catch hiccups in church, you are possessed by the devil until you rid yourself of them.

The old, superstitious cures for curing hiccups actually can work. Drinking a glass of water backwards works well for many people. Taking nine gulps of water while holding your breath is another effective

cure. Holding your breath while reciting the following words three times also appears to be helpful:

> As I went over the bridge,
> The hiccups fell in the water.

The reason these cures work is that in each of them you hold your breath long enough for the air inside your body to balance itself.

See *devil, thumb.*

Hoe: A hoe is a long-handled tool with a thin metal blade. It is used for weeding, loosening earth, and digging up crops. As it is an outdoor implement, it is considered bad luck to bring a hoe into the house.

Holly: Holly is considered a lucky plant and is used extensively in Christmas decorations. The ancient Druids believed holly had special powers, as the evergreen leaves proved it could survive winter. This gave people hope that spring was on its way. The Romans considered holly sacred, and used it as a decoration during their Saturnalia festivals. Christians believe the cross of Christ was made from holly, and the red berries symbolize Christ's blood.

Hanging holly in the house is said to protect the occupants from witchcraft.

Once Christmas is over, many people keep a sprig of holly in the house to protect it from lightning.

It is unlucky to cut down a holly tree. Holly boughs should never be burned while the wood is green, as this might cause a death in the family.

See *Christmas, cross, leaf, lightning, Twelfth Night, witchcraft.*

Holy Water: Holy water is water that is blessed and used in religious services. Fonts were often locked to prevent people from taking water home to heal the sick and protect the house. Holy water had the power to ward off witches and other evil demons. It even forced rats to leave the house. Washing in holy water was considered a good cure for warts.

See *rat, warts, witch.*

Honey: An old superstition says that you can cure an ulcer by putting honey on it. Nowadays, we know that honey has antibiotic properties, so maybe this superstition wasn't a superstition after all.

Honeymoon: The origin of the word "honeymoon" is lost. The most likely reason for the name is the northern European tradition of drinking honey in wine and other beverages during the first month of marriage. Honey has always been a symbol of sexuality, and some people still believe it works as an aphrodisiac.

The honeymoon destination needs to be kept secret. This superstition conjures up feelings of romanticism, secrecy, and the desire to be alone. In fact, this custom began in the days when the man captured the woman and took her someplace where her parents and other family members would not find her. Once the honeymoon period was over, the couple returned home, hoping everyone would accept the new arrangement.

The groom needs to lock the door on the wedding night. If the bride does it, the couple will have an argument during the night.

See *aphrodisiac, honey.*

Horn: In ancient times, horns were emblems of fertility. They were believed to provide protection from the devil, who is, of course, the "horned god." It is unlucky to keep a horn in the house.

A gesture known as "making horns" wards off the evil eye, but is also considered highly insulting. Consequently, it should

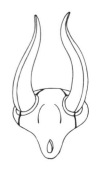

only be used as a last resort when someone has insulted you or tried to take unfair advantage. The horns are always made with the right hand. You make the gesture by folding your middle and ring fingers into the palm and holding them in position with the thumb. The first and little finger should be extended.

See *devil, evil eye, jet, unicorn.*

Horse: For thousands of years, horses were the most convenient way to travel long distances. Consequently, they were prized and valuable possessions, and were protected with amulets, charms, and horse brasses. Horses' tails were frequently plaited with ribbons to ward off witches. Horses are highly intuitive, and many people believe they can see ghosts.

Inhaling the breath of a horse is considered an effective way of curing a multitude of minor ailments, including whooping cough.

It is bad luck to change a horse's name. It is good luck to unexpectedly see a gray horse.

Your fortunes will improve if you spit on your little finger and rub it on a horse

See *amulet, breath, charms, death, ghost, horse brass, physiognomy, spitting, turquoise, white, witch.*

Horse Brass: For thousands of years, the horse was the main means of transport. Consequently, it had to be protected against evil spirits. The earliest horse brasses date back five thousand years, which shows how old this superstition is. Horse brasses are made of metal, and are kept polished to ward off evil and to deflect the evil eye. The designs were symbolic, and many people collect them today. Popular designs were depictions of the sun, crescent moon, acorns, swastikas, and lotus flowers.

See *evil eye.*

Horse Chestnut: Horse chestnuts act as lucky charms that bring good luck, relieve pain, attract wealth, and cure headaches. Horse chestnuts are sometimes called buckeyes. This is because the partly opened pods of the chestnut remind people of deer eyes. Ohio is referred to as the "Buckeye State" because of the many horse chestnuts growing there.

See *charms, headache.*

Horse Racing: Trainers and jockeys are highly superstitious, as luck plays a big part in their careers. Horses frequently win races by fractions of a second, which is enough to make anyone superstitious.

Like other athletes, jockeys have favorite items of lucky clothing they wear, such as underwear of a specific color. Trainers often hang a horseshoe over the barn door. They know it is bad luck to send an opened bag of salt to another racetrack, or to eat peanuts at the track.

It is good luck to pick up a coin at a racetrack if it is lying heads up, but bad luck if tails are up.

Saying "break a leg" to actors and actresses means good luck. However, it is bad luck to say this to a jockey before a race.

See *actors and actresses, athletes, coin, horseshoe, salt.*

Horseshoe: The horseshoe is one of the best-known lucky charms. It is believed to both avert evil and attract good luck. No one knows how or where this belief began, but it may be related to horse worship. Other possible origins are the

horseshoe's crescent shape, which moon worshippers revered, or the fact that it is made of iron, a metal believed to possess magical properties. Iron was also believed to protect people from the devil.

Horseshoes are usually nailed above the front door of a building to protect the occupants from evil spirits. Like many sailors before and after him, Lord Horatio Nelson had a horseshoe nailed to the mast of *HMS Victory* to ensure the good luck of everyone on board.

In Christian mythology, there is a story about how St. Dunstan (c.909–988 CE), Archbishop of Canterbury, used a horseshoe to ward off the devil. When he was young, St. Dunstan worked as a blacksmith. One day, a two-legged animal with hooves visited him and asked to be shod. St. Dunstan instantly recognized the creature as the devil, and pounded the nails into his feet with such force that the devil screamed with pain. Before he left, the devil promised never to enter a house with a horseshoe over the door.

In medieval times, three horseshoes were sometimes nailed to the end of a sick person's bed. These were  said to appease three gods: "One for God, one for Wod, and one for Lok." Although the first of these was Christian, the other two came from Norse mythology. Wod represented Woden, or Odin, the great magician god. Lok represented Loki, the cunning trickster who caused evil to occur. Both of these gods also had to be appeased. Interestingly, the expression "one for luck" refers to Loki.

The most effective horseshoes from a luck point of view are those that are found accidentally. A horseshoe that is bought is much less propitious. If you find a horseshoe, you should bring it home without saying a word to anybody. Remain silent until the horseshoe has been attached above your door. Horseshoes are normally attached above the front door of a house. This ensures that the good luck stays inside.

The horseshoe is normally nailed to the wall with the prongs pointing upwards, to prevent the good luck from falling out. This shape also contains the devil, ensuring he can't get into the house. Some people argue that this placement makes the horseshoe look like the devil's horns, and prefer to have the two points facing downwards. This arrangement, of course, cannot hold the devil, as he would fall out.

Blacksmiths used to be the only people who would attach horseshoes with the prongs pointing downwards. They believed this allowed good luck to flow freely into their workshops. However, many people attach their horseshoes this way nowadays, as a downward pointing horseshoe looks like a magnet that attracts good luck.

The third possibility is to position the horseshoe on its side, with the two points facing right. This forms the letter "C," which stands for Christ. This variation was popular with early Christians, and provides God's blessing on the building and its occupants. Even today, you will occasionally see horseshoes attached to a house sideways.

Horseshoe-shaped ornaments are frequently used as charms that are worn or carried. Brides are often given an ornamental horseshoe on their wedding day. The wedding cake often has a horseshoe incorporated into the design. Confetti is also frequently cut into the shape of a horseshoe.

The good luck produced by horseshoes even extends to their nails. Rings fashioned from horseshoe nails are just as lucky as horseshoes. The fact that there are seven nails in each shoe increases the luck.

See *business, charms, devil, door, horse racing, iron, moon, nail, sailors, seven, wedding cake.*

Hospital: Wednesday is the best day to go into the hospital for treatment. Monday is the best day to leave. The worst day to leave is Saturday. An old superstition says

that if you leave the hospital on a Saturday, you'll soon be back.

Hot Cross Buns: Hot cross buns are small buns, marked with a cross, that are made at Easter to commemorate the Crucifixion. The buns were originally eaten at ancient pagan festivals. The cross was added to create a Christian element and to ward off evil spirits. Hot cross buns were traditionally made on the morning of Good Friday, and some were hung in the house to provide the inhabitants with good luck throughout the upcoming year.

See *cross, Easter, Good Friday.*

Housewarming: Today, a housewarming is considered an opportunity to have a party and to show off your new home. This brings good luck to the home and all the occupants. Originally, housewarming was done to honor and thank the spirits that lived in the house. The center of the home was the hearth, and the fire that was kept burning there was considered sacred. The ancient Greeks and Romans had house gods who were worshiped at the hearth.

Gradually, the house gods were replaced by a variety of imps, fairies, and other spirits. They all had to be honored and looked after to ensure that the family living in the house received good luck and prosperity. This is why the hearth and grate had to be tidied up before the occupants went to bed. A new log would also be put on the fire to keep the house spirits happy. When people moved from one house to another, they would take live embers with them from the old home to start a fire in the new hearth. This was a "housewarming." By doing this, they took their particular spirits with them, and this continued their good luck.

It is considered lucky to carry a small piece of bread and some salt into your new home. This ensures that the family will continue to prosper in the new home. An old broom should not be taken from one house to the next. It is lucky to buy a new broom for the new home.

See *bread, broom, fairy, fire, salt.*

Hunch: To play a hunch means to act on your gut feelings or intuition. Originally, it meant to touch a hunchback to ward off evil and bad luck. This derives from an ancient belief that anything deformed or out of the ordinary is potentially evil. Consequently, when you touch anything

"evil," you are transferring any possibility of bad things happening to you onto the object you touch. For best results, it was important to touch the hunchback's hunch without him realizing it.

See *hunchback.*

Hunchback: Primitive people often believed people with physical deformities could bring luck if they were touched. Since the days of the ancient Egyptians, stroking a hunchback's back was considered an effective way of changing one's own luck.

In Italy today, small plastic figurines of hunchbacks, called Gobbos, are sold as lucky charms. Rubbing a Gobbo's back is believed to provide luck whenever necessary.

At one time, the casino at Monte Carlo employed a hunchback. His job was to make an appearance every time someone who had won a lot of money was about to leave, in the hope that they'd believe the superstition that hunchbacks are a lucky omen, and stay to make a few more bets.[34]

See *charms, taboo.*

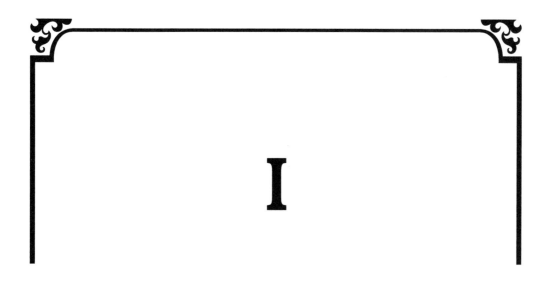

I

Illness: There are many superstitions concerning health and illness. Amulets and charms have long been worn to protect people against illnesses of different sorts. Some of these amulets and charms are intended to provide general good health, while others are used to protect a person from a specific illness.

One all-purpose cure was to take the patient outside at the time of the new moon. A relative had to blow on the patient nine times and then say,

> What I see, may it increase,
> What I feel, may it decrease,
> In the name of the Father, Son
> and Holy Ghost.

In medieval times, the cure for a stye in the eye was to stroke it with a black cat's tail. Each stroke had to be downwards. The tail of a tortoiseshell cat could be used in the same way to cure warts.

The ash tree helped protect people from evil spells, and could also be used to cure rickets and whooping cough. A lock of the person's hair was tied to the tree to effect a cure.

Potatoes were used to reduce the pain and inflammation of arthritis. A potato was cut in half and kept in the sufferer's pocket until it shrivelled away. The pain was believed to be absorbed by the potato, and progressively faded away as it withered.

Posies, or herbs, were frequently carried in pockets to protect the person from illness, as the nursery rhyme attests:

> Ring-a-ring o' roses,
> A pocket full of posies,
> A-tishoo! A-tishoo!
> We all fall down.

Another old remedy is still frequently quoted today: "An apple a day keeps the doctor away."

See *amulet, ash, charms, eye, hair, moon, potato, warts.*

Immaculate Conception: Mythology contains many examples of gods who were born from virgin mothers. Examples include Horus, Krishna, Attis, Adonis, and Dionysus. However, a number of humans also claim to have been born this way.

According to the Bible, Mary of Nazareth conceived Jesus by Immaculate Conception. This is not surprising, as Jesus is considered the Son of God. If you intend to claim divinity, you must have a divine pedigree.

Other people who claimed virgin birth include Plato, Pythagoras, Alexander the Great, Zoroaster, Buddha, Socrates, Pope Gregory, Scipio Africanus, and Appollonius. Even Emperor Nero claimed he was the result of a virgin birth.[35]

It is impossible to verify any of these claims, but obviously someone born this way would be different, and might well possess extraordinary qualities. Belief in the Immaculate Conception of the Virgin Mary has varied at different times over the last two thousand years. It was accepted by the Roman Catholic Church from the sixteenth century on, and became part of the dogma of the Church in 1854. The feast day is December 8.

Recently, biologists were astonished to learn that under certain circumstances, female komodo dragons can produce offspring by a process called parthenogenesis (usually only seen in some fish and insects). This enables an unfertilized egg to develop into a normal embryo without being fertilized by a sperm. Consequently, the offspring produced this way are the result of an immaculate conception.[36]

Incompletion: It is considered bad luck to completely finish a major task, such as building a house. As long as one small thing is left incomplete, the house will not become a target for evil spirits who might enter and cause damage.

Insomnia: Throughout history, many people have suffered from insomnia. Not surprisingly, a number of superstitions have been created to help alleviate this affliction. "Counting sheep" appears to be one that is universally known, but unfortunately does not appear to induce sleep. Neither does taking a brisk walk before going to bed, as this stimulates the body. Listening to the radio or watching TV usually makes it harder for people to fall asleep, though listening to soothing music can help.

The key to a good night's sleep is to relax both the body and the mind. This is hard to do if the person's mind is full of worries and concerns. Unfortunately, insomnia can become a habit. Meditation and self-hypnosis are both useful techniques that can help even chronic insomniacs enjoy a good night's sleep.

See *pillow, primrose, sleep, vervain.*

Iron: Iron has been considered lucky since prehistoric times. People witnessed the supernatural phenomenon of meteors flying through space and landing on the earth. The weapons they made from this mete-oric iron must have seemed like gifts from the gods. Obviously, as the iron came from the heavens, it had to be detested by evil spirits and the devil. People who armed themselves with metal swords and shields were easily able to defeat people without metal weapons. This increased the belief in the powerful, magical properties of iron. This belief held fast even after people started mining iron from the earth during the Bronze Age (c.2000 BCE). (Earth-mined iron lacks the nickel found in meteoric iron.)

Pliny, the first-century Roman author, recorded that people attached iron coffin nails over doors and windows to protect themselves from the evil spirits who roamed the world at night. In the Middle Ages, people would place an iron poker over the cradles of unbaptized babies to protect them from the devil. Even today, some people place an iron object, such as a knife, under a doormat to prevent witches from entering the house.

See *axe, clergyman, cradle, cutlery, devil, horseshoe, knife, miners, nail, pin, ring, sickle, spoon, wedding anniversaries, witch.*

Ironing Board: Ironing boards serve a valuable purpose, but indicate a death in the family if they fall and partially block an open door.

If an iron falls to the floor while you are ironing clothes, it is a sign that a family member will leave the house in the next twelve months.

A wedding will occur in the family if a freshly ironed garment is opened to reveal a diamond-shaped crease in the center.

Itching: Itching is often a warning that things are not what they seem. An itch on the right side of your body is a sign of a favorable outcome. Itching on the left side indicates problems and difficulties.

If someone is telling lies about you, your left ear will itch. If they are saying good things about you, your right ear will itch.

If your right palm itches, you will shortly receive money. You will shortly be paying out money if your left palm itches.

An itch in the right eye indicates good news, but an itch in the left eye is a sign of a disappointment or let down.

You will soon be angry if your nose starts to itch.

An itchy right foot is a sign of travel in your future.

If your body starts itching as you are about to make a major decision, take note of which side it is on. Proceed with your plans if the itch is on your right side, but think again about the proposal if it is on your left side.

See *ear, elbow, eye, left side, letters, lips, money, nose, right side, travel.*

Ivy: The ancient Romans dedicated ivy to Bacchus, as they believed it prevented drunkenness. Ivy is an evergreen plant, which is why it represents everlasting life in Christian symbolism. Partly because of this, ivy is frequently used for funeral wreaths. The ivy also protects the entire funeral party.

Drinking from a cup or bowl made of ivy wood is said to cure children of cramp and whooping cough.

Ivy growing on the walls of a house protects the inhabitants. However, if the ivy dies, it indicates that someone living in the house is about to die, too.

When no one was watching, single women would pluck a single leaf of ivy and say,

Ivy, ivy, I pluck thee,
In my bosum I lay thee;
The first young man who speaks to me,
Shall surely my true lover be.

A young man can see his future partner in his dreams by placing ten ivy leaves under his pillow.

See *corns, cramp, flowers, funeral, wedding.*

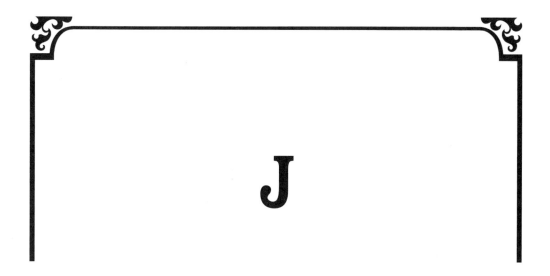

J

Jade: Jade is a semiprecious gemstone. It is considered a lucky stone, especially in the Orient. During the period of the Han Dynasty (206 BCE–221 CE), wealthy families placed pieces of jade in all the body orifices of dead relatives, believing that this would prevent putrefaction. This didn't work, and the ammonia produced by the decomposing bodies changed the color of the jade to chalky white.

Jade has always been popular in the East and many amulets are made from it. Jade butterflies symbolize everlasting love, and it is common for the groom to present one to his bride when they get married. Jade butterflies are also sometimes buried with the dead to ensure that the soul moves on to the next life. A jade padlock is some-times tied around the necks of infants to increase their hold on life. A bat amulet protects anyone who wears it from an early death. Many businessmen hold a jade amulet while conducting important meetings.

The ancient Egyptians also revered jade, and associated it with Maat, the goddess of truth.

When Christopher Columbus and his men reached Central America, they found that the natives used jade to protect themselves from kidney ailments. This belief was already well known in the West. Galen (c.130–201 CE), the Greek physician, had written about this more than a thousand years earlier. Even today, some people wear jade to protect themselves from renal problems.

Many gamblers wear jade, as they believe it will act like a magnet and increase their fortunes. Some people also wear jade ornaments in the belief that it will help them remember their dreams and provide insight into how to resolve personal problems.

See *amulet, bat, butterfly, dreams, gambling, gemstones.*

January: Weather superstitions are extremely common. Fog in January, for instance, is believed to predict a wet spring. Rain in January is a sign of many funerals. It is a sign of a good harvest if oak trees bend with snow in January.

See *funeral, oak, weather.*

Jasper: Jasper has been a popular protective amulet for thousands of years. Roman athletes used it to protect themselves from injury. St. Ephiphanius, the fourth-century Cypriot bishop, claimed jasper drove away poisonous snakes and evil spirits.

Jasper has always been used as an amulet of health. Today, crystal healers use different colored jaspers for a variety of purposes. Green jasper increases confidence and opens the heart chakra. Red jasper eliminates anxiety and stress. Yellow jasper provides protection on a journey. All jaspers are considered beneficial in preventing depression in people after a family bereavement.

See *athletes, gemstones, snake.*

Jaybird: An old superstition explains why you won't see many blue jays, or other jaybirds, during the weekend. Apparently, every Friday they go down to hell to tell the devil the bad things people have done during the week. They also bring the devil twigs to enable him to keep the fires of hell burning.

See *devil, fire, Friday.*

Jet: Jet is unlike most gems, as it is not a crystal mineral. It is a hard form of coal. Jet and amber are arguably the first two minerals to be used as amulets or talismans. Examples of jet amulets have been found in Paleolithic caves in France and Switzerland, and also in ancient Pueblo Indian ruins. The earliest examples are round and have holes drilled through them.

Pliny the Elder (23–79 CE), the Roman historian, recorded that jet could cure hysteria, reveal a predisposition toward epilepsy, and even determine if someone was a virgin.

The early Catholic Church encouraged the use of jet in crosses and rosaries. These were believed to eliminate hallucinations and nightmares created by the devil.

Jet was commonly used in Italy to make amulets of the fig sign or horn sign to ward off the evil eye. The black color, along with the sign, effectively doubled the effectiveness of these amulets.

Queen Victoria (1819–1901) wore jet for the last forty years of her life, as a symbol of her lengthy mourning. Jet became known as the "jewel of widows" and became a popular stone for widows to wear.

Jet has always been used to cure depression. Crystal healers today still use it for that purpose, and also to help heal problems with female reproductive organs.

See *amulet, devil, evil eye, fig, gemstones, horn, talisman.*

Jinx: A jinx is an influence that brings bad luck. Someone who is jinxed is certain that some sort of disaster awaits him or her. Of course, once someone believes that something bad is about to come, he or she will lose confidence and almost ask for some sort of accident to occur. Many people believe that a possession, such as a car, is jinxed if it constantly breaks down or needs undue maintenance.

See *car.*

July: July, the seventh month of the year, was named by Mark Anthony to honor Julius Caesar.

The "dog days" of summer (July 3–August 11) are the hottest days of the year. They were named *caniculares dies* by the ancient Romans, who noticed that Sirius, the Dog Star, which is the brightest star in the sky, rose and set with the sun at this time of year. They thought (wrongly as it turned out) that the Dog Star increased the power of the sun's rays, consequently creating the warmest time of year.

See *sky, sun, weather.*

July 25th: In the United States, many farmers superstitiously consider July 25th to be the best day of the year to sow turnip seeds. July 25th is also the feast day of St. Christopher.

See *St. Christopher.*

June: June has been considered a lucky month since Roman times. A man who

married in June was guaranteed prosperity, and his wife happiness. This is because June was allegedly named after the goddess Juno, who was happily married to Jupiter. Whenever anyone got married in her month, Juno ensured the union was blessed with great happiness. June also has the longest day of the year, and this symbolizes a long and happy marriage.

Farmers say, "If June be sunny, harvest comes early." They also say, "A cold and wet June ruins the rest of the year."

People believed that if it rained on St. Vitus' Day (June 15), they would experience rain for thirty days in a row.

See *agate, marriage, Midsummer's Eve, rain, weather.*

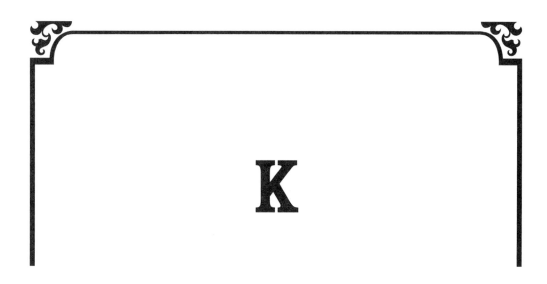

K

Kachina: Kachina are the protective ancestral spirits of the Native American Hopi tribe, who emerge from the earth at the start of the winter solstice and stay until the summer solstice. Kachina dolls, painted in six colors, represent the ancestral spirits. The different colors relate to the six cardinal directions: yellow for north, white for east, red for south, turquoise for west, black for sky, and gray for earth.

Kachina dolls are displayed in the home, and also used as toys by children. This is based on the belief that the spirit represented by the doll will bring good luck to the house if it becomes an integral part of the family.

Key: Keys were traditionally made of iron. Consequently, it made good sense to touch a key whenever danger threatened. Keys were considered lucky, and commonly placed under a child's pillow to keep him or her safe while asleep. It is considered bad luck to drop a key, and even worse luck to accidentally break one. It is also considered bad luck to jangle bunches of keys on Wednesdays. However, jangling keys can avert the evil eye, and this can be done on any day of the week.

Losing keys is considered an omen of some disaster, usually involving a death. A rusty key is a good omen, as it indicates an inheritance.

People turning twenty-one years old are often given cardboard keys to celebrate this milestone of maturity and independence. Alec Kendal mentioned this in his popular song *I'm Twenty-one Today*, which was published in 1912:

> I'm twenty-one today,
> Twenty-one today,
> I've got the key of the door,
> Never been twenty-one before.

When lovers exchange keys, it is believed that they are unlocking each other's hearts. It symbolizes love and happiness.

In Japan, three keys tied together create a powerful lucky charm that attracts love, health, and wealth.

See *Bible, charms, death, evil eye, iron, nose, rust.*

Kiss: The act of kissing someone or something is a gesture of love and affection. Kissing an amulet or charm also provides luck and good fortune. Gamblers kiss lottery tickets and betting slips, hoping this will increase their luck.

It is unlucky to kiss someone on the nose, as this leads to an argument. Likewise, leaning over someone's back to kiss them on the cheek is unlucky, as you risk being stabbed in the back. It's also thought to be highly risky for a single girl to kiss a man with a moustache. If a hair becomes stuck to her lips, she will never get married.

All children know that pain disappears when a parent kisses an injury.

It is considered extremely good luck if a child spontaneously kisses you immediately after first meeting you. This is a sign that you'll enjoy a long and healthy life. However, an unwilling kiss from a child is bad luck. If the parent forces the child to kiss you, you should immediately cross your fingers to avert the bad luck.

See *amulet, charms, children, gambling, lips, mistletoe, nose, St. Valentine's Day, two-dollar bill.*

Knife: The fact that knives were originally made of iron, and can be used for both good and evil purposes, has created a number of superstitions.

Two knives should never be crossed, as this causes arguments and may even attract the devil. While staying in a house in Devon, I was surprised when the lady of the house picked up a knife and

banged the table three times with the end of the handle. She had noticed that two knives had accidentally become crossed while she was gathering up plates and cutlery at the end of the meal. By banging with the handle, she averted the bad luck that would otherwise have come her way.

Cooks should never use a knife to stir food, as "when you stir with a knife, you cook up strife."

Do not pick up a knife you find when you're away from home. Leave it where it is, as it will bring bad luck to whoever picks it up.

It is a common custom to give a small coin to anyone who gives you a knife or a pair of scissors. As the recipient has then, in effect, bought the gift, he or she becomes responsible for any injuries that ensue as a result of using the knife or scissors.

It is bad luck to give a knife as a wedding gift, as it has the power to cut the marriage ties.

It is bad luck to open a pocketknife before handing it to someone. This leads to arguments. If it is already open, put it down so that the other person can pick it up.

Knives need to be treated with great care immediately after someone in the family has died. This is to avoid accidentally stabbing the dead person's soul.

It is considered a good idea to keep a jar of water with a knife in it behind the front and back doors of a house or barn. This scares away the devil and other evil spirits, as they see their reflection in the water along with the knife.

See *coin, cutlery, devil, iron, spoon, water, wedding.*

Knock on Wood: The origin of the superstition of knocking on wood to avert bad luck is lost in time. It probably dates back thousands of years, when people thought gods lived in trees. Knocking on the tree trunk acknowledged the god, who would then provide help. Many Christians believe that knocking on wood comes from the fact the Jesus Christ was crucified on a wooden cross.

See *cross, wood.*

Knot: When people get married they are described as "tying the knot." In ancient Babylon, threads were taken from clothes belonging to both the bride and groom and tied into a knot. This was a form of

magic that demonstrated that the couple were truly one.

Any knots on clothing worn by women giving birth were untied to make the arrival of the baby as smooth as possible for both mother and child. In the Middle Ages, people also opened locks, drawers, cupboards, and doors to ensure that the birth was as smooth as possible.

Knots were frequently untied in houses in which someone was dying. This was because knots could potentially hinder the soul's departure from the house.

In parts of Europe, the bridegroom would go to the altar with one shoe untied. This protected him from witches, evil spirits, and even frustrated rivals who might otherwise cast a spell to make him incapable of "untying" his bride's virginity on the wedding night.

In the Middle Ages, people believed you could prevent a marriage from being consummated by tying a knot in a piece of rope while the wedding ceremony was taking place. The knotted rope was tossed into a river. The marriage would remain unconsummated until the rope was found and the knot untied.

An old party game involved a length of cotton with a knot tied in the middle. A game of "tug-o'-war" would be played until the cotton broke. Whoever retained the piece containing the knot could make a wish, and be confident it would be granted.

In Russia, knots are considered protective, and many peasants carry a knotted length of yarn as an amulet. Fishing nets, which contain hundreds of knots, are thrown over the bride on her wedding day to wish her good luck, long life, and happiness.

See *amulet, baby, birth, death, handkerchief, marriage, nose, ring, rope, sewing, shoelaces, wedding, witch.*

L

Ladder: It is considered good luck to climb a ladder with an odd number of rungs. It's bad luck to fall off a ladder. You may get hurt, but what's worse is that it's a sign you're going to lose some money.

Walking under a ladder is believed to cause bad luck. No one really knows why, but at least three theories have been proposed. The most likely theory is that a ladder forms a triangle when placed against a wall. The triangle symbolizes the Holy Trinity. Consequently, when you walk through it, you effectively insult the Trinity and attract the devil. The second theory concerns the use of the ladder in hangings. The ladder would be propped against a beam to allow the person about to be hanged to climb high enough to reach the rope. A third theory dates back to ancient Egyptian times, when people believed you might see a god walking up or down the ladder while you walked under it.

Fortunately, there are five remedies to avert bad luck if you happen to walk under

a ladder. One is to make a wish while you are walking under the ladder. Alternatively, you could walk backwards through the ladder again, and continue walking backwards to where you started the walk. Or, you could make a fig sign while walking under the ladder. Or else you might choose to say "bread and butter" to yourself. Finally, you could cross your fingers and keep them crossed until you see a dog.

At one time people believed it was bad luck to look through a ladder, or to pass anything through a ladder. Spitting three times can avert the bad luck caused by these actions.

See *bread and butter, devil, dog, fig, grave, luck, money, spitting, V-sign.*

Ladybug: The ladybug, or ladybird, is a small red beetle with black spots. It is a useful in-sect that preys on garden pests. The ladybug is considered a good luck charm all around the world, and it is bad luck to kill one. When you see one, you are supposed to place it on a finger and recite,

> Ladybird, ladybird,
> Fly away home,
> Your house is on fire
> And your children all gone;
> All except one
> And that's little Ann

> And she has crept under
> The warming pan.

After reciting the nursery rhyme, blow on the beetle and the ladybug will fly away. This produces good luck. Similar rhymes are found in most languages.

The house on fire has puzzled researchers, as people said this to witches when attempting to get rid of them. In Germany it is thought the song was originally a charm to help the sun pass through the dangers of sunset. The house on fire symbolized the red evening sky.

It is good luck if a ladybug lands on you. When it flies away again, it will take with it all of your problems and concerns. It is important that the ladybug flies away when it feels like it. All the good luck disappears if you brush or blow the ladybug away (unless, of course, you recite the nursery rhyme before blowing on the beetle).

The ladybug has been associated with the Virgin Mary since the Middle Ages. The name "ladybird" comes from "Our Lady's bird."

Ladybug charms are still worn to attract wealth and success. It is also believed that young girls can count the number of black spots on a ladybug to see how many children they'll have. Consequently, it is sometimes also used as a fertility amulet.

See *amulet, charms, fire, sun, toothache, witch*.

Lamb: The lamb is an important Christian symbol. In John 1:29 we read, "Behold the Lamb of God, which taketh away the sin of the world." John the Baptist is almost always portrayed carrying or accompanied by a lamb. Because of these associations, witches cannot disguise themselves as lambs.

Lambs have always been considered lucky. If the first lamb you see in the spring is black, you can make a wish and be sure it will be granted. Where I grew up, farmers are happy if the first birth of the season is either a black lamb or twin white lambs. Both of these indicate a happy and prosperous year. In most places, a flock of lambs that includes one black lamb is considered extremely lucky (although some people think it's bad luck if the black lamb was the first born). And while it is considered bad luck for a flock to contain more than one black lamb, it is seen as disas-

trous for a ewe to give birth to twin black lambs. To remedy this situation, the twin black lambs need to be killed before they bleat for the first time.

The first lamb you see in spring will tell you how the rest of the year will go. If its head is looking towards you, the rest of the year will be good, but it will be a bad year if the lamb has its head turned away from you.

Your fortunes will improve if you have money in your pocket when you see the first lamb in spring. Turning the money over once ensures you will not lack money in the coming year.

See *dove, money, witch*.

Lapis Lazuli: In ancient Babylon and Egypt, lapis lazuli was considered as valuable as gold. It is a mixture of lazurite, pyrite, and calcite. The violet and blue of the lazurite, flecked with the gold of the pyrite, combine to create a mineral that has been mined for more than six thousand years. Its name comes from two Latin words: *lapis*, meaning stone, and *lazuli*, meaning blue.

Puabi, queen of Sumer some five thousand years ago, wore gold and silver robes studded with lapis lazuli.[37] The Egyptians used lapis lazuli for amulets and cylinder seals. Scarab amulets made of lapis lazuli can be found in museums all around the world.

In the thirteenth century, Albertus Magnus wrote that lapis lazuli, "a blue stone with little golden spots," would cure depression and the quartern fever, which was an intermittent fever that returned every third or fourth day.[38] In the Middle Ages, both men and women carried lapis lazuli to prevent conception and to cure heart problems.

Lapis lazuli is still used today to protect the eyes, throat, bones, and immune system, and to ward off psychic attack. It can also make shy people more outgoing.

See *amulet, evil eye, gemstones*.

Laughter: Laughter is good for your health, but too much laughter is considered a sign that the person's days are numbered. Uncharacteristic laughter from someone who seldom smiles or laughs is a sign of bad luck, and could indicate his or her imminent

death. Friends of mine in Wiltshire frequently told me that people who laughed before breakfast would cry before dinner.

See *Friday the 13th*.

Lavender: Lavender comes from the Latin *lavare*, which means "to wash." It possesses strong anti-bacterial qualities that have been utilized since Roman times.

In the nineteenth century, lavender was used to mask unpleasant smells, and Victorian ladies were immediately suspicious when they entered a room smelling of lavender. In the language of flowers, lavender means "distrust." Lavender was also sewn into heart-shaped bags to freshen drawers and closets.

Today, lavender is used in many space-clearing and magic rituals. Lavender also helps soothes troubled nerves and aids sleep.

See *flowers, magic*.

Leaf: It is considered a sign of a bad winter if trees start shedding their leaves early. If someone manages to catch a falling leaf before it hits the ground, he or she will not catch a cold during the coming winter. In addition, this fortunate person will remain happy for the next twelve months.

It is good luck for dead leaves to blow into a house. However, it is bad luck to carry dead leaves inside.

A fig leaf is a sign of modesty, and was used to adorn paintings and statues, particularly in Victorian times. The Bible says,

And the eyes of them both were opened, and they knew that they were naked; and they sewed fig leaves together, and made themselves aprons. (Genesis 3:7)

A rather complicated method of invoking dreams of your future partner involves collecting nine leaves of the female holly (as they have smooth edges), tying them into a handkerchief with nine knots, and placing the bundle under your pillow.

See *colds, dreams, holly, knot, nine, oak, tree, yellow.*

Leap Year: Leap years occur every four years. They have an extra day, which is known as an intercalary day. This day enables the calendar to remain in agreement with the cosmic order.

It is believed that anything new begun in a leap year will have a good chance of success. Children who are conceived or born in a leap year also have a good chance of achieving significant success in life.

Traditionally, women are able to propose to men in a leap year.

See *February 29th.*

Lee Penny: The Lee penny, named after Sir Simon Lockhart of Lee, consists of a blood-red, heart-shaped stone set into the reverse side of a silver Edward IV groat. The power of the Lee penny was consid-

ered so great that during the reign of Charles I, the burghers of Newcastle were prepared to pay six thousand pounds to borrow it to help them cure a plague of cattle. The Lee penny is still owned by the Lockhart family in Scotland.

See *coin.*

Left Side: The left side has always been associated with bad luck and evil. The Latin word for left is *sinister*. This is why Christ sits on the right hand, or good, side of God. This is also why people throw salt over their left shoulder after accidentally spilling some. They feel that the devil might pounce on them after an accident of that sort. Obviously, he will attack from the left, and being a coward, will also attack from the rear.

This superstition about the negativity of the left side has caused enormous problems over the years for the eight to fifteen percent of the population who are left-handed. They were assumed to have some sort of connection with the devil and evil spirits. However, it was considered lucky to meet a left-handed person, except on Tuesday, when it was highly unlucky. In 1604, Thomas Dekker had a character in his play *The Honest Whore* say, "I am the most wretched fellow: sure some left-handed priest christned (sic) me, I am so unlucky: I am never out of one puddle or another" (Act 2, scene 5).

Black magic is called the "left-handed path," as it is a negative form of magic that is intended to harm people, or force them to do something against their will.

Professional card players are often highly superstitious and pick up their cards with their right hands. Using their left hands would cause bad luck.

Recently, researchers discovered that left-handed people are more efficient at dealing with multiple stimuli than right-handed people. Left-handed people use both sides of their brains for language, making them more bicerebral. This has huge advantages for left-handed people when playing sports. I always hated playing tennis against my left-handed brother, as he could play equally well with either hand. Instead of playing a backhand, he'd simply play the shot with the racquet in his other hand.

Scientists have also found that identical twins are more likely to be left-handed than other people. Older women are more likely to give birth to left-handed children.

See *abracadabra, bed, clothing, days of the week, handshaking, itching, magic, right side, salt.*

Lemmings: Lemmings are small, vole-like rodents that live in the Arctic. Every now  and again they commit mass suicide by jumping off cliffs into the sea. This action was believed to be an indication of a major disaster about to occur.

These mass suicides are unintentional and are caused by hunger. In their search for food, many lemmings embark on mass migrations, and drown while attempting to cross expanses of water.

Leo: Leo is the fifth sign of the zodiac. Its symbol is the lion. Its element is fire, and its gemstone is sardonyx. The keyword for Leo is: I will.

Leos are ambitious, determined, and enthusiastic. They like to do everything in a large way, and express themselves openly, honestly, and confidently. They are proud people who dislike being ridiculed or demeaned. They are generous, magnanimous, and susceptible to flattery. Their enthusiasm means that they sometimes get carried away and exaggerate or distort the truth, as they like to tell a good story. They make good leaders, as they have the ability to inspire and motivate others.

See *astrology, elements, fire, gemstones, zodiac.*

Letters: A letter is on its way to you if you sneeze on a Wednesday, your nose itches, or a spider dangles from its thread immediately in front of you.

It is bad luck for letters to cross in the mail. The only exception to this rule is for Christmas cards.

If you are giving a letter to your lover, make sure that it is handed to his or her right hand. Your love will end if it is placed in the left hand.

If you are writing regularly to your sweetheart, use a special pen for this purpose. Use a different pen for paying bills and writing other letters.

See *itching, sneeze, spider.*

Libra: Libra is the seventh sign of the zodiac. Its symbol is the scales. Its element is air, and its gemstone is opal. The keyword for Libra is: I balance.

Librans are harmonious, noncompetitive, well-balanced people. They tend to be indecisive. Consequently, although they enjoy talking, they dislike arguments and disagreements. Librans enjoy beauty and frequently become involved in creative pursuits. Librans are naturally intuitive.

See *air, astrology, elements, gemstones, opal, zodiac.*

Lightning: Originally, lightning was thought to be an expression of the gods' anger. Consequently, a large range of superstitions developed that were designed to protect and comfort people. Early Christians claimed that the Virgin Mary created lightning to warn people about Satan's thunder. The lightning flash gave people enough time to cross themselves before the thunder. Most superstitions about lightning were forgotten once Benjamin Franklin invented the lightning rod.

The most common superstition about lightning is that it never strikes the same place twice. However, this is not true, as the Empire State Building in New York is struck more than fifty times a year.[39]

Different trees were thought to offer the best shelter to those caught out in a storm. The oak was traditionally thought to be the safest tree, but many people recommended the hawthorn. A rhyme from Sussex also favors the hawthorn:

Beware of the oak; it draws the stroke.
Avoid the ash; it courts the flash;
Creep under a thorn;
it can save you from harm.

Many people believed a stem of hawthorn, especially one cut on Ascension Day, would protect them from lightning.

The ringing of church bells was also thought to protect people from thunder and lightning.

It was important to open windows during a thunderstorm. This allowed any lightning that entered the house to get out again.

As dogs' tails were supposed to attract lightning, it was a good idea to keep well away from the family dog while a storm was raging.

Indians in North America buried people who had been killed by lightning on the spot where the incident occurred. The person was buried face downwards, and the soles of the feet were slit to prevent the person from becoming a ghost.[40]

See *bell, dog, hawthorn, oak, sickle, thunder, thunderstorm, tree, umbrella, vervain, walnut, weather, window.*

Lilac: The lilac is a small shrub that produces pale pinkish-violet or white blossoms. The flowers usually have four petals. A white flower with five petals is called the "luck lilac" or "luck flower." According to a New England superstition, the "luck lilac" should be swallowed by a single girl.

If it was swallowed easily, it meant that the man she had in mind loved her. However, he didn't love her if the flower was difficult to swallow.

See *flowers, white.*

Lily: The lily is believed to have sprung from the tears of Eve as she left the Garden of Eden. In Christian tradition, the lily symbolizes chastity, innocence, and purity. The archangel Gabriel is often shown holding a lily branch in paintings of the Annunciation. Joseph sometimes holds one too, depicting his wife's virginity.

Because of all these associations, it is bad luck to damage lily blooms. If you do, you risk harming all the virgins in your family.

Lilies were thought to provide protection from the devil. They also deterred ghosts and witches. Lilies are frequently used at funerals and weddings to symbolize purity. However, many people refuse to have them inside their homes because their heavy scent is seen as a portent of death.

See *boils, flowers, funeral, ghost, wedding, white, witch.*

Lips: A superstition that can be found all around the world says that itching lips is a sign that you'll shortly be kissed.

See *itching, kiss*.

Lizard: Thousands of years ago, lizards were considered extremely lucky animals, as seeing one was a sign that a poisonous snake was close at hand.

Lizards have also been associated with vision, and lucky charms in the shape of lizards are reputed to be good for the eyes. People who kill lizards are also believed to pay for their sins with failing vision.

Lizards also help unborn babies. Pregnant women who wear lizard charms are believed to give birth to happier, healthier babies than women who don't. It is good luck for a pregnant woman to see a live lizard, as this indicates a long, happy and prosperous life for her unborn baby.

See *baby, charms, snake, wedding*.

Lodestone: Lodestone is magnetic iron ore. It is no longer classified as a *gemstone*, but is still used today as an *amulet* to magically increase the attraction couples feel for each other.

Pliny the Elder (23–79 CE), the Roman historian, credits a young shepherd named Magnes with discovering the metal. Magnes found that the nails of his shoes were attracted to a particular rock on Mount Ida. Lodestone is also known as magnetite, after Magnes the shepherd. Alexander the Great (356–323 BCE) is said to have given a piece of lodestone to all of his soldiers to protect them from evil spirits. As well as warding off the spirits, lodestone was believed to encourage good thoughts and relieve pain.

Lodestone has always been related to love and passion. In China, it was called *t'su shi*, the "loving stone." In Assyria, men and women rubbed a lodestone over their bodies before making love. Even today, prostitutes in Mexico rub a lodestone over their bodies to attract customers.

In the late fourteenth century, John of Trevisa wrote that lodestone could be used to test the virtue of a wife using a procedure that had been well known for one thousand years. A piece of lodestone was placed under the pillow when the wife was asleep. If she was a good wife, she'd immediately embrace her husband. However, if she was unfaithful, the stone would immediately cause her to jump out of bed.[41]

See *gemstones, nail, shoes*.

Lottery: Superstition says that odd numbers are more likely to win lotteries than even ones. It is even better if the series of numbers on the ticket ends with three, seven, or nine.

Love: There are countless superstitions about attracting and retaining love.

It is thought that if you plant marigolds in ground that your desired partner has walked on, his or her love for you will grow as the flowers bloom.

If a young man plucks a twig of laurel from a tree while out walking with his girl friend, and then divides it equally with her, the love will continue to grow as long as they each keep their half.

Love letters should always be written with ink. Writing a love letter in pencil or on a computer indicates a short-term relationship. Love letters should never be mailed on a Sunday. It is bad luck to destroy love letters as long as the relationship lasts. If the relationship has ended, the letters can be destroyed, but only by tearing them into small pieces.

See *flowers, marigold, mirror, peas, rose, St. Valentine's Day, turquoise, yarrow.*

Luck: Our lives are made up of thousands of chance occurrences. As we are so close to these events, we have no way of knowing which ones are likely to change our lives. One evening, in September 1967, I arrived in London knowing no one. The following morning, I was walking down Haymarket and came across two friends from New Zealand. They were going to a party that night, and invited me to join them. At the party I met a young woman called Margaret, who became my wife four years later. Meeting the two friends on the street was obviously lucky for me. Agreeing to come to the party was also extremely fortunate. The fact that Margaret had decided to come to the party was also a stroke of luck. The fact that we met and arranged to meet a couple of days later could also be called luck. Clearly, luck was shining on me that day. If I had walked down Haymarket two minutes earlier or later, I would not have seen my friends, and my future would have been completely different.

The word "luck" is derived from an old Anglo-Saxon verb that means "to catch." Luck is a quality that certain objects possess, but a few, fortunate people seem to have luck around them all the time. These are the people who are described as being "born lucky." These people have no need for charms or amulets, as they somehow attract luck to themselves no matter what they do.

But for many people, luck is something intangible that sometimes works for us and at other times works against us. This is why luck has been anthropomorphized as "Lady Luck." Sometimes she is with us, guiding, supporting, and aiding, but at the next moment—irrational, capricious—she has gone from our side, and we have no way of knowing when she will return. Consequently, she has to be constantly wooed.

People have always believed in luck, and most superstitions have evolved from people's attempts to lure good luck and avert bad luck. Throughout history, people have carried amulets and lucky charms in the hope of receiving good luck, or at the least, preventing bad luck from occurring. Many people still believe that everything that happens to us is fate, despite apparent evidence that we are in control of our actions. These people still believe Shakespeare's immortal words in *Julius Caesar*:

> There is a tide in the affairs of men,
> Which, taken at the flood,
> leads on to fortune;
> Omitted, all the voyage of their life
> Is bound in shallows and in miseries.
>
> (Act 4, scene 3)

Many civilizations have had gods and goddesses of luck. The ancient Egyptians had Bes and Beset. They were squat, bandy-legged, dwarf-like creatures that protected people from harm and bad luck. Fortuna was the goddess of luck to the ancient Romans. The word "fortune" is derived from her name. The term "Lady Luck" is also a reference to her. Fortuna was usually pictured carrying a cornucopia full of good fortune, which was given to those who worshipped her. The Japanese have a fat and cheerful god of luck called Hotei who dispenses good luck from a bag containing an abundance of good fortune.

Millions of dollars a year are spent on lucky charms today, and many people carry objects, such as a lucky coin or a four-leaf clover, in the hope of gaining good luck as a result. Other people perform small rituals, hoping they can evade the vagaries of fate as a result.

No one is immune to this superstition. People who scoff at the idea of lucky charms may well carry a St. Christopher medallion when they travel. When I've questioned people about this, they tell me that they don't really believe in it, but it can't hurt. Few people will walk under a ladder, or open an umbrella indoors. Many people knock on wood to avert fate, and say "God bless you" when someone sneezes.

Many people have a strong belief in the efficacy of their lucky charms. Many sports people possess lucky boots, bats, or items of clothing that they wear whenever playing an important game. Bobby Robson had a lucky scarf, and believed this helped the English football team he managed win the 1990 World Cup.

Even the rich and famous have rituals and charms to ensure good luck. John D. Rockefeller, Sr., had a lucky stone that he carried with him everywhere. Dr. Samuel Johnson, the British writer and critic, always stepped through a door using his right foot.

Lucky charms can be almost anything, but the most popular ones are the four-leaf clover, horseshoe, rabbit's foot, and St. Christopher medal. The luckiest objects to find are horseshoes, four-leaf clovers, and teeth.

See *amulet, charms, clover, coin, horseshoe, knock on wood, ladder, rabbit's foot, ring, St. Christopher, teeth, travel, umbrella.*

Lycanthropy: Lycanthropy is the belief that a person can transform into a wolf. The word comes from the Greek words *lukos*, meaning "wolf," and *anthropos*, meaning "a man." Because the wolf was considered the most ferocious animal in Europe, people who could transform themselves into wolves wielded enormous power.

Although lycanthropy refers specifically to wolves, it has come to mean shapeshifting into any wild animal, such as a leopard or hyena.

See *werewolf, wolf, zoanthropy.*

Lying: Because words were believed to possess enormous power, it was sometimes necessary to lie to preserve the luck embedded in them. Consequently, fishermen lied about the size of their catches. Telling the truth meant the risk of bad luck the next time they went fishing. Fishermen even used false names for their fishing grounds, landmarks, and even their own names and the proper names of the fish they caught. All of this was a form of self-protection, to preserve good luck and avert possible bad luck.

See *fishermen, words.*

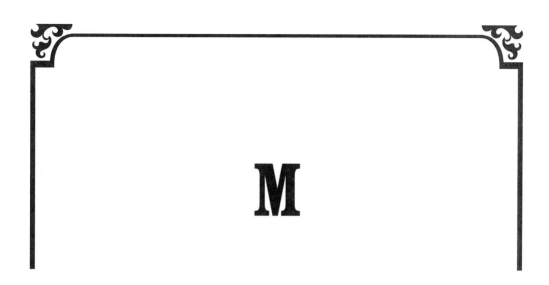

M

Macbeth: Many theater people believe William Shakespeare's famous tragedy was cursed from the outset. It is suggested that Shakespeare probably wrote it to impress King James I, because it is shorter than his other plays and the king had a low boredom threshold. The play is set in the king's home country, Scotland, and contains mentions of witchcraft (the king had written a book on demonology). Legend says that the spells used by the witches in the play were authentic. The real witches took offense at this and cursed the play.

Problems began even before the first performance. Hal Berridge, the boy who was to play Lady Macbeth at the first performance, died of a fever shortly before the play's opening on August 7, 1606, and William Shakespeare acted the role in his place. An overweight, bearded Lady Macbeth must have been a sight to behold.

In a performance in Amsterdam in 1672, the actor playing Macbeth used a real dagger and killed the actor playing Duncan.

In 1721, a nobleman got up during the play and walked across the stage to speak to his friends on the other side. This infuriated the actors, who used their stage swords to drive the nobleman and his friends out of the theater. They returned a short time

later, with the militia, and burned the theater to the ground.

Abraham Lincoln read passages from *Macbeth* to friends while traveling down the Potomac River, on the River Queen, the day the Civil War ended. Five days later he was killed.

In 1947, Harold Norman was stabbed in the sword fight that finishes the play and died as a result of his wounds. His ghost still haunts the Colliseum Theatre in Oldham, where the accident occurred.

In 1953, Charlton Heston suffered burns on his groin and legs on the opening night of an outdoor production of *Macbeth* in Bermuda. The smoke and flames created by the soldiers setting fire to Macbeth's castle also caused the audience to flee in terror.

The Broadway production of *Macbeth* in 1988, starring Glenda Jackson and Christopher Plummer, set a variety of records. Apparently the production went through three directors, six stage managers, five MacDuffs, two set designers, two lighting designers, and six cast changes, as well as a variety of illnesses and injuries including twenty-six bouts of flu, torn and damaged ligaments, and groin injuries.

Professional theater people respect the curse and avoid saying the name of the play inside a theater. Instead, they call it "the Scottish play," "the Scottish tragedy,"

or even "that play." If someone happens to mention the name inside a theater, he has to leave the room, turn around three times, spit on the floor, and then knock on the door of the room and ask for permission to come back in. Variations of this include leaving the theater entirely to perform the ritual, swearing instead of spitting, spitting over both shoulders, or reciting the following words from *Hamlet*:

Angels and Ministers
of Grace defend us!
Be thou a spirit
of health or goblin damn'd,
Being with thee airs
of heaven or blasts from hell,
Be thy intents wicked or charitable,
Thou com'st in such
a questionable shape
That I will speak to thee.
(Act 1, scene 4)

See *spell, theater, witch, witchcraft.*

Magic: Magic is the word used to describe rituals and other activities that are intended to effect change in the universe in ways that do not fit with current scientific thought. Magicians, in effect, are using their will and imagination to exert change. Magic is probably the first way in which ancient people tried to control the strange and frightening world they lived in. The cave paintings of animals such as deer and bison may be good examples of this. By painting them, the artist "captured" them before they were physically caught.

There are two types of magic: black and white. Black magic is used to achieve sinister and egoistic goals. White magic is used for good purposes. Usually, the type of magic is obvious, but sometimes people can go too far and turn what was originally white magic into black magic. An example would be a young man who is performing a magic spell to attract a partner. This is an example of white magic. However, if he performs a spell to attract a specific person to him, he is performing black magic. This is because he's disregarding the thoughts, feelings, and desires of the other person.

See *elemental, left side, pin, prayer, ring, spell, wand, wedding, Wicca, widdershins, willow, women, words.*

Magnetite: Men can wear or carry magnetite to increase their strength, courage, virility, and luck. Women should not wear magnetite at any time.

Magpie: A single magpie is a bad omen. If you saw one, you had to ward off the impending doom by greeting it in a friendly fashion, either by curtseying or raising a hand. Alternatively, you could make the sign of the cross on your chest or cross your thumbs.

A rhyme lists the meaning of different numbers of magpies:

> One for sorrow,
> Two for mirth,
> Three for a wedding,
> Four for a birth,
> Five for rich,
> Six for poor,
> Seven for a witch,
> I can tell you no more.

See *birds, cross, ornithomancy.*

Malachite: Malachite is a copper ore that contains patterns of light and dark green. The ancient Egyptians had malachite mines six thousand years ago, and used it to create amulets and scarabs. They believed that it protected young children. Consequently, it was frequently tied to cradles to protect babies as they slept.

In the Middle Ages, people used malachite to protect themselves from accidental falls, fainting, and hernias. People also wore malachite as a protection. They believed it broke into pieces at the first sign of danger, giving people time to determine the best way to handle the situation.

Malachite is still used as an amulet in Italy. It is usually cut into a triangular shape, with the color banding in the stone forming an eye. This is used to protect people from the evil eye. In Bavaria, necklaces of malachite are used to help overcome the pain of teething. Malachite is believed to eliminate over-tiredness and depression. Wearing a malachite necklace in bed encourages restful sleep.

Malachite is sometimes called the "salesperson's stone," as it provides sales people with confidence, protection, astuteness, and the ability to sell.

Today's technology has created a new use for malachite. It is being worn to protect people from the radioactivity of computers, microwaves, and fluorescent lights.

See *amulet, baby, children, cradle, evil eye, gemstones, scarab.*

Mandrake: The mandrake is a plant with a subdivided root that makes it appear human-like. People believed it shrieked when pulled from the ground. Anyone who pulled up a mandrake had to make the sign of the cross over the plant three times first, or else he would die. In Germany it was considered the devil's plant and was called the

galgenmannchen, or "little gallows man." Anyone who owned one was believed to be possessed by the devil.

Because the mandrake resembles the groin, people thought that eating it would increase sexual desire and fertility. In fact, mandrake is far from being an aphrodisiac, as it contains toxic belladonna alkaloids.

In Genesis 30:14, Reuben, who was Jacob's first wife's son, brought mandrakes home to his mother Leah. Rachel, another of Jacob's wives, wanted the mandrakes to cure her barrenness. Ultimately, though, it was Leah, and not Rachel, who became pregnant.

See *aphrodisiac, cross.*

March: The north and south poles are at their coldest in March. Because the sun is shining directly on the equator at this time of year, this part of the world is at its hottest. According to an old saying,

> When March blows its horn,
> Your barn will be filled
> with hay and corn.

Folklore from Suffolk, England, reminds us that

> March dry, good rye;
> March wet, good wheat.

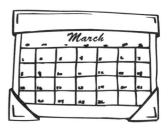

An old American saying goes,

When March comes in like a lion
It goes out as a lamb.
When March comes in like a lamb
It goes out as a lion.

Even though I was brought up in the Southern Hemisphere, I learned this popular rhyme:

March winds and April showers
Bring forth May flowers.

See *April, May, weather.*

Marigold: The marigold gained its name from the Virgin Mary, who was believed to wear one on her breast. Marigolds are attractive golden flowers, yet they need to be handled carefully, at least in the West Country of England where they are called the "drunkard's flower." Apparently, if you look at them for too long, or pick them, you will become addicted to alcohol.

Marigolds are sometimes found in wedding bouquets, as they symbolize fidelity, faithfulness, and long-lasting love.

Marigold flower heads can be rubbed on wasp and bee stings to take away the pain. Inhaling the scent of a marigold is said to ward off infections and cure headaches.

See *bee, flowers, headache, love, wedding.*

Marriage: Superstition provides a number of indications that you will soon be getting married. These include: stumbling while climbing stairs, a live piece of coal falling out of the grate and landing by your feet, and a strange female dog following you home.

You can find out who your partner will be by counting seven stars on seven nights in a row. The first person of the opposite sex you shake hands with after that will become your future husband or wife.

You can also find out how highly the other person thinks of you by blowing once on a dandelion. The quantity of seed heads that are left will tell you how the other person regards you.

See *chimney sweep, cutlery, dandelion, dog, June, knot, moles, plate, star, stumbling, wedding, wedding cake.*

Mascot: Mascots come in a variety of forms. They can be humans, animals, charms, or talismans. Many sports teams use mascots, which are sometimes people dressed up as animals. The origin of this superstition is thousands of years old. Assyrian kings used lions and leopards as mascots when they went into battle. Ancient Egyptian

paintings show cats serving the same purpose. The Roman army also regularly employed animals. One of Vespasian's legions had an eagle mascot. It had been caught in the Austrian Alps and acted as a live replacement for the standard golden eagle that was displayed proudly on the standard of the legion.

See *baseball, cat, charms, eagle, talisman.*

May: An old saying goes, "A cold May gives full barns and empty churchyards." Another version of this says, "A cold, wet May gives a barn full of hay." No wonder that, at least for farmers, this month is called "the merry month of May."

Geoffrey Chaucer (c.1343–1400) coined the expression "May and January" to describe a young woman and her elderly husband. In "The Merchant's Tale" in *The Canterbury Tales*, a woman called May, who is under twenty, marries a Lombard baron called January, who is over sixty.

See *January, May, weather.*

May Day: Come, lasses and lads,
        Take leave of your dads,
    And away to the Maypole hie;
    For every he has got him a she,
    And the minstrel's standing by;
    For Willie has gotten his Jill,
    And Johnny has got his Joan,
        To jig it, jig it, jig it,
        Jig it up and down.

Nowadays, the sight of children dancing around the maypole on the first day of May is considered a charming, old-fashioned custom. But May Day ceremonies were originally performed to receive blessings from the spirits that lived in the tree the maypole was made from. The maypole was believed to ensure fertility for both human beings and cattle.

May Day ceremonies originated with the Roman festival of Floralia, which celebrated Flora, the goddess of flowers. The festival began on April 27 and lasted for several days. During Floralia, women participated in games and races and the winners received garlands of flowers. In time the whole process got out of hand and the winners began receiving entire trees. As this was awkward and cumbersome, poles containing garlands were substituted instead.

See *willow.*

Meat: It's considered a sign of bad luck if a joint of meat shrinks while in the oven.

Conversely, a happy and successful future is indicated if the joint swells.

Raw meat placed over a black eye will reduce the swelling and inflammation.

I haven't noticed this myself, but according to superstition, eating red meat raises the blood pressure and causes bad temper.

See *cooking, eye.*

Memory: You will remember what you have learned, it is said, if you place the books you have been studying under your pillow at night.

Rubbing the head of a bald-headed man before going into an examination will enable you to remember everything you have learned.

Menstruation: There are many superstitions concerning menstruation. Most of these have to do with the blood, which was one of the greatest mysteries. People looked at a menstruating woman with horror and awe, because although she lost blood, she continued to live. Menstruating women had to remain out of sight, as it was thought that they brought potential danger to the whole tribe. Even making eye contact with a menstruating woman was considered dangerous. At one time,

men thought copulating with a menstruating woman would infect them with syphilis or some other disease. People also believed that taking a bath at the time of menstruation would stop the flow of blood, but would cause the woman to contract tuberculosis. Even today, some women believe that any cooking or baking they do at this time will be spoiled, and any fruit trees they touch will die.

See *blood, eye, women, taboo, tree.*

Midsummer's Eve: Midsummer's Eve occurs on or around June 21, the night before the summer solstice. In pagan times huge bonfires were lit on this night to help the sun, as it was starting to lose its strength and power. People leapt through the flames, believing that this would help the crops and the well being of the participants. Sometimes burning torches were carried through the fields to ensure that the crops gained full protection.

Midsummer's Eve is one of the most important times for any magical undertaking. It is a good time to procure charms, especially love charms, as the spirits who fly around at this time imbue them with additional potency. Herbs picked at midnight bring good luck, and provide protection from a wide variety of potential calamities.

St. John's wort is harvested at this time, and hung over doorways to prevent evil spirits from entering. Women who were having difficulty in conceiving could go into their garden on Midsummer's Eve and pick a sprig of St. John's wort. The woman had to be naked for this to work.

Because Midsummer's Eve marks the start of the sun's decline, the forces of darkness are out in force on this night, too. Witches hold meetings and divine the future on this evening. As these events often take place close to walnut trees, people kept well away from them.

Midsummer's Eve was adopted by the Christian calendar and is known as St. John's Eve. The earlier pagan custom of sacrificing animals was abandoned and replaced with a wreath of herbs. These wreaths contained both "good" and "bad" herbs. The good ones were herbs used for medicinal purposes, while the "bad" ones were weeds and plants believed to have evil qualities.

Even the ribbons used to tie the plants together had a symbolic meaning. The white ribbon symbolized strength; the green, knowledge and wisdom; the blue, love; the red, sacrifice; and the yellow, the sun.

It was thought that people who spent the evening on the porch outside a church were able to see ghostly visions of the people in the parish who would die during the next twelve months.

See *charms, church, June, St. John's wort, sun, walnut, witch.*

Milk: An old European superstition promises seven days bad luck to anyone who spills milk. The cow that produced the milk is also likely to produce less milk in the  future, and may even become sick as a result of the spillage. One possible explanation for this superstition is that witches and fairies are attracted to any homes that have milk on the floor.

It is considered good luck to see milk when you first wake up in the morning.

Thunder is believed to sour milk.

See *cow, fairy, seven, tea, thunder, witch.*

Mince Pies: Mince pies (and mince tarts) are considered lucky, and you should never turn one down when it is offered to you. Turning one down brings bad luck that could last up to twelve months.

Try to eat at least one mince pie on each of the Twelve Days of Christmas. Each one guarantees you a month of good luck.

See *Christmas.*

Miners: Mining is a dangerous occupation. Like sailors, miners have many superstitions that need to be heeded before going underground.

It is, for instance, bad luck to see a dove or robin flying near the entrance to the mine shaft. It is also bad luck for a miner to see a rabbit or a cross-eyed man while walking to work. Once leaving home for work, the miner must not turn back, as this could bring bad luck. It is a sign of imminent disaster to see rats leaving a mine.

There are also superstitions that have to be observed once the miner gets underground. It is bad luck to see a cat in the mine. The cat needs to be killed to avert a disaster. Miners must not whistle underground. The remedy for this is to touch iron.

It is bad luck to encounter Tommy Knockers, the spirits of dead miners. Offerings of food are sometimes left for them, to ensure that they don't do anything mischievous.

Many miners avoid washing their backs, as this could cause the roof of the mine to fall in.

Children were told to speak politely and clearly to any miners who happened to pass them while on their way to work. Any apparent lack of respect could create bad luck for the miner.

See *cat, coal, cross-eyed, dove, iron, rabbit, rat, robin, sailors, Tommy Knockers, washing, whistle.*

Mirror: The original mirrors were ponds and pools. People gazed into them to determine their futures. It was a sign of bad luck if the image they saw appeared distorted. People also believed that they saw their souls when they gazed into the water. This belief continued after mirrors were invented.

Almost everyone is familiar with the superstition that some disaster will occur if a mirror breaks. Souls were said to dwell inside mirrors, so any harm done to the soul when the mirror broke would also happen to the person. Yet because mirrors were used to foretell the future, the mirror obviously knew it was going to be broken. It was thought that the gods must have caused the accident to occur, to prevent the owner of the mirror from knowing the terrible things that were going to happen.

Over time, these disastrous consequences were softened to a mere seven years of bad luck. The choice of seven as the number of years is because of the myth that the entire body is completely

renewed every seven years. Of course, back then, it would take seven year's savings to earn enough to replace a good mirror.

A common superstition says that if a young woman holds a mirror over a well, she will see an impression of her future husband in the reflection. You can also place a mirror under your pillow to encourage dreams of your future partner.

A baby should not be shown its reflection in a mirror until it is at least one year old. If it sees its reflection before then, you or the baby will die young.

It is bad luck for a bride to look at herself in a mirror while wearing her wedding dress before the wedding. This risks cancellation of the wedding.

Until a hundred years ago, it was not uncommon to cover mirrors in a room that someone had died in. This was because people believed that if they saw themselves in the mirror, they too would die. Some people cover bedroom mirrors when they go to bed at night. This is to make sure that their soul does not travel in the night and become trapped inside the mirror.

Napoleon Bonaparte was highly superstitious about mirrors. On one occasion he accidentally broke the glass on a portrait of his wife Josephine, and thought she had died. He was unable to sleep until

a messenger returned with the news that she was alive and well.[42]

See *baby, bottle, breakages, bride, death, moon, obsidian, scrying, unicorn, wedding, wedding dress, witch.*

Mistletoe: Mistletoe is a poisonous, parasitic plant, yet it has a long history of providing people with protection against evil spirits. Because it grows on trees and never touches the ground, ancient people considered it sacred. Mistletoe was placed at the entrances of people's homes to prevent evil spirits from entering. As this is also the place where visitors are welcomed, often with a kiss, the mistletoe gradually became known more for kissing than for protection. This custom began in Saxon times. Originally, one berry was removed with each kiss, and no more kisses could be claimed after the last berry had been plucked.

It was thought that if a girl was kissed seven times in one day under the mistletoe, she would be married within a year. A girl who stood under the mistletoe but did not receive a kiss was doomed to remain without a husband for at least one year. A girl who gets married without ever having been kissed under the mistletoe will never have children.

Kissing under the  mistletoe is not only for lovers. You should kiss anyone and everyone possible while the mistletoe is hanging. This brings good luck to everyone in the house for a whole year.

The ancient Druids revered mistletoe for its magical properties. They cut it with a golden sickle during the summer and winter solstices. The mistletoe was caught in their robes to prevent any from falling to the ground, where it would lose its magical qualities.

Mistletoe is also known as all-heal, and is renowned for its healing qualities. A tea made from mistletoe is believed to help sufferers from epilepsy, heart disease, nervousness, toothache, and St. Vitus' dance. A sprig of mistletoe in the house is said to guarantee domestic harmony and to increase fertility. It also wards off evil spirits.

It is good luck to cut mistletoe at Christmas, but bad luck to cut it at any other time. It is extremely bad luck to cut down any tree that is bearing mistletoe.

See *children, Christmas, kiss.*

Moles: Moleomancy, or molescopy, is the art of determining someone's character, and sometimes future, by the placement of moles on his or her body. The darker the mole is, the more significance it has. Moles on the left side of the body are considered unlucky, and those on the right side lucky. There is one exception to this. A woman with a mole on her left breast will have a wide choice of marriage partners. Girls with moles on the right breast will overindulge in a variety of ways, bringing disgrace to their families. A large number of moles on either breast indicates many children. Someone with many moles will ultimately become wealthy.

The placement of the moles can be interpreted in many ways. Here are the traditional gypsy interpretations:

Eyes: confident and serious.
Ears: destined to achieve wealth.
Nose: sensuous and lustful.
Cheeks: kind-hearted and friendly.
Mouth: passionate.
Chin: thoughtful and generous.
Neck: ultimate wealth.
Shoulders: keen on learning.
Arms: suspicious and cautious.
Armpits: ups and downs in life.
Elbows: talented but procrastinates.
Wrists: creative and entrepreneurial.
Hands: modest and successful.
Fingers: anxiety and stress.
Back: obstacles and setbacks.
Buttocks: laziness and lack of motivation.
Chest: amorous nature.

Stomach: egotistic and self-indulgent.
Navel: success in all undertakings.
Genitals: long-term, happy relationship.
Hips: responsible and faithful.
Thighs: hard work pays off.
Knees: caring and supportive.
Legs: lack of confidence.
Ankles: strength of character.
Feet: disappointment.

Moleomancy was practised by the ancient Egyptians, Greeks, and Romans, but was most popular in medieval Europe. It was a popular method of divination, but was also used to confirm whether or not someone was a witch.

See *birthmark, devil, divination, marriage, witch.*

Money: It is good luck to fold your money toward you, as this means more money in the future. If you fold your money away from you, money will slip away.

Two-dollar bills are considered unlucky. Apparently this superstition began with people placing two-dollar bets on horse races. Because these bets were usu-

ally lost, the two-dollar bill became an indicator of bad luck.

It is good luck to find money, but you must attempt to return it to its rightful owner first to receive the luck.

A coin placed in the right-hand pocket of a new coat always brings luck. You should also keep a penny in your purse or wallet to attract luck.

An old saying advises, "Never pay out on a Monday or you'll pay out all week."

See *coin, itching, ladder, lamb, numbers, purse, soot, spider, spitting, star, tomato, tongue.*

Moon: In astrology, the moon is the most important heavenly body next to the sun. It represents the emotional and unconscious aspects of our personality.

The moon exerts a strong effect on all of us. There are more babies born at the time of the full moon than at other phases of the moon. There are also more accidents, and a greater risk of problems for people undergoing operations at this time.

Seeds sown at the time of the waxing (growing) moon grow better than seeds planted at other times. In fact, everything grows better when the moon is waxing. This includes love and business as well as plant life.

The best time to start anything new is at the time of the new moon. The best time to make a wish is outdoors under a new moon. It also brings good luck to bow or curtsey three times to the new moon. It is  bad luck to point at a new moon, as this insults the man in the moon.

Lovers are more romantic at the time of the full moon. According to superstition, gazing at the full moon for too long can make you mad. The word lunatic comes from the Latin *luna*, which means "moon." The werewolf is a man who turns into a wolf at the time of the full moon.

It is possible to have a dream vision of your future partner by speaking to the first new moon of the year. You need to gaze at the moon and say,

> All hail to thee, dear moon,
> all hail to thee,
> I prithee kind moon, please reveal to me,
> [He / She] who is my life partner to be.

Shortly after this, you should see your future partner in a dream.

Moonlight adds to the potency of spells. An old belief says that you can put someone under your spell by using a mirror to reflect moonlight into his or her closed eyes.

The moon can also be used to predict the weather,[42] as the following rhyme attests:

> Pale moon doth rain,
> Red moon doth blow,
> White moon doth neither
> Rain nor snow.

Moonlight is also believed to dull the blade of a razor.

See *boils, children, dog, dreams, eye, fairy ring, Good Friday, illness, mirror, moonstone, periwinkle, quartz, sailors, spell, sun, Wednesday, werewolf, wishing well.*

Moonstone: The moonstone is sacred in India and is believed to bring good luck to anyone who wears it. It is a popular gift for lovers, as it arouses the passions and enables couples to visualize their futures together.

The moonstone has been associated with the lunar cycle since Roman times, making it a popular amulet for women. It is used to enhance fertility, relieve menstrual pain, increase lactation, and ease the pain of childbirth. The moonstone is frequently used in love spells performed when the moon is waxing (increasing in size). It is also used during the waning moon to provide glimpses of the future.

The expression "once in a blue moon" comes from the moonstone. Indians believe that every twenty-one years the sun and moon create a special juxtaposition to each other, and at this time blue moonstones can be found on the seashore.

The moonstone is also used to protect travelers and to enhance natural psychic abilities.

See *amulet, gemstones, moon, spell, wedding anniversaries.*

Mother Shipton: The prophecies of Mother Shipton are still being published and believed by the credulous. In fact, there never was a real Mother Ship-ton, although her book says she was born in a cave in Knaresborough, Yorkshire, in 1488.

Mother Shipton first became famous in 1641, when her prophecies were first published. They were amazingly accurate, and included the lives of Thomas Cromwell and Cardinal Wolsey. Strangely, all of the predictions occurred between the time of her alleged death and 1641.

In 1862, a London publisher called Charles Hindley issued a book of Mother Shipton's prophecies. These included the telegraph, steam engine, submarine, and many other Victorian inventions. One of the predictions said the world was going to end in 1881. Charles Hindley admitted his work was a hoax in 1873. Despite his well-publicized confession, in 1881 many super-stitious people left their homes to spend the last days of their lives in contemplation and prayer in the countryside.

Murder: Because murder is the most serious of all crimes, it is not surprising that a number of superstitions surround the subject. It is considered extremely unlucky to witness a murder, or to discover a victim of murder. People used to believe that the body would bleed when touched by the murderer. Another common belief was that the eyeballs of the victim retained an image of the murderer long after death had occurred.

See *diamond, dimple.*

Mushroom: The halluci-nogenic effect of fungi has always been known, and used by shamans and warriors preparing for battle. The Hebrews considered mushrooms sacred and only priests were allowed to eat them.

Mushrooms were considered a delicacy in Roman times, but there was always the problem of determining whether or not they were edible. Emperor Claudius (10 BCE–54 CE) had this problem solved, as he used a food taster to eat some of his food first. Unfortunately, the mushrooms his taster tried one night produced no immediate effects. Consequently, Emperor Claudius ate them, and both he and his taster died. It is widely believed that his second wife, Agrippina, who wanted her son Nero to have the throne, deliberately poisoned her husband.

Along with oysters, mushrooms have always been considered aphrodisiacs. The aphrodisiacal effect was increased if the mushrooms were picked at the time of the full moon.

Primitive people treated mushrooms with great respect, as it was so difficult to determine whether they were safe to eat. Even experts on mushrooms need to remember the old saying, "There are old mushroom hunters and bold mushroom hunters, but there are no old, bold mushroom hunters."

See *aphrodisiac, moon.*

Music: Musicians are just as superstitious as other people. Gustav Mahler refused to call his ninth symphony by its number and named it *Das Lied von der Erde* instead. This was because several other composers, including Beethoven and Schubert, died after completing their ninth symphonies.

Orchestral players dislike recommencing a piece at the same place where it stopped, if there has been a substantial delay. Usually, they will play a few notes from another piece first to avert any bad luck, and then return to the original piece.

It is considered bad luck to keep a violin in the house if no one can play it.

Singers, like most performers, are highly superstitious. Judy Garland sang *Over the Rainbow* at every live performance, as she felt it gave her good luck.

Plants are believed to grow more quickly when music is played in the background. Cows are also believed to produce more milk when music is played in the milking shed. There is no scientific evidence for either of these beliefs.

See *cow, plants.*

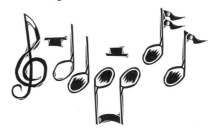

N

Nail: Because nails are made of iron, they are believed to possess magical properties. The first amulet I ever saw was a ring made from a horse-shoe nail.[44] Horseshoe nails are considered powerful amulets that ward off witches. It was said that you could test someone for witchcraft by hammering an iron nail into a footprint that the person had left behind. If the person was a witch, he or she would return to remove the nail.

Hammering nails into the walls, especially into the lintel over a door, is thought to help protect the house by warding off evil spirits. The protection is enhanced if the nails are old and rusty.

Finding a nail when you are out and about is a sign of good luck, and carrying it around with you wards off the evil eye.

It is especially good luck to find a rusty nail. You should hammer it into the framing surrounding your kitchen door to provide protection. The best place for this rusty nail is at eye level. The hammering is done in a special way. Place the nail in position and drive it into the frame with four strikes of your hammer. Say out loud, "Once for luck" after the first strike, and "once for health," "once for love," and "once for money" after each successive strike.

Nails were used to cure a variety of ailments. The nail was placed in contact with the affected part of the body, and then hammered into the ground. The ailment was thought to be transferred to the next person to walk over the nail.

See *amulet, evil eye, Good Friday, horseshoe, iron, lodestone, nightmares, toothache, witch.*

Names: "What's in a name? That which we call a rose by any other name would smell as sweet" (*Romeo and Juliet*, Act 2, scene 2).

Despite William Shakespeare's famous words, names are of vital importance. People have recognized the magic in names for thousands of years. Many parents want their sons to have strong names. They also tend to choose gentle, feminine names for their daughters. This is because, consciously or unconsciously, parents believe the child will exhibit these characteristics. Some names carry more power and influence than others. The name you were given by your parents is not simply a convenient way to identify you, but an important part of your personality.

Some people dislike their given names so much that they change them. John Wayne's given first name was Marion. He frequently mentioned the problems this name caused him. Josef Stalin's original name was Džugašvíli, which is derived from "dross" and means "waste matter."

The name Stalin means "man of steel." It is easy to see why he chose that name.[45]

Actors frequently use a stage name to create a particular image for themselves. Authors sometimes use a pseudonym for a variety of reasons. Mary Ann Evans used the name George Eliot because she believed her writing would be taken more seriously if she used a man's name. People also change their names for religious reasons. Cassius Clay became Muhammad Ali.

Marriage is another common reason for a name change. It is considered bad luck for a woman to speak or write down her married name before the wedding, as this might end the relationship before the wedding takes place. It is also thought to be risky for a woman to marry someone with a surname that starts with the same letter as her maiden name. However, it is extremely good luck to marry someone with the same surname. This is said to provide the woman with healing powers that will benefit her future family.

It is considered good luck to have seven letters in your name. Thirteen letters is considered bad luck.

It was considered bad luck to mention the name of someone who has died without adding, "May he (or she) rest in peace." Some people still say this.

It is believed to be bad luck to name a child after a dead older sibling. This is because the newborn child will likely share the same fate.

A Jewish tradition says it is unsafe to name a child after a living relative. This is because it risks shortening the life of the older person. Another Jewish tradition is to change the name of a sick person. The new name effectively creates a new person, and hopefully the sickness will remain with the old person who has ceased to exist.

At one time, it was important that no one outside the immediate family knew what name a child would be given until he or she was christened.

It is bad luck to give a child the same name as a family pet. This is because it is feared that anything bad that befalls the animal will also affect the child.

It is good luck to name your child after someone famous, as the child will receive some of that person's luck. It is also good luck to name a child after a saint, martyr, or prophet, for the child will receive divine protection.

The names of ships also possess magical qualities, and it is bad luck to change the name of a ship. This is believed to increase the risk that the ship will be lost at sea.

See *ships, wedding.*

Napkin: Folding a napkin after finishing a meal is a fairly ordinary activity that most people tend not to think about. However,

there is one situation in which it is considered bad luck to do this. This is when you visit a house for the first time for a meal. If you fold your napkin after the meal, you are effectively folding up the friendship and will never dine at the house again. This superstition does not apply if you happen to be staying at the house and eating several meals there.

See *waiter.*

Needle: It is bad luck to see a needle on the ground and not pick it up. Before lending a needle to a friend, you should prick yourself with it first. This guarantees that the friendship will continue. If a pregnant woman finds a needle, she will have a girl baby. If she finds a pin, she'll have a boy.

If a needle breaks while being used, it is either a sign of a wedding or a good luck omen for the wearer of the garment that is being repaired.

Young women trying to influence a particular person to fall in love with them practiced a form of black magic with a candle and seven needles. The needles

were pushed into the candle, which was then set alight. As the candle burned, the young woman would say prayers to the Virgin Mary. By the time the candle had completely burned, the man in question would be helplessly in love with the woman. He would also be impotent with anyone except her.

See *candle, coin, magic, pin, sewing, thumb, wedding.*

Nest: It is considered a sign of a good summer ahead when rooks are seen building their nests high up in the trees.

If a bird finds some of your hair and uses it in constructing a nest, you will apparently suffer from headaches until the nest falls apart.

See *hair, headache.*

New Year: The New Year marks an important time in the calendar. It is important to have plenty of food and drink in the cupboards, as this symbolically shows that you will have plenty to eat and drink during the forthcoming year. Some people refuse to throw anything out on New Year's Eve, as they fear they may accidentally toss out the family's good luck with the rubbish.

Wearing new clothes on New Year's Day is a good idea, as this shows you'll receive more new clothes during the year.

All outstanding debts should be paid by New Year's Eve to ensure that no unexpected debts arise during the following year. It is bad luck to work hard on New Year's Day, but it is considered good luck to think about work and career during that day.

Staying up until midnight to welcome in the New Year is a popular pastime nowadays. This custom used to be called "ringing in" the New Year, as church bells were rung at midnight. Originally, partying until the New Year arrived was done to drive off any evil spirits. Consequently, it was supposed to be a noisy as well as a joyful occasion. To ensure that this happened, any bottle of alcohol that was open had to be completely consumed.

Babies born on New Year's Day will always be surrounded with good fortune and luck.

See *April Fool's Day, baby, bell, calendar, clothes.*

Nightmare: The "mare" in nightmare is not related to horses. The word comes from Morrigain, the Irish queen of the

elves, who was believed to be a succubus. A succubus is a lecherous demon who visits sleeping men and has sex with them. (Incubus is the term for similar demons who prey on sleeping women.) Consequently, sexual dreams were believed to be actual experiences.

Nightmares were believed to be caused by the devil, who managed to infiltrate people's dreams in a deliberate attempt to cause stress and worry. Fortunately, there were remedies for people who regularly experienced nightmares. One method was to place your shoes under the bed with the toes pointing outwards. All forms of crosses were effective, too. These methods ranged from sleeping with your hands folded on your breast to placing your socks in the shape of a cross at the end of the bed.

Alternatively, you could wear a necklace of red coral beads to ensure that you had a peaceful night's sleep. Red coral was also said to ward off the evil eye.

A nail taken from a grave and placed in the doorframe of the bedroom should also protect you from nightmares.

See *cross, devil, dreams, evil eye, nail, shoes, vervain.*

Nine: Nine has always been considered a lucky number. "A stitch in time" is believed to "save nine" later. A cat has nine lives. The fact that human pregnancy lasts nine months clearly demonstrates the potency and power of this number. Nine is also three times the sacred number three. Nine is also considered remarkable because no matter what number it is multiplied by, the sum of the digits in the total always add up nine.

Single women counted the number of peas in every pod they shelled. If they found nine peas in a pod, the pod would be hung over the front door. The first eligible man to walk through the door would be the future husband.

When people are extremely happy, they are said to be on "cloud nine." This means that they are far above any weather conditions on earth and can receive all the benefits of the sun. Someone who is extremely well dressed is said to be "dressed to the nines." A "nine-day wonder" describes someone who gained enormous, but fleeting, success.

The cat-o'-nine-tails was a cruel whip used to punish offenders in the British army and navy. The fact of the nine "tails" was not accidental. Because of the magical power of nine, it was believed that anyone receiving punishment from this whip

would become a commendable soldier or sailor afterwards.

John Heydon wrote about the number nine in his *Holy Guide* (1662):

> If writ or engraved on Silver, or Sardis, and carried with one, the wearer becomes invisible, as Caleron, the brother-in-law of Alexander, did, and by this means lay with his Brother's concubines as often as he did himself. Nine also obtaineth the love of Women. At the 9th hour our Saviour breathed his last...It prevails against Plagues and Fevers; it causes Long life and Health, and by it Plato so ordered events that he died at the age of nine times 9.

See *nose, numbers, pea, sailors, three, waves, weather, words.*

Noises: Strange noises, such as creaking or rapping sounds, in the night are always considered a bad omen. Three raps on the wall of a bedroom signify a death in the family, but not necessarily of the person who hears the sounds.

See *death.*

Nose: Primitive people revered the nose, as it was so intimately connected with the breath. The nose was sometimes pierced

with a ring to prevent evil spirits from entering the body.

The size of a man's nose was at one time believed to indicate the size of his sexual organs. In physiognomy, the study of determining character from physical appearance, the nose is said to reveal the person's hidden qualities. A long nose denotes a strong personality. The person will be ambitious, proud, and shrewd. A small nose indicates someone who is imaginative and impulsive. Someone with a nose that is broad at the base will be optimistic and sensual. A thin nose indicates someone who is aesthetic and intuitive. An aquiline nose denotes someone who likes to dominate the situation. A pointed nose belongs to someone who is naturally curious. A straight nose indicates loyalty and a positive approach to life. An upturned nose indicates a happy, optimistic approach to life.

Nosebleeds are traditionally a sign of bad luck. Blood coming from the right nostril is thought to be a sign of an impending death in the family. However, it is a good omen if just one drop of blood comes from the left nostril. This indicates a large sum of money.

One traditional method of curing a nosebleed was to tie a knotted red ribbon around the neck. This is an example of sympathetic magic, with the red symbolizing blood, and the knots symbolizing clotting. An alternative method was to tie a thread around the little finger of either hand. You might prefer to drop a key down your back.

A more radical method of curing a nosebleed was to tie a dead toad or frog in a silk bag around the neck. Yet another method was to wear a skein of silk that had been knotted by nine virgin girls.

See *blood, breath, fly, frog, itching, key, kiss, knot, nine, red, ring, thread, werewolf.*

November: November is named after *novem*, the Latin word for nine, as it was the ninth month of the year in the Roman calendar.

The English poet Thomas Hood (1799–1845) described November well in his poem "No":

No warmth, no cheerfulness,
no healthy ease,
No comfortable feel
in any member—
No shade, no shine,
no butterflies, no bees,
No fruits, no flowers,
no leaves, no birds—
November!

A warm November is thought to promise a bad winter. Thunder in November is a sign that crops will do well in the following year.

See *thunder, weather.*

Numbers: Pythagoras and his followers believed that numbers had mystical significance. Most occult systems contain systems of number correspondences, relating numbers to a wide range of esoteric ideas and concepts. The most extreme example of this is the Kabbalistic gematria.

Today, there are still many superstitions about numbers. A good example is the belief that both good and bad luck occurs in threes. People often say, "Third time lucky." Some performers, such as acrobats, deliberately fail twice before succeeding, as they know the applause will be so much greater when they "finally" succeed.

Even numbers can be divided and reduced in value. Because of this, odd numbers are considered luckier than even numbers. William Shakespeare referred to this in *The Merry Wives of Windsor* (Act 5, scene 1): "This is the third time; I hope good luck lies in odd numbers. There is divinity in odd numbers, either in nativity, chance, or death." Thirteen is the most obvious exception to this belief.

Forty is believed to be a dangerous age for husbands. Most people have heard of the "number of the Beast...six hundred threescore and six" (Revelation 13:18), better known as 666. This is considered the devil's number.

Counting can be considered both lucky and unlucky. An example of good luck from counting is an old cure for warts. All you have to do is count the warts and tell that number to a stranger. This makes the warts disappear. However, it is considered unlucky to count your money, your children, or other possessions. This tempts fate, which attracts bad luck.

A common superstition concerns the idea that you'll die when "your number comes up." Even today, some people believe that God, destiny, or the fates somehow decree how long they will live. Years ago, I helped a man who had almost been run over by a bus. "My number wasn't on it," he told me.

Many people have lucky numbers that are in some way associated with them. It might be their day or month of birth, or any other number that seems to give them luck.

See *children, devil,* individual numbers, *money, numerology, warts.*

Numerology: Numerology is the art of determining someone's personality and future trends by examining their full name and date of birth. It was practiced by the ancient Babylonians and Egyptians, making it one of the oldest divinatory arts. Pythagoras is credited with modernizing it more than twenty-five hundred years ago.

The most important number in numerology is the Life Path number. This reveals what the person should be doing with his or her life in this incarnation. It is derived from the person's date of birth, reduced to a single digit. For example, for the birth date of June 25, 1965, add 6 + 25 + 1965 to get 1996. When adding those numbers together (1 + 9 + 9 + 6), you get 25, and 2 + 5 = 7. This person would have a Life Path number of 7.

There are two exceptions, as 11 and 22 are considered Master Numbers in numerology. The presence of these numbers indicates that the person is an "old soul" who has lived many times before this current life. Consequently, 11 and 22 do not get reduced further.

The next most important number in numerology is called the Expression. This reveals a person's natural abilities, and is derived from the person's full name at birth, turned into numbers and reduced to a single digit (or Master Number). The letters of the name are turned into numbers using this chart:

1	2	3	4	5	6	7	8	9
A	B	C	D	E	F	G	H	I
J	K	L	M	N	O	P	Q	R
S	T	U	V	W	X	Y	Z	

Here is an example:

JOHN DUNCAN BROWN

1+6+8+5   4+3+5+3+1+5   2+9+6+5+5

2 + 0   2 + 1   2 + 7

2 + 3 + 9

1 + 4

5

John's Expression number is 5.

The third most important number is called the Soul Urge. It is sometimes called the Heart's Desire, and reveals a person's inner motivations. It is derived from adding up the vowels in the person's full name at birth and reducing them to a single digit (or Master Number). Just to complicate things, Y is usually classified as a vowel. However, if it is pronounced when the name is said, it is classified as a consonant. For example, the Y in Yolande is a consonant, but the Y in Kaye is a vowel.

John Duncan Brown, in the example above, has a Soul Urge of 7.

There are keywords for each number:

1—Independence, attainment

2—Cooperation, tact, diplomacy

3—Creative self-expression

4—Limitation, restriction, order

5—Freedom, variety

6—Responsibility, love, service

7—Analysis, wisdom, spirituality

8—Ambition, material freedom

9—Humanitarianism, visionary, universal love

11—Illumination, idealism

22—Master builder, ultimate success

See *divination*.

Nuns: While it is believed to be bad luck to unexpectedly see a clergyman, it is good luck to see a nun walking toward you. It is especially lucky to see three nuns walking toward you. However, it is bad luck to come across a nun, or nuns, walking away from  you. To avert the bad luck, you should cross your fingers and spit on the ground.

See *clergyman, fishermen*.

Nut: Nuts symbolize fruitfulness and life itself. Consequently, they have always been considered lucky. A good crop of nuts is a sign that a large number of babies will be born in the area during the year. It is dangerous to pick nuts on September 14. This is thought to be the day the devil gathers nuts.

In Roman times, newly married couples were presented with bags of nuts, as it was believed that these would increase their fertility. Rice tossing gradually replaced this tradition.

You can determine whom you will marry by roasting chestnuts in an open fire. Place as many chestnuts as there are possible partners in the fire. The first one to pop indicates the person you will marry.

Married couples can do a similar exercise by placing two chestnuts in the fire. If they move apart or crackle, the relationship is not going well. However, if the chestnuts stay together, so will the couple.

See *devil, fire, rice.*

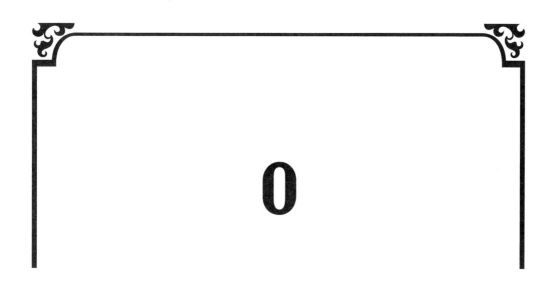

O

Oak: The ancient Druids venerated the oak tree and credited it with magical powers. The fact that it seems to be struck by lightning more often than other trees added to its mystique, and also made it sacred to Thor, the Norse god of thunder. Funnily enough, another superstition says that keeping a few acorns in the house will protect it from lightning.

Couples who are having difficulty conceiving are advised to hug an oak tree. This is believed to cure hernias as well.

King Charles II (1630–1685) hid in an oak tree after the Battle of Worcester (September 3, 1651). When he was restored to power in 1660, his followers wore oak leaves to proclaim their allegiance. May 29, King Charles' birthday, became known as Royal Oak Day. This was also the day he entered London after his restoration.

Oak and ash trees were used to predict the weather, depending on which one was in leaf first:

> If the oak's before the ash,
> Then you'll only get a splash;
> If the ash precedes the oak,
> Then you may expect a soak.

Many of the doorways in New York City's Grand Central Station contain depictions of oak branches. They were placed there to provide symbolic strength to the passengers who were about to leave on a lengthy cross-country train ride.

See *acorn, ash, colds, January, leaf, lightning, thunder, toothache, tree.*

Obsidian: Obsidian is a semi-transparent, brownish-black natural glass. Obsidian has been used to make scrying mirrors for thousands of years. A true obsidian mirror is believed to appear smoky at first, and then become clear when it is gazed into. John Dee (1527–1608), astrologer to Queen Elizabeth I, had an obsidian mirror that he called his "jet shewstone." He used it to contact the angelic kingdom.

Obsidian is used today to focus energy and encourage clear thinking. It also absorbs negative energy and prevents indecisiveness. It can also help heal digestive problems.

See *gemstones, mirror.*

October: October was the eighth month in the Roman calendar, and is named after the Romans' word for eight, *octo.*

A warm October is said to be a sign of a cold February. If leaves wither on the trees and fail to fall to the ground in autumn, it indicates a frosty winter with a great deal of snow.

See *February, weather.*

Omen: Omens are signs and warnings about the future. They can be either good or bad. An example of a good omen is someone born with a caul. A bad omen might be stumbling while going downstairs. Omens occur purely by chance. They appear to be random messages, and because of this, they are easily missed.

See *caul, cutlery, red, ring, stumbling.*

One: One is considered a lucky number, as it is indivisible, and when multiplied by itself remains the same. One is associated with God, the intellect, purity, and the sun. Children born on the first day of the month are believed to be enterprising, independent, and lucky.

See *numbers, sun.*

Oneiromancy: Oneiromancy is the art of interpreting dreams, both to predict the future and to gain insight into the subconscious mind of the dreamer. Dream interpretation has been practiced for thousands of years. People used to believe that dreams were messages from God, rather than messages from one's own subconscious mind.

In the Bible, Joseph interpreted many dreams, both his own and other people's. He interpreted the Pharaoh's dream about seven well-fed cattle and seven malnourished cattle as a prediction of seven good years followed by seven lean years. This enabled the Pharaoh to put aside food in the good years so that everyone had enough food to eat during the famine that was to come (Genesis 41:15–36).

Sigmund Freud and Carl Jung revived interest in dream interpretation. They used them to uncover repressed emotions and explore the subconscious mind.

See *dreams*.

Onion: There are many superstitions concerning onions. If you want to see your future marriage partner in your dreams, all you need do is place an onion under your pillow. If you are trying to determine between two marriage prospects, you should write their names on two onions, place them on a windowsill, and see which one sprouts first.

The onion's pungent odor is believed to ward off witches and evil spirits. It also provides general protection.

Carrying an onion around with you is said to be good for your health, and en-

sures that you do not catch a cold. During the plague, onions were frequently hung up in rooms to help preserve good health.  Even today, some people still place an onion in the room of someone who is sick, believing that it will help drive the illness away.

Keeping a piece of raw potato in your mouth while cutting onions will stop your eyes from weeping. Holding a matchstick between your teeth also works.

An old superstition claims that eating onions is good for your heart. This is an example of sympathetic magic. Because onions are sharp to the taste, you need to be strong to eat them.

Apparently, onions can even act as weather forecasters:

> Onion's skin very thin,
> Mild winter coming in.
> Onion's skin thick and tough,
> Coming winter cold and rough.

See *colds, dreams, eating, potato, weather, witch*.

Onyx: The Greeks have a legend to explain where onyx came from. Venus, the goddess of love, was sleeping on the banks of the Indus River. Cupid used one of his enchanted arrows to manicure her fingernails. The nail parings dropped into the river, and were transformed into onyx.

Originally, onyx was thought of favorably, but its reputation disappeared in the Middle Ages. Sir John Mandeville, the fourteenth-century adventurer, wrote, "He who wears it at the neck or on the back will see devils; it causes many frivolities, it brings anger and disagreement, but it gives hardiness."[46] Onyx was also believed to separate lovers and create marital problems.

Camillus Leonardus, the sixteenth-century Italian physician, wrote that onyx created nightmares and stirred up quarrels and disagreements.[47]

Today onyx is considered much more favorably, and is used to alleviate stress, worry, and nervousness. It also provides energy and stamina.

See *gemstones*.

Opal: An ancient legend says that opals were formed when the god of storms became jealous of the beautiful rainbow god. He finally smashed the rainbow. As the pieces fell to earth, they were transformed into opals.

Opal consists mainly of silicon oxide. It also contains a small amount of water, which gives it a unique gleam of color, known as "fire."

The ancient Romans called the opal the "cupid stone," and related it to love, hope, and longevity.

However, wearing an opal is thought to bring bad luck. This superstition began during the Black Death that ravaged Europe in the fourteenth century. A woman in Venice caught the disease and continued wearing her favorite opal in her sickbed. The people who looked after her commented on how brilliant the stone looked. After her death, they noticed that the stone had lost its luster. This made them think that the opal had caused the disease, and word spread quickly about how unlucky the opal was. Today, we know that it was probably changes in body temperature that caused the opal to react in the way it did.

Alfonso XII (1857–1885), King of Spain, presumably did not know of this superstition. He gave his wife, Maria, an opal ring on her wedding day. She died two months later. Alfonso then gave the ring to his sister, who died a few days later. The opal was then presented to his sister-in-law, who died three months later. Finally, King Alfonso wore the opal himself as a tie-pin. Less than two weeks later, he died. The deaths were probably due more to a cholera epidemic than to the opal, but the damage had been done. The opal was now considered the stone of death.

Queen Victoria didn't accept this superstition, and wore many pieces of jewelry that were set with beautiful opals. The back of the gown she wore at her coronation was fastened with an opal brooch. During the processional, the brooch opened, and the embarrassed guests saw more of the queen than they had expected to. Needless to say, this incident seemed to provide further evidence of how unlucky this stone was.

Opal is the birthstone for October. Nowadays, it is considered a lucky stone for people born in October, but bad luck for everyone else.

See *birthstone, death, engagement, gemstones, rainbow.*

Orange: Orange is considered a lucky fruit. If a young man gives an orange to his girlfriend, it is believed to increase their love for each other. A curious superstition says that if a young man wants to win a girl's heart, he has to prick an or-ange all over with a pin, and then go to sleep with the orange held firmly in his armpit. The next day he has to offer the orange to the girl. Her affection will grow if she accepts it, and then eats it.

The orange blossom is possibly the best-known floral fertility symbol. Soldiers returning home from the Crusades introduced it to Europe. Decorating a bride with orange blossoms is a French tradition that was introduced to Britain in the early nineteenth century. The white blossom symbolizes innocence, and the fruit signifies fruitfulness. Consequently, brides carry orange blossoms, not only for good luck but to ensure that the couple will have children.

See *children, pin, wedding.*

Orchid: Orchids are considered aphrodisiacs. This belief probably came from the flower's physical ap-pearance. Some orchids possess a pair of tubers that have been related to testicles. The name "orchid" comes from the Greek word for testicles, *orchis.* Men ate the larger tuber of an orchid when they wished to have a male child, and the smaller tuber when they desired a female child.

See *aphrodisiac, flowers.*

Ornithomancy: Ornithomancy is a form of divination that uses the song, appearance, and actions of birds to predict the future. Ornithomancy was extremely popular in Greco-Roman times, and is still practiced in rural areas around the world.

Sailors believe that seeing an albatross is a sign of good luck. However, harming an albatross attracts bad luck.

Here are some other common beliefs about birds:

Seeing a crow is a sign of bad luck.
Seeing a dove is extremely favorable for
   lovers.
Seeing an eagle is a sign of success after
   a long struggle.
Seeing a magpie is a sign of bad luck.

See *albatross, crow, dove, divination, magpie, sailors.*

Owl: The owl is often considered wise, as its wide head and large, front-facing eyes make it look intelligent. Consequently, the owl is often considered a symbol of wisdom.

Owls have an interesting history from a superstition point of view. The ancient Greeks liked owls, but the Romans did not. The Romans thought the owl's nocturnal habits were suspicious, and felt that it might have links with the devil and evil spirits. They believed that the hoot of an owl signified death, especially as the deaths of Julius Caesar, Augustus Caesar, and Agrippa were all predicted by the hooting of an owl. The Romans also believed that witches could change into the form of owls, and in this guise drank the blood of babies. Owls are also associated with witches because of their nocturnal habits and haunting cry.

It is considered bad luck to hear an owl's hoot in the daytime. Seeing an owl in the daytime is even worse, as it is an omen of death or major misfortune. If an owl hoots near your home, you should toss some salt into the fire to avert bad luck. In Welsh folklore, a hooting owl is a sign that one of the young girls in the village has lost her virginity. If you walk around a tree containing an owl, it will turn and watch you. If you keep on circling the tree, the owl will eventually ring its own neck.

An owl perching on the roof of a house in the daytime is thought to be a sign that one of the occupants will shortly die.

An owl's feather makes a highly effective protective amulet. If you find one, keep it in a safe place, and use it whenever necessary.

See *amulet, baby, death, devil, familiar, feather, fire, salt, witch.*

Oyster: Oysters have been considered aphrodisiacs for thousands of years. The Romans gorged on them at feasts because of this. This superstition may have developed because of a perceived similarity between oysters and the female genitals.

An old American superstition says never to eat oysters in a month without an "r." As these months are May, June, July, and August, the superstition may have developed in the days before refrigeration, when it was a risky matter to eat an oyster that might have been exposed to the heat of summer. However, in England it is considered good luck to eat an oyster on St. James' Day (August 5). This ensures that the person will never lack sufficient food.

See *aphrodisiacs, pearl.*

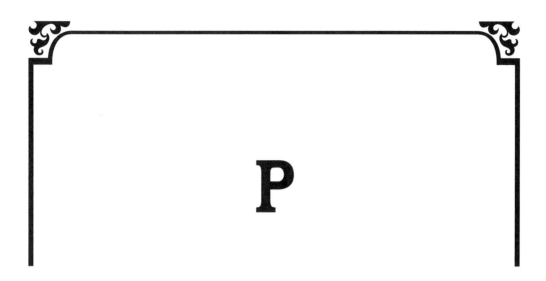

P

Palmistry: Palmistry is the art of studying both the shape of, and the lines on, people's hands to determine their character and predict future trends. Chirognomy, or chirology, is the name given to the study of the shape of the hand; chiromancy studies the lines and markings on the palm. Like most forms of divination, palmistry reveals opportunities and possibilities, but

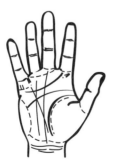

because everyone has free will, it cannot tell you exactly what will happen.

Palmistry probably began in India some four thousand years ago. It gradually spread eastwards to China and Japan, and west to Persia, the Middle East, and Europe. Aristotle is reputed to have written a book on palmistry for Alexander the Great.

Palmistry is mentioned three times in the Bible: "Behold, I have graven thee upon the palms of my hands; thy walls are continually before me" (Isaiah 49:16); "He sealeth up the hand of every man; that all men may know his work" (Job 37:7); "Length of days is in her right hand; and in her left hand riches and honour" (Proverbs 3:16).

The tradition of crossing a gypsy's palm with silver dates from the fifteenth century, when the Christian Church claimed that gypsies were in league with the devil. To counter this, the gypsies explained that the devil was afraid of both silver and the sign of the cross. Consequently, if you made a sign of the cross over a gypsy's hand with silver, you would be protected. Naturally, the gypsy retained the piece of silver.

Nowadays, scientists are looking at palmistry from both a psychological and a medical perspective. Research scientists at the Kennedy-Galton Centre at the University of London are starting to confirm knowledge that palmists have known for thousands of years. It would seem that palmistry's greatest years are still ahead.

See *cross, devil, finger, hand.*

Pancake: Shrove Tuesday, the last day before Lent, is often called "Pancake Day," as pancakes are traditionally prepared and eaten on this day to ensure good luck for the next twelve months. As a bonus, if you eat pancakes on this day, you will not run out of food or money either. The

pancakes apparently need to be eaten before eight o'clock in the evening to ensure the good luck. Eating them after that time brings bad luck. Lent used to be an austere time of year, and Pancake Day was the last chance people had to enjoy themselves before Lent began.

Part of the fun of Pancake Day was to force prostitutes out of their homes, and to throw specially trained cocks at each other so that they would fight. When these two activities were stopped, people started "tossing" pancakes instead.

See *cock.*

Parsley: The best time to plant parsley, according to superstition, is on Good Friday. However, young women who want a baby can plant parsley at any time, as this improves their chances of becoming pregnant. An old saying says, "sow parsley, sow babies." Women should not plant parsley unless they want to become pregnant. However, eating parsley will, at least according to superstition, prevent the pregnancy from occurring.

According to legend, only sinful people can grow good parsley. This story probably began in Roman times, when parsley was planted on graves.

Another superstition concerning parsley says that it's bad luck to transplant it, as this will result in a death in the family.

It is also considered bad luck to give or receive parsley as a gift.

See *aphrodisiac, baby, death, Good Friday, grave.*

Pea: The humble pea has always been considered lucky. Finding a pod containing one pea is extremely lucky. Pods containing nine peas are equally fortunate. They can be thrown over the right shoulder while making a wish. Nine peas in a single pod are thought to cure warts. They are rubbed on the wart, and then thrown away while saying "wart, wart, dry away."

The pea is also a useful plant for people seeking love. If a single woman finds a pod containing nine peas, she can place this over the lintel of her front door. The first single man to walk through the door will become her husband. (A variation of

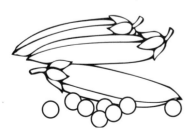

this says that the man who walks through the door will have the same first name as her ultimate husband.)

See *love, nine, warts.*

Peacock: Both the Greeks and the Romans considered the peacock sacred, and only priests were allowed to handle these sacred birds. It was a punishable offence for other people to touch the birds, or even to possess a feather.  The eyes on the peacocks' tails were considered a sign that the gods were constantly alert and watching what humans were doing.

However, other ancient people were more suspicious of the many eyes that peacocks possessed. They thought that the eyes belonged to the devil, or were an example of the evil eye. They worried that people might be fooled by the magnificent plumage and take a feather home, placing themselves at risk of the evil eye. In Islam, it's believed that a peacock allowed Iblis, the devil, to enter Paradise, thus causing mankind's fall from grace.

However, not all the Greeks considered the peacock sacred, as the story of Zeus and his affair with a mortal girl shows. One day, Zeus came down from

Mount Olympus while his wife, Hera, was asleep. When she woke up and found he wasn't there, she immediately raced to earth to see what Zeus was up to. Zeus, who was in the process of seducing Io, a young mortal woman, heard her coming and quickly transformed Io into a cow. Hera was not fooled, although she pretended to be. She commented on how beautiful the cow was, and asked if she could have it for her herd. In those days, most of the gods kept herds of cattle in various parts of the earth. Zeus couldn't say no without facing awkward questions. Hera took the cow, and asked Argus Panoptes, a giant with one hundred eyes, to look after it. Argus faithfully kept at least one eye on the cow at all times. However, Zeus asked Hermes to free the cow, so Io could be restored to human form again. Hermes succeeded in this by playing his flute, and finally bored the giant to sleep with endless stories. Hermes then killed the giant and cut off his head. Io, still in the form of a cow, galloped off in search of her father. Hera sent a gadfly to tor-

ment her, and Io finally galloped to the Bosphorus, swam across it, and eventually ended up in Egypt where she regained her human form. Hera was upset about the death of Argus, the giant, and had his eyes placed into the tail of a peacock to remind people of his horrible death. The peacock thus became an unlucky bird, with eyes in its tail that reminded people of Argus' sad fate.

Over time, peacock feathers became associated with funerals and death. This came about when people noticed that peacocks' feathers did not fade or lose their shiny lustre. This was seen as a sign of immortality or resurrection. Early Christians decorated the walls of the catacombs with depictions of peacocks and their feathers to illustrate their faith in the resurrection. Even today, when the pope is carried in his *sedia gestatoria*, or portable chair, his attendants on each side carry two large fans, known as *flabella*, made of peacock feathers, or ostrich feathers with eyes attached.

Even today, some people are superstitious about allowing peacock feathers into their homes, as they consider them an omen of death.

However, the opposite tradition applies in Japan, China, and India, where peacock feathers provide protection. In India, it is common to see fans made out of peacock feathers. These have as many

of the eyes as possible on display, and they are used to provide protection.

See *actors and actresses, death, evil eye, feather, funeral.*

Pearl: A pearl is created when an irritant, such as a grain of sand, enters a bivalve  mollusc such as the oyster. The mollusc, unable to reject the irritant, constructs a secretion around it that becomes a pearl. Cleopatra (69–30 BCE) is supposed to have drunk a dissolved pearl in a toast to Mark Antony. This was to demonstrate the incredible wealth of Egypt. The effort was duly noted, as the pearl was worth more than the entire feast put on in his honor. Sir Thomas Gresham replicated this gesture some sixteen hundred years later when he used a dissolved pearl, valued at fifteen thousand pounds, to toast Queen Elizabeth I.

The ancient Romans revered pearls, and used them in many ways. Both men and women wore them, and even items of furniture were studded with pearls to create feelings of opulence and abundance. Emperor Caligula had slippers totally encrusted with pearls. Pliny the Elder, the Roman historian, wrote that pearls were dewdrops from heaven that fell into the sea and were captured by oysters.

The pearl became so popular during the Renaissance that some royal families decreed that only members of royalty could wear them.

There are many superstitions about pearls, the most important being that as it is symbolically a tear of the oyster, people in love should not wear it. If they do, they are likely to shed many tears. Although you should not give a pearl to someone in love, it is good luck to give one to a baby, as this ensures a long life. Pearls are also valued because they are seen to provide serenity, purity, virtue, and peace of mind.

Pearls are also reputed to have aphrodisiac qualities, and sleeping with a pearl under the pillow is believed to help childless couples conceive.

Pearl is the birthstone for June.

See *aphrodisiac, baby, birthstone, engagement, oyster, toast, wedding anniversaries.*

Pendulum: A pendulum is a weight attached to a length of chain or cord. It is used for dowsing or divination. When I was growing up, my mother always used her wedding ring attached to thread to determine the sex of any unborn babies in the family.

See *aquamarine, baby, wedding ring.*

Penny: The humble penny, or one-cent coin, has always been considered lucky, and many people carry one around with them as a lucky charm. Some people toss a penny into the water whenever they travel by boat. This is to appease the gods of water and to ensure a safe arrival at the destination.

See *charms, coin.*

Periwinkle: The periwinkle is a trailing evergreen plant, with flowers that look similar to violets. It is usually grown over doorways and windows because it is believed to ward off bad luck and evil spirits.

Only virtuous people, who are pure in heart, can cut the periwinkle. Even then, it should be done only on the first, ninth, eleventh, or thirteenth night after the new moon.

See *flowers, moon, violet.*

Petrified Wood: Petrified wood is a form of fossil. Ancient trees that spent thousands of years in water gradually dissolved and were replaced with minerals from the

water, forming petrified wood. Because of this association with water, petrified wood has often been used as an amulet to protect people from drowning.

Petrified wood is also believed to promote a positive mental attitude and to help in all forms of healing.

See *amulet, drowning, tree, water, wood.*

Petticoat: An old belief says that the father of a girl who wears petticoats that show beneath her dress loves her more than her mother does.

Phobias: A phobia is an abnormal, irrational fear that often has its cause in superstition. Triskaidekaphobia, fear of the number thirteen, is a good example. Other common phobias include claustrophobia (fear of confined space), acrophobia (fear of height), nyctophobia (fear of the dark), phobophobia (fear of fear), and thanatophobia (fear of death).

See *thirteen.*

Phrenology: Phrenology is the art of determining someone's character by feeling and interpreting the bumps on the skull. The first person to practice phrenology was Dr. Franz Joseph Gall (1756–1828), a Viennese physician. Along with Dr. J. G. Spurzheim, his colleague, Gall wrote the first book on the subject, called *The Physiog-*

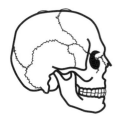

nomical System. They believed that raised areas, or bumps, on the skull reveal a person's talents and skills.

Phrenology was extremely popular in the nineteenth century. More than fifty phrenology organizations were formed in the United States to promote this new fad. Ralph Waldo Emerson, Edgar Allan Poe, Mark Twain, and Walt Whitman all were keen supporters of phrenology. Naturally, this new "science" had its detractors, too, and these included John Quincy Adams, former president of the United States. When Dr. Spurzheim died, his autopsy was held at Harvard University and people were invited to see his remarkable head for themselves.

By the start of the twentieth century, interest in phrenology had declined enormously, and today only a few people practice the art. There have been a number of attempts to revive interest. In 1935, a machine called a psychograph was invented to read the bumps on the head. Books are occasionally still published on the subject, but it has not helped the cause that no phrenologist has yet been able to determine an honest person from a dishonest one by interpreting the bumps.

Physiognomy: Physiognomy is the art of determining someone's character from his or her face. In China it is known as *Siang Mien,* and is often used to predict the future. The Chinese categorize the face into eleven types. A wide forehead, a thin nose with fleshy nostrils, pronounced earlobes, and a round chin are all highly positive traits in *Siang Mien.* Someone who possesses two or more of these traits is destined to achieve great success.

The ancient Greeks related different faces to different animals. For instance, someone with an equine face had the appearance and traits of a horse. He or she was assumed to be sincere, reliable, generous, and easy to get along with.

See *horse, nose.*

Picture: It is considered bad luck for a picture to fall off a wall for no apparent reason. This is especially the case if the glass covering the picture breaks. Some

people believe that if the picture is a photograph of a living person, he or she will die as a result.

You can send a curse to someone by hanging his or her picture on a wall backwards and/or upside down.

See *glass.*

Pig: Pigs are thought of in different ways in various parts of the world. They were worshipped in ancient Egypt, and are considered lucky animals in China. The ancient Cretans considered the pig sacred, as a sow suckled Jupiter.

However, Jews and Arabs refuse to eat pork as they consider the pig "unclean." Even the Bible reviles pigs:

> And the swine, though he divide the hoof, and be cloven-footed, yet he cheweth not the cud; he is unclean to you. Of their flesh shall ye not eat, and their carcass shall ye not touch; they are unclean for you. (Leviticus 11:7–8)

In most parts of the world it is also considered unlucky for a pig to cross your path.

Many sailors have a deep fear of pigs and refuse to call them by name, instead referring to them as porker, curly-tail, or grunter. Pig is a taboo word. If a sailor comes across a pig while heading to his ship, he should immediately turn around and return home. This seems a particularly strange superstition, and might derive from the story of the Gadarene swine, which di-

rectly connects pigs with drowning. When Jesus landed at Gadarene, he met a man with "an unclean spirit." Jesus ordered the legion of unclean spirits out of the man and into a herd of some two thousand pigs that were feeding nearby. The pigs "ran violently down a steep place into the sea, (they were about two thousand;) and were choked in the sea" (Mark 5:13).

Fortunately for the poor pig, some people have shown them respect. Sir Winston Churchill, who was highly superstitious, said,

> A cat will look down to a man.
> A dog will look up to a man.
> But a pig will look you straight in the eye
> And see his equal.

See *drowning, sailors, taboo.*

Pigeon: It is bad luck for a single white pigeon to settle on a rooftop. However, it is good luck for pigeons of other colors to settle there. It brings good luck to the occupants of a house if a group of pigeons settles on the roof. It is considered good luck to feed pigeons, and you will probably make new friends as a result.

If your lover has left you, you can encourage him or her to

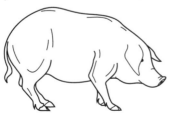

return by piercing the heart of a dead pigeon with pins.

See *birds, pin.*

Pillow: A pillow filled with hops will cure insomnia and ensure a good night's sleep.

See *insomnia.*

Pin: The old saying "see a pin, pick it up, and all day long you'll have good luck" comes from the belief that iron, or anything made from it, keeps evil spirits away. The full version of the rhyme goes,

> See a pin,
> Pick it up,
> And all day long
> You'll have good luck.

> See a pin,
> And let it lie,
> You'll want a pin
> Before you die.

Here are two more versions of the second verse:

> See a pin,
> And let it lay,
> Bad luck will follow you
> All day.

> See a pin,
> And let it lie,
> All day long
> You'll have to cry.

Pins that have been used in the making of a wedding dress are particularly lucky, but it is bad luck to accidentally leave any pins in the finished garment.

One form of black magic is to stick pins into a wax effigy of someone you dislike. This causes physical suffering to the person you are targeting, but you need to think carefully before attempting anything like this. All magic has consequences, and the "threefold law" says that everything you send out comes back to you threefold.

Hairpins were considered just as lucky a find as ordinary pins. Leo Durocher (1905–1991), the famous baseball player and manager, collected thousands of hairpins as luck amulets.

See *amulet, baseball, coin, iron, magic, orange, pigeon, thumb, wedding dress.*

Pisces: Pisces is the twelfth sign of the zodiac. Its symbol is two fish swimming in opposite directions. Its element is water, and its gemstone is aquamarine. The keyword for Pisces is: I believe.

Pisceans are gentle, imaginative, dreamy people who may give the mistaken impression that they're living in a fantasy world.

However, they are thoughtful, philanthropic, and highly creative. They are sensitive, easily hurt, and inclined to worry. Pisceans are inclined to be indecisive and can be imposed upon by others. Pisceans are naturally intuitive and can develop this talent to a high degree.

See *aquamarine, astrology, elements, gemstones, water, zodiac.*

Pixies: Pixies are not the same as fairies. Pixies are little people who are always dressed in green. They love dancing in magic circles. Pixies are believed to be the souls of babies that died before they were baptized. The king of pixies gives each pixy a specific task to do. Some of these tasks are beneficial for all mankind, but others are mischievous, such as playing practical jokes and leading people astray.

People used to leave a bowl of water by their chimneys for the pixies.

See *baby, chimney, fairy, green.*

Plants: Plants have been credited with a large variety of beneficial qualities, rang-ing from creating luck to curing illness and providing protection from evil spirits. Many plants have specific superstitions attached to them, but there are also more general beliefs that apply to the entire plant world.

The most common of these beliefs is that it is bad luck to sleep in a room containing plants because they will use up all the oxygen.

Another superstition says to tell your plants about any important occurrences happening in the family. If the plants are not told, they are likely to die. If someone in the family dies, the plants should be adorned with a piece of black cloth to allow them to mourn with the family.

See *flowers, music, sleep, spitting.*

Plate: If you accidentally break a plate, you can guarantee two more breakages will occur in the near future. Fortunately, you can avoid any further damage to your crockery by deliberately breaking two valueless items of pottery or glassware.

It is particularly bad luck for a bride to break a plate at her wedding reception. This is a sign that her marriage will be unsuccessful.

See *bride, marriage, three, waiter, wedding.*

Pointing: Pointing at someone is considered rude today. This is because of an old belief that pointing at people is a supernatural way to kill them. Even today, pointing the bone at someone is a death sentence in many parts of the world. The bone is either a real bone, between six and nine inches long, or a similar length of wood, which is pointed at someone while a curse is chanted. People who are pointed at believe in the curse, and effectively will themselves to die. Usually the victim dies within a week. In the past, pointing a forefinger, wet with saliva, was also a way to curse someone.

The first and second fingers of the right hand are used when giving a blessing. They can also be used to avert a curse or spell. Point these two fingers at the person who is cursing you, and the spell will immediately cease to have any effect.

See *finger, spell.*

Potato: When the potato was first introduced to Europe in the sixteenth century, it was believed to work as an aphrodisiac. That belief did not last for long. A new superstition began, as people assumed that

carrying a potato around in one's trouser pocket would cure rheumatism.

Potatoes were also believed to cure warts. You had to slice a potato in half and rub it against the wart. The element of belief ensured that this cure sometimes worked.

Another superstition claimed that you could darken your hair by rinsing it in water that had been used to boil potato peelings.

It was said that potatoes should be planted on Good Friday to protect against evil spirits and the devil. The first person in a family to eat a new potato is entitled to a wish.

See *aphrodisiac, devil, Good Friday, hair, illness, onion, warts.*

Prayer: Prayer is an act of communicating with the divine. It is an essential part of worship in many religions, and has been practiced for thousands of years.

During the Middle Ages, the Christian Church tried to abolish magical charms, as these were associated with paganism, witchcraft, and magic. It was said to be acceptable to recite a prayer, but evil to recite a charm in an attempt to cure an illness or ward off potential danger. The

Church did not succeed in this attempt to replace charms with prayers. In fact, they confused the situation so much that many prayers were used as charms. In addition, to obtain the utmost protection, many people made use of both church and magic.

Christian leaders taught that saying prayers at the start of the day would protect against witches and the devil. People believed that witches were unable to recite certain prayers, including the Lord's Prayer, and this was sometimes used as a test during the witch trials.

It is considered unlucky to kneel at the foot of the bed to say good-night prayers. However, it is considered good luck to say them while kneeling at the side of the bed.

See *charms, devil, magic, quartz, seven, witch, witchcraft.*

Praying Mantis: It is bad luck to kill a praying mantis, which is considered holy because of its apparent attitude of prayer. It is considered a sign of good luck whenever a praying mantis appears, although the luck will quickly disappear if the insect is harmed in any way.

If a praying mantis lands on your arm, you can expect to meet an important person. You will receive recognition or an honor if a praying mantis lands on your head.

See *prayer.*

Pregnancy: Many superstitions have developed about how to ward off harm to a fetus and mother during the nine months of gestation. It was believed that if the mother-to-be gazed at the moon, the child would have mental problems. If she spun or knitted, the poor child would one day be hanged. If she stole anything while pregnant, the child would grow up to be a thief. If she saw a corpse, the child would have a pale complexion. In Scandinavia, it was believed that if a pregnant woman stepped over a cat she'd give birth to a hermaphrodite. Even talking about the baby before it was born was potentially dangerous, as this could attract fairies who might steal or harm the fetus.

It was believed that the pregnant woman's cravings would reveal themselves as physical marks on the baby's body. If, for instance, she craved strawberries, the child would be born with a strawberry birthmark. Fortunately, this would not occur if the craving was satisfied.

Even the pregnant woman's dislikes could appear as a birthmark. If the woman disliked cats, her baby would be born with a birthmark in the shape of a cat.

The best time to conceive was thought to be midday, when the sun was highest. Women who wanted to conceive stood a better chance of doing so if they spent plenty of time with pregnant women. Wearing an item of clothing belonging to a pregnant woman also helped.

See *baby, birthmark, cat, corpse, fairy, moon, sun, thief.*

Prenatal Influences: Many people still believe that the emotions of a pregnant woman can adversely affect her unborn baby. The mother's stresses, fears, anger, and shame are all believed to potentially harm the child. This is not the case, as the umbilical cord possesses no nerve fibers, making it impossible for the mother's emotions to harm the baby.

See *baby, umbilical cord.*

Primrose: The primrose is a spring flower that is known as "the keys of heaven." It was sacred to the mother goddess Freya. During the Middle Ages, people believed the primrose could unlock or open hidden treasures or secrets. The primrose is  also believed to "unlock" spring, and even the sight of a primrose is said to alleviate feelings of gloom and melancholy created by a long winter.

It is considered bad luck to bring one or two primroses into the house, or to give such a small number as a gift. Bunches should contain at least thirteen primroses. These not only bring good luck, but also ward off evil spirits and cure insomnia.

See *flowers, insomnia, thirteen.*

Prophecy: The word "prophecy" comes from the Greek *prophetes,* which means "one who speaks before." Many prophecies are believed to have been predictions made through divine guidance or intervention.

People who are about to die are believed to have the gift of prophecy, as they have already started to part the veil to gain a glimpse of the future.

Pumpkin: The pumpkin pie eaten at Thanksgiving is a remembrance of the pumpkins the Native Americans taught the early American settlers how to grow, but it is also related to the days when the pumpkin was a harvest symbol. Early Irish immigrants probably brought this tradition to America.

Pumpkins are frequently carved into hideous faces at Halloween. When illuminated with a candle, they scare off the evil spirits who are out and about on this special night.

These lanterns made from pumpkins are called jack-o'-lanterns, after the hero of an old Irish story. Jack cleverly tricked the devil out of stealing his soul, but was still unable to enter heaven because of the disreputable life he had led. He was condemned to wander the world in darkness. The devil eased his burden by giving him a piece of coal from hell to light his lantern.

Because of their association with warding off evil, Good Friday is considered the best day to plant pumpkins.

A superstition from Maine says pumpkins are good for the eyes.

See *candle, coal, devil, eye, Good Friday, Halloween.*

Purse: It is important to place a coin in any purse that you intend to give away as a gift. This ensures that the person who receives the purse will have good luck and will never run out of money.

See *coin, money.*

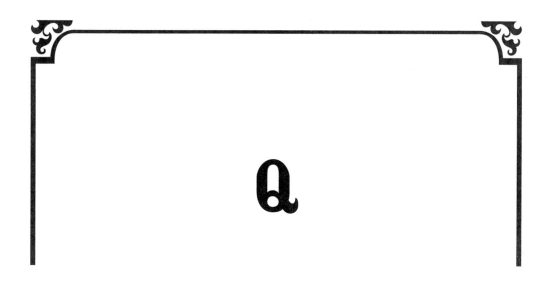

Q

Quartz: Quartz can be found almost everywhere, making it one of the most commonly found minerals. Large quartz crystals were found in the Egyptian temple of Luxor, showing that mankind has used this crystal for at least eight thousand years.

The ancient Greeks believed that anyone who held a piece of quartz in their hands while praying would have his or her prayer answered. This was because the gods were not able to turn down a prayer when faced with the magical power of quartz.

Quartz is said to enhance mental concentration, which may explain why it is used in crystal balls. Quartz has been used for healing and magical purposes for thousands of years, and is still popular today.

A piece of quartz placed beside a bed is believed to eliminate unpleasant dreams.

Quartz is known as the "stone of power," as it amplifies energy fields and is an excellent source of purification. Clear quartz provides energy and stamina. Rose quartz is pale pink in color. It alleviates jealousy and fear, and promotes fertility. As it also is thought to attract people, it is frequently used in spells to attract love.

Many people like to "bathe" their quartz crystals in the light of the full moon, as they believe this increases the protective and luck-providing qualities of the crystal.

Milky quartz is used as a protection against any form of negativity.

Smoky quartz eliminates feelings of doubt, despair and depression. It creates feelings of positivity and well being. It is also used to heal wounds, both psychic and actual.

Rose quartz is a cheerful stone that creates feelings of loyalty and love.

See *gemstones, moon, prayer.*

Quince: In ancient Greece and Rome, quince symbolized love, fertility, and happiness. It was sacred to Aphrodite and Venus. In Greece, newly married women brought quince into the house to symbolize a long and fruitful marriage.

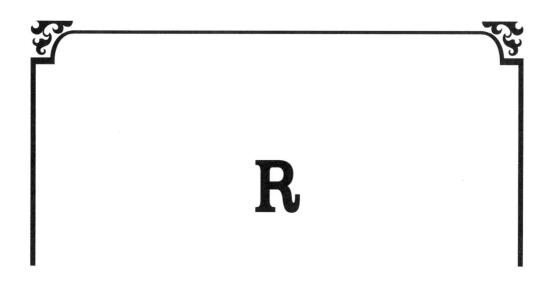

R

Rabbit: It is considered bad luck if a rabbit runs across your path. In the nineteenth century, miners would return home if this occurred, as they believed it indicated a mining disaster.

Some people use rabbits to predict good and bad luck. They believe it is good luck for a rabbit to cross your path from left to right, but bad luck if it runs from right to left.

To ensure a lucky month, the first words you should say on the first day of each month are "white rabbits."

See *Easter, hare, miners, sailors, ships.*

Rabbit's Foot: The rabbit's foot is arguably the most popular of all lucky charms. The origins of this charm are unknown, but there are a number of possibilities. As rabbits are born with their eyes open, the charm may originally have been used to provide protection against the evil eye. Rabbits are renowned for their fecundity. Consequently, as feet are considered phallic symbols, the rabbit's foot may originally have been a fertility symbol.

Hundreds of years ago, people were terrified of the spirits who lived underground. Rabbits obviously possessed special powers, as they were able to live underground and raise their offspring there in apparent safety. People noticed the strange way in which rabbits moved, with the hind

legs touching the ground before the front ones. The also saw rabbits digging their burrows with their hind legs. Rabbits also warn other rabbits of impending danger by thumping a hind leg. These facts made people think that the rabbit's luck was stored in its back feet.

Actors are amongst the most superstitious of people. Many years ago, they used a rabbit's foot to apply makeup. When powder puffs were developed, the rabbit's foot was no longer required, but actors kept them as lucky charms.

Samuel Pepys (1633–1703) wore a "hare's foote" as a lucky charm. On December 31, 1664, he wrote about his good fortune and good health over the previous twelve months. He wrote that he was "at a great loss to know whether it be my Hare's foote, or taking every morning of a pill of Turpentine, or my having left off the wearing of a gowne."[48]

Nowadays, most lucky rabbit foot charms are made from the rabbit's front feet. But these are unlikely to produce luck, as traditionally only the rabbit's left hind foot was lucky. In fact, if you want to be really lucky, the left foot has to be severed by a cross-eyed person at full moon.

Sailors believed witches could take the form of rabbits and hares. Consequently, these were considered evil animals that should be destroyed. It was bad luck to see a rabbit, or even mention its name, before going to sea.

In Wales, newborn babies had their foreheads brushed with a rabbit's foot. This was believed to give them good luck in later life. A rabbit's foot was frequently hung over the cradle to provide protection.

See *actors and actresses, amulet, charms, cradle, cross-eyed, evil eye, hare, sailors, witch.*

Racial Superiority: The belief that one race of people is superior to another is a pernicious superstition that has caused enormous damage throughout the history of mankind. This superstition is still widely prevalent, causing endless hatred and prejudice against others.

Rain: Because rain is essential for a good harvest, a large number of rituals and ceremonies have been developed to entice rain. Of course, almost as many rituals have been performed over the years to discourage rain. Lighting bonfires, burning ferns, or dipping religious relics in holy water are all reputed to cause rain. One well-known remedy for too much rain is to recite the old nursery rhyme:

> Rain, rain, go away,
> Come again another day.

In 1687, John Aubrey mentioned this rhyme as a method to "charme away the rain." He also said that charms of this sort dated back to antiquity. Strattis (409–375 BCE) wrote that when clouds obscured the sun, children would call out: "Come forth, beloved sun!"[49]

In Cornwall, it's considered good luck if it rains during a funeral, as this is a sign that the deceased has reached heaven. This may be related to another old superstition, which says, "Happy is the bride that the sun shines on, and the corpse that the rain rains on." Another superstition I heard in Cornwall is that coins washed in rainwater can never be stolen.

Two saints are vitally interested in rain. Saint Bernard causes rain that goes on and on, and Saint Barnabas makes it go away again.

Many people believe that their corns and rheumatism tell them when it's going to rain. Some people also believe that washing their eyes in rainwater helps cure eye problems.

Carrying an umbrella is considered an excellent way to keep the rain away.

See *April, charms, clouds, coin, corpse, December, eye, fox, funeral, June, St. Swithin's Day, seagull, sky, sun, umbrella, water, weather.*

Rainbow: Rainbows are considered lucky, and many people make a wish when they see one. Every child knows the old story about the crock of gold that can be found at the end of the rainbow. As Noah saw a rainbow near the end of his time on the ark, some people believe it is a sign that God will never flood the entire world again. Early Christian legends say that the rainbow is actually the archangel Uriel, who looks after thunder, lightning and storms. Rainbows are sometimes also used to help predict the weather. To see a rainbow in the afternoon is a sign that the next day will be fine. However, a rainbow in the morning means wet weather on the following day. A rainbow at lunchtime indicates a sudden burst of rain. It's a sign of good weather to see a perfect rainbow after it has rained. You should never point at a rainbow, as this is a symbolic request for more rain.

It is especially good luck to see both ends of a rainbow.

See *gold, lightning, opal, storm, thunder, weather, wish.*

Rat: It has always been considered a bad omen for rats desert a ship. This superstition apparently began with an old belief that rats contained the souls of people who had died. Because of what they had gone through in their previous lives, people thought that rats could predict future disasters. Conversely, it is considered a good omen for rats to board a ship.

It is considered a sign that someone in the family is about to die when rats leave a house. A death is also considered imminent if rats start gnawing at bedroom furniture. If rats leave one house and move into another, it brings good luck to the occupiers of their new home.

One old superstition says you can get rid of rats by catching one, painting it, and then setting it free. This odd-colored rat will confuse the other rats, who will immediately leave the area.

An interesting superstition says that children's baby teeth should be thrown away while asking rats to send stronger ones to replace them.

Because mice and rats can smell their human enemies, a belief grew up that it was best to set traps while wearing gloves so that the vermin would not sense the human presence. This superstition has long been discredited.

Many gypsies call rats "long tails," as it is thought to be bad luck to say their real name out loud.

See *death, evil eye, holy water, miners, sailors, ships, teeth.*

Raven: Ravens have always had a bad reputation and are believed to have foreknowledge of disasters and tragedies, particularly death. It is considered a sign of sickness or death if a raven makes its distinctive croaking sound while flying over a house. Their call is sometimes heard as "corpse, corpse," which is not an encouraging message for anyone lying ill in bed.

The most famous superstition about ravens concerns the birds living in the Tower of London. It is believed that if they leave, the royal family will die and the United Kingdom will collapse. In the early 1920s, only one raven was left at the Tower of London and new ravens had to be captured and introduced to the Tower. Nowadays, the ravens at the Tower of London have their wings clipped to ensure that they don't fly away. People still believe that anyone who kills one of these ravens will die as a result.

See *birds, death, familiar.*

Red: Red is the color of blood, so it is believed to possess strong supernatural energy that scares away witches and demons. Red thread has been used in spells to cure bleeding noses and rheumatism. Farmers used to tie red thread around the horns or tails of livestock to protect them from witches.

At one time it was considered bad luck to meet someone with red hair, as the person was assumed to have a violent temper. It was especially unfortunate to meet a red-haired person on New Year's Day. Fishermen did not like to go to sea with red-haired or ginger-haired crewmates, as they considered it a bad omen. Red-haired children were believed to be the progeny of unfaithful mothers.

Red is thought to provide good luck to young girls. A red ribbon tied in a girl's hair is believed to provide protection until she reaches puberty.

See *fishermen, hair, New Year, nose, omen, rheumatism, St. Valentine's Day, white, witch.*

Rheumatism: Rheumatism is a painful affliction, and a huge number of folk cures have been attempted in the hope of finding relief. Common cures involved carrying a rabbit's foot, potato, or rowan twig in your pocket. Red thread could be tied around the neck, or around painful areas. Bees were encouraged to sting affected joints. Placing a pillow filled with hops under the sufferer's bed was also believed to cure the problem. Copper rings and bracelets are still worn today to help effect a cure.

By far the most bizarre cure for rheumatism was the Welsh tradition of repeatedly burying the naked victim vertically in a churchyard for two hours until the symptoms disappeared.

See *bees, potato, rabbit's foot, red, ring, rowan, serpentine, turtledove.*

Rice: Confetti is usually thrown at newly married couples today, but until recently, rice was used instead. Rice symbolizes fertility and prosperity, and expresses the feelings and good wishes of the couple's friends and family. Rice also provides food for any evil spirits who might wish to deprive the couple of happiness. It was thought that by the time the evil spirits had eaten the rice, the couple would have moved away. The ancient Romans threw nuts and sweets at the bride and groom, and other cultures

have thrown a variety of other items. The symbolism of these objects is always the same: fertility and happiness.

See *nut*.

Right Side: The right side has always been considered more fortunate than the left. Ancient fortunetellers, who frequently used the flights of birds and the movements of clouds to help make their predictions, drew on this belief. Greek augurs faced the north. Movements from the west (left) were thought to indicate bad luck, while movements from the east (right) indicated success and good luck. (It was especially fortunate to see an eagle, heron, or falcon.)

Plato and Aristotle explained that because the sun set in the west, good luck departed in that direction also. And because nighttime was seen as the time for witches and evil spirits, the setting of the sun in the west was another indication of bad luck coming from the west, or left side.

This is also the origin of the belief of getting out of bed on the right side. As gods were thought to live on the right side, and evil spirits on the left, it was important to get into bed on the right side, and exit it on the right side when you woke up.

Many people believe that they should start any forward movement using their right foot, as this will provide good luck and lead them to success.

See *bed, birds, clothes, clouds, eagle, itching, left side, sun, witch.*

Ring: The ancient Egyptians were the first people known to wear rings. The earliest rings were made of knotted cord or wire, and were used as protective amulets rather  than as items of adornment. The knot confused any potential enemies, as it symbolically tied them in a knot.

Iron rings were common in Roman times. Originally, senators were the only people allowed to wear gold rings, but by the third century CE all freeborn men could wear a gold ring. Women did not appear to have faced restrictions of this sort, and all reasonably well-off women wore gold rings.

Plutarch (c.46–c.120 CE) recounted a superstitious use of signet rings in his *Life of Timoleon*, a famous Greek general. On one occasion, Timoleon and his troops had to ford a river to attack the enemy. Timoleon's officers started arguing about who would be the first to enter the river. Timoleon collected all the officers' signet rings in his cloak. The rings were thoroughly mixed and one drawn out. This ring bore a depiction of a trophy. This was considered such a good omen that the squabble was forgotten, and the soldiers crossed the river and defeated the enemy.[50]

In medieval times, magicians created magical rings to act as amulets and talismans. Cornelius Agrippa (1486–1535) included instructions on how to make these in his *Three Books of Occult Philosophy*.[51]

Cramp rings also became popular after King Edward II (1284–1327) was brought one from Jerusalem. They were worn for therapeutic purposes, and gained their power by being consecrated by the king, usually on Good Friday.

A ring is comprised of a circle, which has no beginning and no end. Consequently, it is considered a sign of everlasting life. A ring also encloses good luck, and could be said to be a miniature magic circle. Wedding rings symbolize continuity and completeness.

This is why sailors traditionally wore an earring through an earlobe. They thought it brought them both good luck and a long life. Piercing the ear also enabled any negative spirits trapped inside the body an opportunity to escape.

Large rings, such as those worn by the clergy, symbolize authority.

See *amulet, circle, cramp, ear, elephant, engagement, gold, Good Friday, iron, knot, luck, magic, omen, sailors, serpent, serpentine, talisman, topaz, wedding, wedding ring*.

Robin: The robin has always been considered a lucky sign. An early Christian tradition says that a few drops of Christ's blood created the robin's distinctive red breast. It has also been suggested that the robin was accidentally pricked when it tried to remove the thorns from Christ's forehead.

It is believed that anyone who hurts a robin will receive the same injury as punishment. In addition, anyone who kills a robin will experience an immediate and permanent decline in his or her wealth.

There are three situations in which the sight of a robin is unwelcome. It is a sign of imminent death if a robin flies into a home or a church, or settles near a mine shaft.

It is good luck to see the first robin of spring, and you should make a wish when you see it. This luck is increased if the robin is flying upwards. It is also considered lucky to find a robin's nest containing eggs, as long as the nest is not disturbed. You will enjoy good luck for a whole year if robins build a nest close to your home.

Early American colonists mistook the American thrush for the robin. This was not surprising, as apart from the fact that it is much larger, it has similar markings and even has a red breast. All of the good luck associations attached to the European robin were given

to the American one, and remain to this day.

See *birds, death, eggs, miners, St. Valentine's Day, wish.*

Rope: Lumbago is a painful rheumatic pain in the muscles of the lower back. People engaged in sedentary occupations are most prone to this, but it can afflict anyone. The remedy is to discard your belt and replace it with a length of hempen rope.

See *knot.*

Rose: The rose is the ultimate symbol of love. Ancient drawings of the rose have been found in the caves of Knossos in Crete. The island of Rhodes was named after the flower.

In Greek mythology, Chloris, the goddess of flowers, found the dead body of a young nymph and created the first rose from it. Aphrodite, the goddess of love, was responsible for the flower's beauty, and Dionysus, the god of wine and fertility, added the scent. Apollo warmed the bud to enable it to open. Another myth says that Cupid created the first roses. He tripped while carrying nectar to the gods on Mount Olympus. Roses immediately bloomed on the ground where the nectar had fallen.

The Romans adored the rose and used it extensively. It was woven into garlands, and worn by brides and grooms. Rose petals were strewn everywhere during processions and banquets. Guests at celebrations wore rose crowns to prevent drunkenness.

The Romans associated the rose with discretion and secrecy. A rose was suspended from the ceiling whenever a confidential meeting took place. This custom is still remembered in the term *sub rosa*, which means "under the rose." The secrecy aspect of the rose still applied in Tudor England, and many ceilings contained a rose pattern or single rose in the center. Secret meetings were announced by the passing of roses.

Early Christians refused to allow roses inside their churches, as they associated it with the debauchery of the Romans. However, they gradually added their beliefs to the story of the rose. Apparently, all roses were red until the Virgin Mary rested her cloak on a rose bush. When she did this, the flowers turned white to indicate her purity. After this, the rose became sacred to Christians, as it symbolized the wounds of Christ (red) and the purity of the Virgin Mary (white).

Muslims believe that roses were created by sweat from the brow of Mohammed. Consequently, the rose became a sacred flower and was linked with the journey of the soul. It is likely that the beautiful rose windows in European cathedrals are related to this idea.

Dreaming of roses is considered a sure sign of love and good fortune. Roses have different meanings, according to color, in the language of flowers. White roses symbolize chaste love, red roses symbolize passion, and yellow roses symbolize jealousy.

See *bride, church, flowers, love, St. Valentine's Day, umbilical cord, wedding.*

Rosemary: "There's rosemary—that's for remembrance" (*Hamlet*, Act 4, scene 5).

Because rosemary is sacred to friendship and remembrance, it used to be tossed onto coffins at funerals as a sign that the mourners would not forget the deceased. Brides and grooms drank rosemary in wine at their wedding receptions to symbolize their love and fidelity.

Rosemary was also believed to provide protection against illness, and to ward off the evil eye as well as witches and demons. A sprig of rosemary, worn as a lucky charm, was believed to provide good fortune and opportunities for expansion.

Rosemary leaves can be rubbed on the chest to cure colds. They can also

apparently be rubbed on the scalp to cure or prevent baldness.

See *baldness, coffin, colds, evil eye, funeral, wedding, wine, witch.*

Rowan: The rowan, or mountain ash, is a tree with strong protective qualities. Planted in the garden, it was thought to provide protection from witches and evil spirits. Nailing rowan branches to a building also provided similar protection. Two small pieces of rowan, tied together with red ribbon to form a cross and carried in a pocket, was considered an effective personal amulet that ensured protection. In Scotland, crosses of rowan were placed over doors and windows to ward off evil spirits and witches. The use of rowan to ward off witches led to a rhyme:

> Rowan tree or reed
> Put the witches to speed.

Rowan trees are frequently found in graveyards, because it is believed that they ensure that the dead will enjoy a peaceful, undisturbed sleep. They also eliminate any likelihood of haunting.

See *amulet, cross, graveyard, tree, witch.*

Ruby: Ruby is the red variety of corundum. It is a legendary stone in India. Statues of Buddha usually have a small ruby on the forehead, as red symbolizes the reincarnation of Buddha. If an offering of a ruby was made to Krishna, the person was expected to be reborn as a king (if the stone was small), or as an emperor (if the stone was large).

In early Christianity, the ruby was considered the most valuable of all the stones God created. God is believed to have ordered Aaron to wear a ruby on his neck in addition to in his breastplate of gemstones.[52]

The ruby has always been seen as a lucky stone that imparts joy and happiness. In fact, the more rubies you own, the greater your happiness should be. Wearing a ruby also puts fear into the hearts of your enemies, protects you from excesses of all kinds, and preserves good health.

It is also believed that the ruby will change color when the fortunes of its owner are about to decrease. A ruby belonging to Catherine of Aragon (1485–1536), the first wife of Henry VIII, is believed to have changed color when he was considering divorcing her.

Ruby is the birthstone for July.

See *birthstone, gemstones, wedding anniversaries.*

Rue: Rue is an acrid herb that was planted close to farm buildings to ward off any potential predators. It symbolizes regret and sorrow. If you were angry with someone, you could toss a handful of rue at him or her and say, "may you rue the day." In *Hamlet*, William Shakespeare called rue the "herb of grace." He had Ophelia say, "There's rue for you; and here's some for me. We may call it 'herb of grace' a Sundays" (*Hamlet*, Act 4, scene 5).

Rum: A superstition from Maine says that pouring rum on the head prevents baldness. In some cases it makes the hair curly as well.

See *baldness, hair.*

Rust: Oddly enough, it is a good omen for your keys or cutlery to become rusty. This means that someone is saving money that you will ultimately inherit.

See *cutlery, key.*

S

Sage: Sage is considered a lucky plant that improves wisdom and memory. It has been used to heal wounds and prevent colds. Before toothpaste was invented, many people cleaned their teeth by rubbing them with a sage leaf. Sage can even be used, it is said, to avert the evil eye.

Sage is also used to aid fertility and ease the pain of childbirth. Women who have trouble conceiving are advised to go to bed for four days and drink a juice made 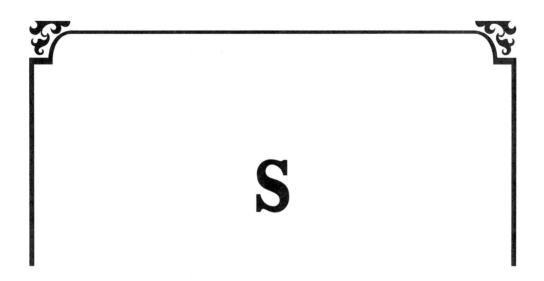 from sage. After this, conception should occur easily and a healthy child will be the result.

Sage is also believed to absorb any negativity or evil influences, mak-ing it a useful plant to have in your home. However, as it's considered unlucky to grow sage in your garden, you should obtain it from someone else.

You can write a wish on a sage leaf and then send it out into the universe by burning it. If you believe strongly enough, your wish will come true.

See *baldness, colds, evil eye, teeth, wish.*

Sagittarius: Sagittarius is the ninth sign of the zodiac. Its symbol is the archer. Its element is fire, and its gemstone is amethyst. The keyword for Sagittarius is: I see.

Sagittarians are friendly, open, optimistic people with a positive, enthusiastic approach to life. They are honest and loyal, but have a tendency to be outspoken at times. They are independent people who enjoy having room and space around them. Consequently, they are frequently interested in sports and travel.

See *amethyst, astrology, elements, fire, gemstones, zodiac.*

Sailors: Sailors have always been amongst the most superstitious of people. This is not surprising when you consider the perilous nature of their work, especially hundreds of years ago when they had to rely entirely on their own skill to sail their craft using the sun, moon, stars, and winds. Every time they set off from land, they had no idea if they would return home again.

Sailors had a perfectly natural fear of drowning, and amulets were used to protect them from this fate. Gold earrings were worn, and sailors also carried cauls for protection. Sailors believed that touching their wives' genitals before leaving on a trip also provided protection. This was called "touching the bun."

Stones containing natural holes in them were tied to the bows of boats to protect both the boat and its occupants. These stones were known as "holy flints." They symbolized the womb, which relates to fruitfulness, and by association, good luck.

Sailors had to be careful when travelling from home to their ship. It was bad luck to come across any member of the clergy, someone who was cross-eyed, or a person with red hair. Sailors stepped on to their ship using their right foot, to avert the potential bad luck that using their left foot might cause. At the end of the voyage, sailors also stepped off the ship using their right foot.

It was bad luck if the voyage started on a Friday, or on any of the inauspicious days of the calendar. It was also bad luck if the new moon fell on a Saturday, or the full moon occurred on a Sunday.

It was bad luck to have dogs, horses, pigs, or rabbits on board the ship. However, cats were extremely lucky. It was bad luck for rats to leave the ship, as this indicated that the ship was about to sink. The albatross was a sign of good luck, but terrible things were expected to happen if it were killed. (Sailors believed the albatross to be the soul of a drowned sailor.) Seagulls were not to be harmed either, to prevent misfortune. Three seagulls flying close together over a ship indicated someone on board would shortly die.

Sailors love dolphins, too. A pod of dolphins playing around the ship in good weath-er is thought to be a sign that a storm is on its way. Seeing dolphins in bad weather indicates that the storm is about to end. Whales are also considered lucky, except when close to shore. This is considered a sign of bad luck ahead.

It was believed to be bad luck to have a woman on your boat, but it was good luck for a baby to be born on board. It was good luck to quarrel with your wife before setting sail, but the disagreement could not be forced. It had to be an argument that happened without forethought.

A boat had to be pulled out of the water bow first. It was considered bad luck to pull it out stern first.

Sailors could also bring good luck to others. A young woman could receive good luck by touching a sailor's shirt collar, especially if he wasn't aware of what she was doing.

See *albatross, amulet, baby, calendar, cat, caul, coal, coin, cross-eyed, dog, drowning, figurehead, fingernail, fishermen, garlic, hair, horse, horseshoe, miners, moon, nine, ornithomancy, pig, rat, rabbit, ring, St. Elmo, seagull, shell, ships, star, storm, sun, tattoo, women, whistle, wind.*

St. Christopher: St. Christopher is the patron saint of travelers, and many people believe that a medallion or amulet depicting him will protect them. The legend of St. Christopher is an appealing one. His original name was Offero. He befriended a hermit who taught him about Christianity. After Offero was baptized, the hermit told him to live by a river and carry people from one side to the other. One night, he carried a small child across the river. The infant grew larger and heavier with every step Offero took. When they finally reached the other side, the child told Offero that he was Jesus, and the weight was all the cares of the world he was carrying on his shoulders. Jesus told Offero to change his name to Christopher, which means "Christ-bearer" in Greek.

There is considerable doubt that St. Christopher ever really existed, and in 1969 the Roman Catholic Church removed him from their list of saints. However, this seems to have made no difference in his popularity.

In 1968, the United States Navy failed in its attempt to put several Vanguard rockets into orbit. The contractors blamed this failure on the absence of St. Christopher medals on the rockets. A medal

was attached to the next rocket, and it performed perfectly.[53]

In recent years, young couples have exchanged St. Christopher necklaces as a token of their love. These necklaces protect the wearers during travel, and also proclaim the couple's love to the world. If the relationship ends, the necklaces are returned.

St. Christopher's feast day is July 25th. See *car, July 25th, luck, travel.*

St. Elmo's Fire: In sailing ship days, St. Elmo's fire was a particularly good omen. The fire consisted of luminous lights flashing on the masts of ships after a storm, and sailors believed St. Elmo had helped them survive the hazardous weather conditions.

St. Elmo was a fourth-century Syrian bishop who kept on preaching during a thunderstorm and was hit by lightning. He survived this, and carried on preaching.

Sailors still revere St. Elmo today, and he is also believed to help pregnant women with the pains of giving birth.

See *sailors, ships.*

St. John's Wort: The Romans called St. John's wort the "devil chaser," and hung it in their homes for protection. The plant was named after John the Baptist, and its flowers were burned on Midsummer's Eve in honor of him. Translucent spots of red can sometimes be seen in the leaves of St. John's wort. The flower petals also produce a crimson resin when rubbed. These are said to be spots of John the Baptist's blood.

An intriguing superstition for women having problems conceiving says for them to take off all their clothes on Midsummer's Eve and, while naked, pick a sprig of St. John's wort from their garden.

Placing St. John's wort under your pillow was believed to encourage dreams in which you would see your future husband or wife.

St. John's wort is frequently used as an anti-depressant. The proper name for this plant is *hypericum perforatum.* The active ingredient in hypericum is hypericin, which stabilizes and balances the serotonin levels in the brain. Serotonin directly affects our feelings of well being and happiness. Hypericin is also used to treat insomnia, nervous disorders, and premenstrual tension.

See *dreams, flowers, Midsummer's Eve.*

St. Stephen: St. Stephen was the first Christian martyr (Acts 6–7). The Jewish authorities charged him with speaking against the Temple and the Law, and condemned him to death by stoning. Because this is a particularly painful way to die, people suffering chronic headaches call on him to help relieve their suffering.

See *headache.*

St. Swithin's Day: An old tradition says that if it rains on St. Swithin's Day (July 15) it will rain for the next forty days. Conversely, the weather will be fine for forty days if it does not rain on his day.

St. Swithin (d. 862 CE), a Saxon Bishop of Winchester, was buried, at his request, with the poor people in the common churchyard. However, once miracles started occurring at his grave, the monks erected a beautiful shrine for him inside the cathedral. Apparently St. Swithin wept when they tried to move him inside, and this caused forty days of continual rain. The heavy rain was interpreted as St. Swithin's disapproval of the move, which was then abandoned. People came to believe that if it rained on St. Swithin's day, the rain would last for forty days.

Apples apparently should not be picked or eaten before St. Swithin's Day. The apples are blessed if it rains on this day.

See *apple, grave, rain.*

St. Valentine's Day: One of the most popular days of the year is February 14, St. Valentine's Day. On this day most people think about love and the special person in their life. The origins of  this day are lost in history, but it appears to have developed from Lupercalia, a pre-Christian Roman festival that was held in honor of Pan and Juno. The main purpose of the celebration was to ensure fertility and bountiful crops. This festival was celebrated on the evening of February 14, and on the following day. As part of the celebration, young men drew the names of girls from a large urn to discover who would be their partner for the festival.

In the fourth century, the Christian Church became concerned about this "pagan" festival and tried to abolish it, without success. They compromised, and renamed the day after St. Valentine, an early Christian martyr.

It is highly likely that St. Valentine never existed. The early Church lists a number of martyrs with that name, and celebrated the lives of seven of them on February 14. However, no one knows if any of them had anything to do with love and romance. Naturally, there are stories connected to each of them. My favorite concerns a man named Valentine who was imprisoned because he helped the Christians who were being persecuted at the time. While in prison, he performed a miracle by restoring the sight of the jailor's blind daughter. The night before his death, he sent her a farewell letter that

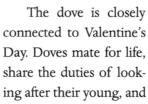

was signed, "from your Valentine."

The dove is closely connected to Valentine's Day. Doves mate for life, share the duties of looking after their young, and are mentioned favorably in the Bible. Also, during the Middle Ages, people believed that birds mated on Valentine's Day.

As a result of this, many people believe that the first bird a young girl sees on Valentine's Day will help her identify her future husband:

If she sees a blackbird, she will marry a clergyman.

If she sees a robin redbreast or a bunting, she will marry a sailor.

If she sees a goldfinch, she will marry an extremely wealthy man.

If she sees a yellowbird, she will marry a man who is comfortably well off.

If she sees a sparrow, she will marry a farmer and live happily in a cottage.

If she sees a bluebird, she will marry a happy man, but live in poverty.

If she sees a crossbill, she and her husband will argue constantly.

If she sees a woodpecker or wryneck, she will never marry.

If she sees a dove, she will marry a kind and good man.

If she sees a flock of doves, she will have an exceedingly long and happy marriage.

Red is the color associated with Valentine's Day. Not surprisingly, sales of red roses increase enormously at this time of year. Red roses were sacred to Venus, the goddess of love and beauty, and Bacchus, the god of wine and happiness. Roses are also associated with Cupid, who is believed to have been the cause of their appearance in the first place. According to legend, he was carrying a vase of nectar to the gods on Mount Olympus. Unfortunately, he tripped and spilled the nectar on the ground. Immediately, roses started growing on the spot.

The Puritans brought Valentine's Day to America in 1629. However, life was hard and there was not a great deal of time for activities that were seen as frivolous. Consequently, it took about a hundred years for Valentine's Day to be celebrated in the United States. Valentine's Day cards followed soon afterwards.

It is bad luck to sign a Valentine's Day card. Naturally, this also defeats the object of the card.

Another common superstition says that the first person of the opposite sex that you meet and kiss on this day will be your Valentine for the next twelve months.

If a single woman goes for a walk early in the morning on Valentine's Day, she can expect to gain information about her future marriage. If the first person she meets is a woman, she will not get married that year. However, if the first person she meets is a man, she will become engaged within three months.

See *amethyst, dove, kiss, love, red, robin, sparrow.*

Salespeople: Salespeople experience rejection on a regular basis. Even though they know they themselves are not being rejected, a series of rejections can make it hard for them to continue calling on potential customers. Consequently, many of them carry lucky charms, especially lucky coins. Some wear the specific clothes that they wore when they made a good sale. This might include a complete suit of clothes, but is more often a special tie or pair of socks.

See *charms, clothes, coin.*

Salt: Salt is one of the necessities of life, as it preserves food. It has been valued and treasured throughout human history. The word salary comes from the Latin

sal, which means "salt." This is because Roman soldiers were often paid in salt. The incredible value of salt also made it responsible for terms such as "salt of the earth" and "he has earned his salt."

Salt makes up approximately one percent of the human body. It can be tasted in our blood, sweat, and tears. Because of the taste of salt in tears, salt is sometimes connected with sorrow. Salty foods are often served after a Jewish funeral to help the mourners replace the salt they lost through their tears at the funeral service.

The devil is believed to detest salt, as it is incorruptible, immortal, and linked to God. Salt is a preservative, which makes it a natural enemy of anyone or anything that seeks to destroy. If a superstitious person accidentally spills some salt, he must immediately toss a pinch of salt over his left shoulder. This is because the devil is likely to attack from the rear, and will also attack from the left, or sinister, side. The presence of salt will immediately scare off the devil before he has time to cause any difficulties.

If you are about to undertake an important task, you might find it helpful to carry a small amount of sea salt in your pocket to provide you with good luck, and to avert any possible bad luck.

Reginald Scot, author of *The Discoverie of Witchcraft* (1584), did not believe in any form of superstition. He wrote, "To recount it good or bad luck, when salt or wine falleth on the table, or is shed, is altogether vanity and superstition."

Leonardo da Vinci used the symbolism of spilt salt in his painting *The Last Supper*, by having Judas knock over the saltcellar.

See *blood, curse, devil, Friday the 13th, funeral, horse racing, housewarming, left side, virginity.*

Santa Claus: Santa Claus is one major superstition that retailers and parents actively encourage. Santa Claus is thought to be a fat, happy man who lives at the North Pole, with his wife and an army of elves who build toys to deliver to good children on Christmas Eve. On Christmas Eve, Santa Claus puts on a bright red suit and cap, loads a sleigh with toys, and harnesses his reindeer. He rides the sleigh from house to house delivering toys by climbing down chimneys. He manages to travel throughout the world and return home before Christmas

morning. Although Santa Claus and his sleigh are usually invisible, the harness bells the reindeer wear can sometimes be heard.

This happy superstition is probably derived from St. Nicholas, a fourth century bishop in Asia Minor, who handed out gifts to the poor at Christmas time.

See *bell, chimney, Christmas Eve, Christmas Stocking.*

Sapphire: The sapphire is a corundum gem that can be colorless, or alternatively, any color except red. It is usually blue. (Red corundum is called ruby.) The blue color of sapphire relates it to coolness, chastity, and innocence. Because of these qualities, Pope Innocent III (1160–1216) required his bishops to wear rings with sapphire settings.

Sapphires are also believed to improve concentration and clarity of thought. They have also been used to remove boils and assist with eye problems. Modern day crystal therapists use sapphire to treat anemia and disorders of the blood.

See *blood, chastity, eye, gemstones, ruby, wedding anniversaries.*

Saturday: Saturday is the worst day of the week on which to start a new job. People who start new jobs on a Saturday do not keep them for long.

Scarab: The ancient Egyptians prized the scarab beetle, and wore depictions of it as an amulet. This was because the scarab represented Re, the sun god, who was the source of all life. A process of sympathetic magic imbued the scarab with the same qualities.

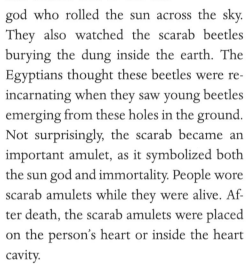

The Egyptians watched the scarab beetles roll pellets of dung across the ground, and related this to the sun god who rolled the sun across the sky. They also watched the scarab beetles burying the dung inside the earth. The Egyptians thought these beetles were re-incarnating when they saw young beetles emerging from these holes in the ground. Not surprisingly, the scarab became an important amulet, as it symbolized both the sun god and immortality. People wore scarab amulets while they were alive. After death, the scarab amulets were placed on the person's heart or inside the heart cavity.

The Egyptians manufactured hundreds of thousands of scarab amulets during their civilization. Production is still continuing, as people still wear scarab amulets as luck charms today.

See *amulet, beetle, carnelian, heart, malachite.*

Scissors: Scissors need to be handled with care, as any accident or mistake "cuts" into your luck. It is unlucky to drop a pair of scissors. If you do, someone else should pick them up for you. If no one is available, you should step on the scissors before picking them up. Before using them again, you should warm them in your hands to avert any possible bad luck.

Scissors are not a good choice when choosing a gift for a friend. This is because they could "cut" the friendship. Give scissors only to people who know they have to give you a small coin in exchange to effectively pay for them.

Scissors make powerful protective amulets, as they are made of metal and can cut. Consequently, scissors were sometimes opened to resemble a cross and placed under doormats, to deter witches and other evil spirits.

See *amulet, coin, cross, witch.*

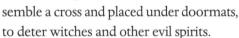

Scorpio: Scorpio is the eighth sign of the zodiac. Its symbol is the scorpion. Its element is water, and its gemstone is topaz. The keyword for Scorpio is: I desire.

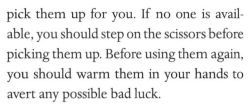

Scorpios are forceful, determined, secretive, and emotional. They are naturally intuitive, and instinctively know what makes other people work. However, they keep their own motivations and true nature a secret. Scorpios are patient people who wait for opportunities and then act quickly, using surprise to their benefit. Scorpios usually know what they want, and they invariably achieve their goals in the end.

See *astrology, elements, gemstones, topaz, water, zodiac.*

Scrying: Scrying is the ability to see into the future using a reflective surface, such as a crystal ball, mirror, cup of liquid, or pond. The scryer gazes at the surface until he or  she enters a trance-like state, which allows thoughts, images, or scenes of the future to appear. Michel de Notredame (1503–1566), better known as Nostradamus, is arguably the best-known scryer of all time. Dr. John Dee (1527–1608), astrologer to Queen Elizabeth 1, employed scryers to communicate with the angelic kingdom.

See *divination, mirror.*

Seagull: Seagulls are considered unlucky birds, as they were believed to be the reincarnation of drowned sailors. It has always been considered unlucky to kill one. It is a sign of death for three seagulls to fly over someone. However, it is good luck for sailors to see gulls sitting on the water.

It is generally considered a sign of rain when seagulls fly inland. When the seas become stormy and fish are hard to find, gulls fly inland in search of food, making them highly effective weather forecasters. An old saying relates to this:

Seagull, seagull get on to sand
It'll never be fine while you're on land.

Seagulls do not usually have a good reputation. However, there is a Sea Gull Monument in Salt Lake City, Utah. In May 1848, the Mormons planted their first crop and were horrified when a plague of locusts arrived and started eating it. The settlers fell to their knees and prayed. Miraculously, thousands of seagulls arrived and made a feast of the locusts. This saved enough of the crop for the pioneers to survive.

See *fish, rain, sailors.*

September: In Europe, thunderstorms in September are traditionally considered a sign of good crops the following year. In California, it is believed that a wet September indicates a drought the following summer.

See *thunderstorm, weather.*

Serpent: Ancient people watched snakes shedding their skin and thought they  were immortal. Consequently, snakes became symbols of longevity and represented the god of medicine, a tradition that exists to this day. Snake amulets can be found in a variety of forms. Rings and bracelets have always been popular, especially ones depicting a snake swallowing its own tail, which is an amulet against all forms of sickness.

See *amulet, ring, snake, virginity.*

Serpentine: Serpentine is an oily green mineral that often looks like snake's skin. In fact, this is how it got its name. In ancient Egypt it was used to make scarab amulets. In Italy, it is used as an amulet to protect the wearer from snakebites and insect stings.

People suffering from rheumatism or heart or lung diseases frequently wear serpentine.

See *amulet, gemstones, heart, rheumatism, scarab.*

Seven: Seven has always been a highly auspicious and lucky number. Seven is unrelated to any of the other numbers from one to ten, and is indivisible. Numerologists have always been fascinated with it because of this. It took God seven days to create the world. There were seven "planets" in the ancient world (Mercury, Venus, Mars, Jupiter, Saturn, Moon, and Sun). There are seven seas, and there were seven wonders of the ancient world. There are seven days in the week, the seventh of which is traditionally the day of prayer and rest. There are also seven virtues, seven deadly sins, and seven ages of man. The menorah, sacred candelabrum of the Jews, has seven branches depicting the seven heavens.

The seventh son of a seventh son (and the seventh daughter of a seventh daughter) is believed to be a highly lucky person. He or she also frequently possesses strong intuitive abilities and powers of healing. If the sum of a person's full date of birth is divisible by seven, he or she will always be lucky.

The "seven-year itch" is believed to tempt people who have been in a relationship for that length of time to look for new conquests. This idea is derived from the ancient belief that major changes in life occur every seven years.

When you are in "seventh heaven," you experience the ultimate in joy and happiness.

See *horseshoe, mirror, numbers, prayer.*

Sewing: It is believed to be bad luck to start sewing a garment on a Friday. How-ever, this superstition does not apply if the garment is started and finished on the same day. Saturday and Sunday are not good days for sewing. It is also considered unlucky to wear a garment while someone is sewing it. It's an indication of a quarrel if the seamstress threads knots while sewing.

If a seamstress pricks her finger and allows blood to stain the garment she is working on, it is said that the future wearer of the garment risks an early death.

Fortunately, there is also good luck connected with sewing. It is a sign of good luck if you accidentally drop the needle on the floor. However, it is bad luck if it sticks into the floor. If a needle breaks while a dress is being made, the wearer of the dress will receive a kiss as a result. If the sewer loses a thimble while making a garment, the ultimate wearer will receive good luck. Naturally, this is not the case if the sewer is the person who will ultimately wear the garment.

See *blood, death, Friday, Friday the 13th, knot, needle, thimble, umbilical cord.*

Sex: The number of superstitions concerning sex is incredible. It's not surprising, either, given that sex was a taboo subject to talk about not very many years ago.

One of the most common superstitions is that men with large hands and feet possess correspondingly large penises. Likewise, women with large mouths are thought to possess large vaginas. Almost as common is the belief that too much masturbation will make you go blind.

Apparently, if a man has sex with a woman while she is menstruating, he will either lose all his hair or become impotent.

Hippocrates (c.460–c.377 BCE) was the most famous physician of his day. He and his contemporaries believed that sperm from one testicle created boy babies, while sperm from the other created girls. Consequently, it was thought that you could choose the sex of your baby by tying off the testicle that created babies of the sex you did not want.

Male potency was associated with the generative power of the sun. This is why, even today, dark-skinned men and men from countries that are hot are considered more passionate than other men.

Hair was also considered an indication of sexual potency, and consequently hairy men were assumed to be more virile than men with less body hair.

See *aphrodisiac, hair, sun, taboo.*

Shadow: Thousands of years ago, people believed their shadows were their souls. Consequently, they thought they would die if anyone attacked their shadow with ill intent. You certainly didn't want anyone, or even an animal, to walk over your shadow, in case they sucked the life's blood out of it in the process.

I remember as a child deliberately standing in a larger person's shadow on an extremely hot day. An elderly aunt told me never to stand in anyone's shadow, as it was important to be your own person. I wasn't sure what she meant at the time, but as I still remember the incident, it must have had an effect on me.

Even today, some people consider it bad luck for their shadow to touch an open grave or a coffin. This meant they would soon be inside a coffin themselves.

It was important to remain alert for evil forces that might try to steal your shadow. Someone without a shadow was believed to have sold his or her soul to the devil.

On Christmas Eve, people used to look at the shadows cast on the wall by the fire. If any of the shadows appeared headless, it was a sign that the person would be dead before the next Christmas Eve.

See *Christmas Eve, coffin, devil, fire, grave.*

Shamrock: People of Irish descent consider the shamrock a sign of good luck. At one time, shamrocks were exchanged when a couple became engaged. Nowadays, many people wear charms in the shape of a shamrock.

See *charms.*

Sheep: Sheep have always been considered lucky animals, as they are associated with the Good Shepherd. Sheep are believed to remember the Nativity each year at midnight on Christmas Eve, when they all face east and bow their heads.

It is considered a lucky sign to encounter a flock of sheep on the road, especially if you make your way through them to get past. This can be a useful thing to remember when driving on country roads in New Zealand. The origin of this belief dates back to when people lived in isolated communities. The sight of a shepherd and his flock meant that fresh meat would be available.

Even today, some shepherds are buried with a tuft of wool. This means they'll be excused attendance on Judgment Day, as no good shepherd would ever leave his flock.

See *Christmas Eve.*

Shell: Shells have been used as lucky charms for thousands of years. A sound like waves pounding on a beach can be heard when a shell is placed to the ear, and people thought this demonstrated a connection between people on land and those at sea. This made it a lucky charm that ensured sailors would return home safely.

See *charms, ear, sailors.*

Ships: Sailors are highly superstitious, and this extends to the vessels that they sail in. The superstitions begin when the ship is launched. Today, a bottle of champagne is broken over the bow. It is considered bad luck, however, if the bottle does not break on the first throw. In the past, human and animal blood sacrifices were made. The Vikings even crushed prisoners beneath the keels of their longships as they were launched. The Greeks and Romans used red wine instead. They also gave ships female names, so that the ships could ef-

fectively become brides to the sea gods, Neptune and Poseidon. Ships are still considered feminine today.

It is considered bad luck for a clergyman, or any man of the cloth,

to join a ship. This belief dates back to the story of Jonah, a prophet who took a ship that was heading west when he should have gone east to Nineveh. God created a storm to punish Jonah. The ship and the entire crew would have been wrecked if Jonah had not asked the sailors to toss him overboard. As soon as they did this, the storm ended.

Gradually, sailors came to connect Jonah with all members of the clergy. They reasoned that the devil would be keen to board a ship containing a clergyman, as he could easily be drowned once the ship was well away from shore. Once on board the ship, there was no knowing what other mischief the devil would get up to. Consequently, it was much better for everyone if clergymen stayed on shore.

Another superstition is that women are not welcome on board a ship, as they could cause jealousies to occur amongst the all-male crew. The origin of this is an ancient belief that the woman might be a witch who could cause enormous problems for the ship and crew.

Rabbits should not be taken on board either. Interestingly, eggs can be taken on board during the day, but it is bad luck to bring them on board after sunset.

Figureheads were used to provide the ship with good luck. Large eyes painted on each side of the bow provided protection from malicious spirits. A ship's cat was believed to provide good luck.

The name of a ship should never be changed. This always leads to a disaster of some sort.

You should never whistle on board a ship, unless you want wind. Most of the time, whistling creates storms.

It is considered unlucky to break up an old boat or ship. This is why, even today, you can find the wrecked hulks of old boats around the coastline, especially close to fishing villages.

See *cat, clergyman, coin, devil, eggs, eye, names, rabbit, rat, sailors, St. Elmo's fire, storm, whistle, wind, wine, witch, women.*

Shivering: An involuntary shiver is said to be a sign that someone is walking over the spot where you will ultimately be buried. Shivering when you first get out of bed is a sign that you'll experience bad luck all day long.

See *shudder.*

Shoelaces: It is good luck to find that your shoelaces have formed a knot. This means that good luck will remain with you throughout the day.

It is considered a sign that someone is talking about you if you find a shoelace undone. They are speaking badly of you if it is the left shoelace, but saying good things if it is the right shoelace.

You can make a silent wish for yourself while tying up someone else's shoelaces.

Both shoelaces need to be the same color. It is bad luck to wear shoelaces of different colors. This is particularly the case if you wear one brown and one black shoelace. Black is the color of death, and brown is the color of the earth in the graveyard.

See *death, graveyard, knot, tinnitus, wish.*

Shoes: Shoes are considered lucky. This is where the custom of tying an old boot to the back of the bridal car came from.

It is thought to be bad luck to put shoes on a table, or to leave them crossed on the floor. It is particularly dangerous to walk with only one shoe on, as this is likely to lead to the death of one of your parents. It's also bad luck if a shoelace becomes undone as you embark on an errand.

It's good luck to stand on the toes of a new pair of shoes. I remember doing this at school, and recently saw my granddaughter standing on a friend's new shoes to give her luck.

A good cure for nightmares is to place a pair of shoes at the entrance of your bedroom, with one shoe pointing into the room and the other out. This confuses the devil, who is responsible for bad dreams.

See *baby shoes, clover, cramp, cross, death, devil, lodestone, nightmare, shoelaces, table, theater, wedding dress.*

Shrove Tuesday: Shrove Tuesday is the day before Ash Wednesday, which is the first day of Lent. Shrove Tuesday is also known as Pancake Day because of the ancient tradition of tossing pancakes on this day. Every person needs to make and toss their own pancakes before eating them. The pancakes need to be eaten no matter what state they are in after the tossing, to ensure that the person will enjoy good luck in the future.

Shudder: A popular superstition that many people still believe in is that if they shudder for no apparent reason, someone is walking over the exact spot where their grave will ultimately be.

See *shivering.*

Sickle: A sickle is a short-handled tool with a semicircular blade. Farmers use it for

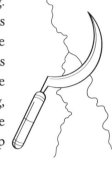

cutting and trimming. Like other implements made of iron, the sickle provides protection. As the sickle protects the house from lightning, it should be kept by the chimney with the tip pointing upwards.

See *chimney, iron, lightning.*

Silver: Silver is considered feminine and is associated with water and the moon. In western magic, a silver crescent symbolizes the moon. Because of these magical elements, silver cannot be enchanted, but it increases the power of any amulets, charms, or talismans made from it.

At one time it was believed that the only way to kill a vampire, werewolf, or witch was to shoot him or her with a silver bullet. This belief is still perpetuated in the movie industry.

Silver has always been considered lucky, and people tend to collect and hoard silver coins to ensure their future prosperity.

See *amulet, baby shoes, charms, cramp, moon, talisman, vampires, water, wedding anniversaries, werewolf, witch.*

Singing: Probably the most common superstition about singing is the belief that if you sing before breakfast, you will cry before the day is over. This superstition probably began with the thought that you might be tempting fate if you appeared overly happy early in the day. Happiness has to be earned. Consequently, you should do at least some work before starting to sing.

It is also considered unlucky to sing in bed, while playing cards, or while baking bread. If you sing at the dining table, you will receive a disappointment in business or love. However, it is lucky if you happen to unconsciously sing while having a bath. And it is extremely lucky for two people to unintentionally start singing the same song at the same moment.

See *bread*.

Six: There are six sides to a cube, making six the number of harmony and balance. The cube also depicts matter and the three dimensions.

The Star of David, the six-pointed star created by two overlapping triangles, is one of the most famous of all talismans. It also symbolizes both the Jewish religion and the nation of Israel. In the original Hebrew, the Star of David is called the Shield of David, as it shielded people from negative energies.

Six is also related to the six days of creation, and in 666 becomes the number of the Beast.

Six is considered an unlucky number for thieves and confidence men.

We all possess a "sixth sense," the term used to describe our intuition or our ability to know something without using the usual five senses.

See *numbers, talisman*.

Sky: Red sky at night is a sign of good weather on the following day. Red sky in the morning is a sign of bad weather later on in the day. A dark blue sky is a sign of impending wind. A clear blue sky indicates good weather.

A bright yellow sky at sunset is a sign of wind. A pale yellow sky at sunset indicates rain.

In the winter, it is a sign of frost if the night sky appears full of stars. But in the summer, a starry night sky is a sign of good weather on the following day.

See *clouds, July, rain, star, thunder, turquoise, weather, wedding, widdershins, wind*.

Sleep: Benjamin Franklin is credited with the saying "Early to bed and early to rise makes a man healthy, wealthy and wise." Henry Fielding, the English novelist, wrote, "An hour of sleep before midnight is worth two hours thereafter." As everyone is different, these sayings are true for some people but not for others. The biggest advantage of going to bed before midnight is that you will probably spend more hours asleep.

A common superstition is that you should always sleep with your head pointing north. Apparently, this aligns your body with the earth's magnetic waves, allowing you to enjoy a more peaceful and restful sleep.

Even the wedding night has a superstition concerning sleep. The first person to fall asleep that night will also be the first one to die.

Until recently, plants were removed from hospital rooms at night, as people believed that the plants would absorb all the oxygen in the room.

Superstitious people believe that the soul can leave the body during sleep, making this state a potentially dangerous one. This is why a sleepwalker should never be woken up suddenly, in case the soul has temporarily left the body and hasn't had time to return. An ancient poem il-

lustrates the mixed feelings people have about sleep:

> Now I lay me down to sleep,
> I pray the Lord my soul to keep;
>   If I should die before I wake,
>   I pray the Lord my soul will take.

See *plants, right side, wedding.*

Sleepwalking: An old superstition says that it's dangerous to wake someone who is sleepwalking. This is due to a belief that the soul leaves the body during sleep (which explains dreams in which a person travels freely around the world). If you wake a sleepwalker, it is feared, the soul will be absent and the person will die.

See *dreams.*

Smoking: There is little need nowadays to use superstition to discourage smoking, as reports on the effects of smoking provide discouragement on a regular basis. Children used to be told that smoking stunts growth, and many people still believe this to be true.

Snail: There are two main superstitions concerning snails. The first is the belief that it is bad luck for a snail to enter your home. 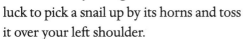 The second says it is good luck to pick a snail up by its horns and toss it over your left shoulder.

Snake: People have considered the snake a symbol of evil for so long that no one knows where or when it began. A snake was the villain in the Garden of Eden. Snakes are also believed to possess supernatural powers. People erroneously believe snakes hypnotize their prey, spit venom using their forked tongues, and never die before sunset. Snakes are not charmed by music, either. Snake charmers create the swaying motion in snakes by the movements of their hands and heads.

It is considered bad luck for a snake to cross in front of you. It is also bad luck to dream of snakes.

There is no truth in the belief that snakes travel in pairs.

See *familiar, jasper, lizard, serpent, unicorn, wedding.*

Snapping Fingers: Snapping your fingers is believed to cause good luck. This derives from the old belief that making a noise will frighten away evil forces. Snapping your fingers while whistling is a good idea, as it frightens  away any evil forces who might be attracted by the whistling.

See *finger, whistle.*

Sneezing: Numerous cultures believed that the soul could escape from the body during a sneeze. Blessing people after they sneezed would protect them until the soul returned. Saying "God bless you" or "Gesundheit" ("good health") to someone when they sneeze can also stop him or her from sneezing again. It also brings good luck to you. It is bad luck not to say these words.

A myth that goes back to Roman times is the belief that if a woman sneezes at the moment of orgasm, she will not become pregnant. Leaping backwards seven times while sneezing was also believed to work.

Sneezing once or three times is believed to be bad luck, but sneezing twice provides good luck. However, young children have a better superstition: "Once a wish, twice a kiss, three times something better."

It is said to be a good sign for a sick person to sneeze, as this indicates that he or she will recover.

The first sneeze of a baby is highly important. People used to believe that idiots couldn't sneeze. Consequently, a baby's first sneeze brought great relief to the parents. In Scotland, it was believed that babies were enchanted by a fairy spell, which was broken by the first sneeze.

In seventeenth century Europe, it was considered good manners to take off your hat while sneezing. In 1627, Joseph Hall, the Bishop of Exeter, wrote that a man could not be considered a friend if he failed to remove his hat when he sneezed.[54]

An old rhyme about sneezing says,

> If you sneeze on a Monday,
> you sneeze for danger;
> Sneeze on a Tuesday, kiss a stranger;
> Sneeze on a Wednesday, sneeze for a letter;
> Sneeze on a Thursday, something better;
> Sneeze on a Friday, sneeze for sorrow;
> Sneeze on a Saturday,
> see your sweetheart tomorrow;
> Sneeze on a Sunday, and the devil will
> have domination over you all the week!

It is good luck to sneeze between noon and midnight, but there is no benefit gained from sneezing between midnight and noon.

It is bad luck to sneeze while getting dressed in the morning. This is a sign that bad luck will follow you throughout the day.

It is good luck for the entire household if the family cat sneezes. It is also good luck if two people sneeze at the same time.

While working on this book, a friend told me a superstition that I had not come across before. He believed it was bad luck to turn your head to the left while sneezing, but good luck to turn to the right.

See *baby, cat, fairy, Friday the 13th, letters, hat.*

Snow: When snow sits and doesn't melt, it's a sign of more snow yet to come.
See *weather.*

Soap: In Scotland, it is believed to be unlucky if the soap slips out of your hands while you are washing them. It is also considered unlucky to give soap as a gift, as this might "wash the friendship away."

Socks: It is good luck to accidentally put on a sock inside out. It is also fortunate to inadvertently put on odd socks. However, in both cases you need to wear them as they are for the rest of the day to preserve the luck.

It is bad luck to toss out old socks without washing them first. This is because unwashed socks are impregnated with your personal energy, and you do not want this to disap-pear. Even worse, someone who doesn't like you could use your old socks to create a spell that might harm you.

See *spell*.

Soot: Soot falling down the chimney is a sign of money coming. It's also telling you that it's time to have your chimney cleaned.

See *chimney, money*.

Sorrow: It is extremely bad luck to pretend you are grief-stricken or to cry when you don't mean it. If you pretend to cry, you can guarantee that genuine sorrow will not be far away.

Spade: It is bad luck if the handle of your spade breaks while you are working in the garden. This is a sign that your hard work will produce next to nothing, and your crops will be disappointing. You can avert this possibility by burying the broken spade in the garden for twenty-four hours before throwing it out.

It is also considered bad luck if a spade you have just stuck in the ground falls over. This means that this year's crops will not be as good as the previous year's.

Spades need to be kept in a barn, garage, or shed. They should not be carried indoors, as this is an omen that a spade will shortly be required to dig a grave for someone living in the house.

It is bad luck to try to attract someone's attention by waving a spade at the person. This could mean that the person will die. If someone waves a spade at you, immedi-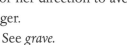ately toss a handful of earth in his or her direction to avert the danger.

See *grave*.

Sparrow: The humble sparrow has suffered over the years from the legend that he betrayed Christ in the Garden of Gethsemane. Later, at the cross, a sparrow called out, "He lives, he lives," telling the soldiers that Jesus had not died. God punished the sparrow by tying an invisible thread around its feet, which is why the sparrow hops rather than walks.

See *cross, St. Valentine's Day, swallow*.

Spell: A spell is a ritual or procedure performed to create a specific change in a situation. Anyone can perform a spell,

but spells are traditionally associated with witches and wizards. Incantations or specific words (sometimes nonsense words) and rhymes are usually chanted to create the spell. Special ingredients are sometimes used, and powerful spirits are sometimes called upon to help perform the necessary magic.

Spells can be either good or evil. A good spell might be to help someone's health improve, while an evil spell might be to coerce someone into a specific course of action.

See *ankh, bread, charmers, elemental, Macbeth, magic, moon, moonstone, socks, tinnitus, urine, water, widdershins, witch.*

Spider: Seeing a spider is usually a lucky sign. In England it indicates money. Consequently, if a spider is found in an inappropriate place, such as on a table or running over your clothing, it is picked up and taken to a more appropriate place. If the spider dies during this process, all the money will be lost. Conversely, money will be gained if the spider survives. The tradition of associating spiders with money dates from Roman times, when people

wore spider amulets to attract success in business. Small spiders are frequently called "mon-

ey spiders," and it's considered extremely bad luck to kill one.

Spiders have always been welcome in people's homes, as they catch flies in their webs, which helps to prevent disease. An old rhyme says, "If you want to live and thrive, let the spider run alive."

Spiders also provide protection, and there are many legends to support this. One from the Christian tradition says that Jesus, Joseph, and Mary were hiding from Herod's soldiers in a cave. A spider spun a web at the entrance and the soldiers did not bother to search inside, as they assumed no one had entered it for some time. Similar stories are told about King David, Mohammed, and Frederick the Great.

See *amulet, fly, letters, money, weather, wedding.*

Spider Web: Spider webs are an omen of future prosperity. Unless it is strictly necessary, it is better to leave them where they are. Removing spider webs also removes potential wealth.

Spitting: Ancient people considered saliva a product of their soul. Therefore, spitting was, in effect, an offering to the gods, who would reciprocate by protecting you. Saliva was considered a potent charm against witchcraft and the devil. The Greek poet Theocritus (c.310–250 BCE) wrote, "Thrice on my breast I spit to guard me safe from fascinating charms."

Jesus used saliva in some of his miraculous cures (Mark 7:32–37, Mark 8:22–26, John 9:1–7).

Some people still spit on the first money they receive each day from a business transaction. This is thought to attract good luck, and ensure that more money will come in. Fishermen spit on their nets and bait for good luck. Spitting in a hole before planting a plant in it also brings good luck. Spitting on a ball before starting a game with it increases your luck. People sometimes spit when passing a place they believe to be dangerous. They might also spit for luck when seeing a white horse or someone who is lame.

See *charms, devil, fingernail, fishermen, horse, ladder, money, plants, urine, warts, witchcraft.*

Spoon: Only a few hundred years ago, spoons and knives were considered precious personal possessions. Knives were considered masculine and spoons feminine.

It is an indication of a pleasant surprise if you drop a spoon and it lands with the bowl facing upwards. If it lands face downwards, you will shortly be disappointed.

It is a sign of a wedding if two spoons are unintentionally placed in a cup.

See *cutlery, knife, spooning, wedding.*

Spooning: Simple people were at one time called "spoons" because they were seen as shallow, like a spoon. Gradually, the name came to mean anyone who engaged in light-hearted, amorous play. People who did this were described as "spoony." Kissing, cuddling, and affection between a young, unmarried couple came to be called "spooning."

In Wales, it became a custom for a young man to present a hand-carved wooden spoon to his fiancée. The couples' initials would be carved on this spoon to symbolize their engagement.

See *engagement, spoon.*

Spring Cleaning: Spring cleaning should be completed by the end of May. It is unlucky to spring clean the house after that.

Squirrel: Many people consider squirrels to be pests, but apparently it is good luck if one crosses your path heading from left to right. Of course, it is bad luck if it travels from right to left. The bad luck can be

averted by staying in the same area until another squirrel crosses your path, heading from left to right. Alternatively, you can snap your fingers and say "bread and butter."

See *bread and butter, December.*

Stairs: An ancient belief says that it's bad luck to pass someone going in the opposite direction while using a staircase. The remedy is to cross your fingers to avert the bad luck.

The origin of this superstition goes back to Jacob's dream of a ladder going from earth to heaven (Genesis 28:12–16). Angels went up and down this ladder to perform their tasks. It was considered sacrilegious to inadvertently obstruct an angel performing the Lord's work.

Tripping while on a staircase can cause either good or bad luck, depending on which way you are going. It is a lucky sign if you trip while going upwards, but bad luck if you are heading down.

It is also considered bad luck to change your mind and turn back when you are halfway up or down a staircase. To avert

this, you need to continue the flight to the top or bottom, and then turn around. An alternative method is to pause for a few moments, and then whistle as you retrace your steps.

See *whistle.*

Star: The ancients believed it was unlucky to point at a star. This was because they thought that stars were supernatural beings looking down on the world.

Many people believe that they have a special star that guides and protects them. Napoleon said, "(My guiding star) never deserted me. I see it on every great occurrence, urging me forward. It is my unfailing omen of success!"[55]

Of course, if you have a guiding star, you also have an evil star. When your star is on the ascendant, your luck improves, but life becomes a struggle when your star is on the descendant.

A good cure for poverty is to wait for a shooting star, and then say the word "money" three times as it is falling. Money should come your way after performing this.

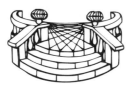

Another common superstition about shooting stars is that each one indicates a soul going to heaven.

A charming superstition about stars concerns making a wish when you see the first star after dark. This tradition is recorded in the popular nineteenth century American nursery rhyme:

> Star light, star bright,
> First star I see tonight,
> I wish I may, I wish I might
> Have the wish I wish tonight.

See *marriage, money, sailors, sky.*

Stork: Every year, storks come back and build a new nest on the same site as the previous year. As storks can live up to seventy years, they return to the same site many times. Storks bring good luck to whoever owns the property the nest is built on. This belief goes back to Roman times. The stork was sacred to the goddess Venus, and when storks built a nest on the roof of your home, you received a blessing of love from Venus. When a stork flies over a home, it is a sign of an imminent birth.

From this belief came the custom of telling small children that storks brought babies to their new homes. People still sometimes say "the stork came" to indicate a new addition to the family.

See *birds, birth.*

Storm: Storms have always provoked fear, and were at one time thought to be the anger of the gods. An Austrian superstition says that tossing a handful of meal out a window, while telling the gods to cease, is enough to quiet the gods.

Particularly violent storms, or unseasonable storms, were believed to presage some important worldly event, such as the death of a sovereign or an important leader. If a storm occurred while criminal trials were being conducted, it was considered a sign that more criminals than usual would receive the death penalty.

Sailors do not like to cut their fingernails or hair while at sea, as this is believed to encourage storms. Whistling also apparently creates storms.

A Scottish superstition says that if a storm breaks out while a coffin is being lowered into the grave, the deceased has sold his soul to the devil.

See *bell, candle, coffin, death, devil, drowning, fingernail, grave, hair, rainbow, sailors, ships, swan, whistle, wind, window, wine, witch.*

Stumbling: Stumbling has always been considered a bad omen. It is an indication of bad luck, and a sign of misfortune or disaster ahead. It is thought that, in a sense, the fates cause the person to stumble as a final warning. Stumbling in the morning is a sign that bad luck will occur during the day. Stumbling near a grave is particularly bad, as it indicates that the person will shortly be in a grave also. William Shakespeare alluded to this when he had Friar Lawrence say in *Romeo and Juliet,*

> How oft tonight
> Have my old feet stumbled at graves.
> (Act 5, scene 3)

Stumbling while climbing upstairs is lucky, but it is unlucky if you are going downstairs.

See *grave, marriage, omen.*

Sugar: It is considered bad luck to spill sugar. Sugar used to be an expensive commodity, and because of this, spilling it affects your financial situation. The remedy

is to clean up the mess right away, and knock three times on wood.

See *knock on wood.*

Suicide: It was believed that the soul of anyone who committed suicide was condemned to roam the earth forever, unable to progress to the next world. Various methods were used to prevent the spirits of these people from returning to haunt the area in which they had lived while alive. Burying the bodies at a crossroads, rather than in consecrated ground, was thought to confuse the spirits. Sometimes a stake was used to pin the corpse to the ground.

It was said that if a pregnant woman walked over the grave of someone who had committed suicide, she would miscarry.

See *corpse, crossroads, death, diamond, ghosts, grave.*

Sun: Early humans were in awe of the sun and considered it a god. They followed its movements with great interest and performed rituals to encourage it, especially during winter when they felt that the sun was losing power. Bonfire festivals are the surviving relics of these rituals.

Because the sun rises in the east, this direction became associated with resurrection. It was considered lucky to be born at sunrise, and unlucky to be born at sunset. It was even considered lucky to stir pots from east to west, in a clockwise direction.

It has always been considered bad luck to point at the sun.

See *circle, eagle, Easter, fox, July, ladybug, Midsummer's Eve, pregnancy, rain, right side, sailors, sex, sunstroke, umbrella, virginity, Wednesday, widdershins.*

Sunstroke: People used to believe that white-skinned people were more likely to be affected by the sun than darker-skinned people. In actuality, there is no difference whatsoever. All people can suffer from sunstroke.

See *sun.*

Swallow: The arrival of swallows in spring and their departure in fall has been an endless source of fascination. The appearance of swallows told people that summer wasn't far away. Seeing a swallow in the air was a sign of good luck. The ancient Greeks thought that swallows did not fly away at all, but buried themselves at the bottom of ponds so that they could hibernate with the frogs and turtles. This belief may have come from the fact that barn swallows build their nests with mud.

Swallows arrive each year at the Mission San Juan Capistrano near San Diego, California. They usually arrive on March 19 (St. Joseph's Day) and leave again on October 23 (San Juan's Day).

It is said to be good luck if swallows build a nest on your house. This protects your house and everyone living in it. The best place for the nest is in the eaves. However, it is bad luck if a swallow builds a nest on a house, but then leaves it unexpectedly. This means the house will be destroyed by fire.

An old Christian legend says that a swallow called out "dead! dead!" at the Crucifixion of Jesus to prevent the Roman soldiers from hurting Jesus even more. Because of this, it is bad luck to hurt a swallow or damage its nest.

Swallows were believed to carry special magical stones in their bodies. One is red, and is thought to cure insanity. The other is black, and provides good luck. If you place either, or both, under your tongue  you will be able to sway people with your eloquence.

Swallows are said to cure problems with the eyes. If you have such problems, you need to wait until you hear a swallow sing in spring, and then wash your eyes in running water while silently saying a prayer. The swallow will fly away, taking your eye problems with it.

See *birds, eye, fire, sparrow, tongue, weather.*

Swan: It is unlucky to kill a swan, even unintentionally. Anyone who kills a swan is expected to die within a year. Swans are normally found in pairs. Consequently, a single swan is a sign of an imminent death.

Swans are believed to be able to hatch their eggs only during a thunderstorm. Also, if they appear to be sleeping during the daytime, it is a sign of a storm brewing. If swans fly into the wind, it is a sign of a violent storm in the next twenty-four hours.

Apollo, the Greek god of music, was said to have given his soul to a swan. Because of this, swans were believed to sing as they thought about the wonderful things Apollo had arranged for them when they died. This is why a creative person's final work is said to be his or her "swan song."

See *eggs, storm.*

Sweater: It is good luck to accidentally put a sweater on back to front. If you put your arms into the sleeves of a sweater before pulling it over your head, you will never die of drowning.

It has always been considered bad luck to use dark thread to mend a light-colored sweater.

See *drowning.*

Swimming: Many sailors have never learned how to swim. This may seem strange, but comes from the belief that the sea will claim whomever it wants. Therefore, superstitious sailors often develop an attitude of "why flounder around in agony any longer than necessary?" They also believe that if one person is rescued, the sea will quickly find another victim.

See *sailors.*

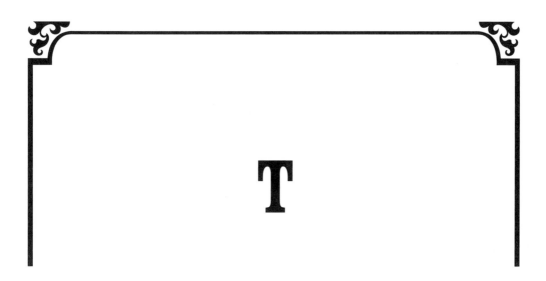

T

Table: Young women should never sit on a table or at the corner of a table, as this means that they'll never marry. It is considered bad luck for children to crawl under a table. If they do, the remedy is for them to crawl under the table again, in the opposite direction. It is also unlucky to change your position at the table once a seat has been assigned to you. People who lie down on a table, it is said, will die within a year.

If someone accidentally upsets his chair when rising from a table after a meal, it is a sign that he has lied during the conversation.

It is extremely unlucky to place a pair of shoes on the table. This can presage a death in the family.

See *chair, children, shoes, thirteen.*

Taboo: Something that is forbidden or prohibited is described as being "taboo." Sigmund Freud wrote a book called *Totem and Taboo*, and described taboo as "the oldest human unwritten code of law ... taboo is older than gods and dates back to a period before any kind of religion existed."[56] Consequently, many unfortunate people became outcasts because of taboo. Superstitious people were afraid of others who were deformed, such as hunchbacks, or of people who were believed to be witches or possess the evil eye. Some taboos were temporary. Menstruation and childbirth are good examples of this. Lesser-known temporary taboos included the many superstitions that were practiced on the days fishing vessels went out to sea, and activities such as wassailing, which were performed at certain times of the year.

See *evil eye, fishing, hunchback, menstruation, pig, sex, wassailing, witch.*

Talisman: Talismans are objects that provide special benefits, such as power, protection, or energy, to their owners. They can be made from almost any material, and are frequently inscribed with words or pictures. They are frequently made at cosmically significant times, in order to harness the power and energy of the universe. Amulets are made to provide protection, but talismans are usually intended to attract a particular benefit to the person who made or owns it.

See *amulet, jet, ring, six.*

Tattoo: Tattoos have become fashionable nowadays, but until recently sailors were the only group of people in the West who traditionally wore tattoos. This was based on the superstition that tattoos protected the wearer from bad luck and evil influences. Consequently, many of the tattoos worn by sailors were good luck symbols, such as hearts, flowers, and crosses. The tattoo, in effect, became a permanent protective amulet. Interestingly, in the days when flogging was common, many sailors had Jesus Christ on the cross tattooed on their backs in the hope that this would make the person wielding the lash use it more gently.

The word "tattoo" came into the English language in the eighteenth century. When Captain James Cook discovered the Hawaiian Islands, he found that the natives carved their bodies and called it *tatou.*

See *amulet, cross, flowers, heart, sailors.*

Taurus: Taurus is the second sign of the zodiac. Its symbol is the bull. Its element is earth, and its gemstone is emerald. The keyword for Taurus is: I have.

Taureans are practical, patient, and determined. As they are naturally cautious, they think before acting. Consequently, they are often accused of being stubborn or obstinate. Taureans love comfort, luxury, and beauty. They insist on the best of everything. They are generous, but like to keep a "nest egg" back just in case it is needed. They are loyal and devoted to their friends.

See *astrology, earth, elements, emerald, gemstones, zodiac.*

Tea: If you stir the tea in your teapot, make sure to stir it clockwise. If you stir it counterclockwise, you will inadvertently stir up a quarrel. You should never stir tea for someone else, as you risk falling out with him or her.

If a woman puts milk into her cup before the sugar, it is thought that she will never marry. If a woman allows a man to pour her more than one cup of tea on the same occasion, she will become attracted to him. If two women pour tea from the same teapot, one of them will become pregnant within a few months. If you allow the lid of a teapot to remain open, you will shortly receive visitors.

See *baldness, fly, milk.*

Tea Leaves: If tea leaves float on the surface of a cup of tea, you will shortly receive visitors.

Tasseography is the art of tea-leaf reading. It began in China, and was introduced to Europe by traveling gypsies. Loose tea is used for tea-leaf reading. The cup of tea is drunk, leaving about a dessertspoon of liquid behind to enable the leaves to be swirled around in the cup. The cup is held in the left hand, swirled three times in a clockwise direction, and then quickly placed upside down on the saucer. The cup is left facedown for several seconds and then turned over. The arrangement and pattern of the tea leaves in the cup is then interpreted. Sometimes the images are clear and easily recognized, but more often the psychic has to use his or her clairvoyant powers to discern the meanings of the leaves.

See *tea.*

Teeth: Amulets made from the tooth of a predatory animal are considered powerful, as the people who wear them hope to gain some of the strength and power of the animal. A tiger's tooth amulet, for instance, would be considered extremely powerful. In some parts of the world, tiger's claw and tooth amulets are

considered helpful for gamblers. In China, the tiger is considered "the gambler's god."

The most common superstition concerning human teeth is that of the tooth fairy, who brings a coin to a child who has just lost a baby tooth. Usually, the tooth is placed under the pillow, but sometimes it is placed in a container beside the bed.

Another superstition says that it's bad luck for a baby to be born with any visible teeth. It's also an indication that the child will become a murderer.

It's good luck to have gaps between the front teeth. This is supposed to ensure luck, prosperity and a great deal of travel.

It is considered an indication of an upcoming death in the family if you dream of teeth.

See *amulet, coin, comb, death, dreams, fairy, gambling, luck, rat, toothache.*

Theater: There are countless theatrical superstitions. Actors and actresses are highly superstitious people, and it has been suggested that if there were no superstitions about a particular venue, they would invent some.

It is bad luck to whistle in a dressing room, to open an umbrella on stage, to see

a cat walking across the stage during rehearsal, or to repeat the last line of a play at rehearsal.

However, wigs and squeaky shoes are considered good omens. To fall over on stage is also a sign of good luck, as it means that the production will enjoy a long run.

See *actors and actresses, cat, shoes, umbrella, whistle.*

Thief: Thieves are just as superstitious as anyone else, and many of them believe that they will not be caught if they carry a toad's heart with them when committing their crimes. Thieves can also escape detection by carrying a lump of coal in a trouser pocket. Thieves believe that if they successfully steal something on Christmas Day, they can continue stealing for the next twelve months with no risk of being caught.

It is extremely unlucky for anyone to steal from a church.

See *cards, playing; Christmas; church; coal; heart; pregnancy.*

Thimble: Thimbles are often given "for luck." However, it is bad luck to be given three of them, as this means that the recipient will become an old maid and never marry.

It is good luck for the owner of a garment if a seamstress loses a thimble while working on it. However, this doesn't apply if the seamstress is working on her own garment.

See *sewing, three.*

Third Time Lucky: See *three.*

Thirteen: The superstition of unlucky thirteen has existed ever since people learned to count. Ten fingers and two feet totalled twelve, which left the next number feared, unknown, and unpredictable. Fear of the number thirteen is known as triskaidekaphobia. Because of this fear, many buildings have no thirteenth floor, most airlines have no row thirteen, and many streets contain no house with this number.

There is a story in Norse mythology that refers to the fear of number thirteen. Twelve gods were invited to a banquet in Valhalla. Unfortunately, Loki, the spirit of evil, heard about the event and crashed the party. As a result of this, Balder, the favorite of the gods, was killed. This was attributed to thirteen people attending the banquet.

Witches' covens traditionally have thirteen members.

Thirteen people were present at the Last Supper, and most people try to avoid having this number of people seated around a table. In France, it is possible to hire an extra person if you discover that your dinner party totals thirteen. An old legend says that the first person to get up from a table containing thirteen people will die within the year. The remedy for this is to have everyone stand at the same time. Charles Mackay, author of *Extraordinary Popular Delusions and the Madness of Crowds* (1841), wrote, "If thirteen persons sit at a table, one of them will die within the year; and all of them will be unhappy. Of all evil omens this is the worst."[57]

Charles Dickens, in *A Christmas Story* (1850), alluded to the superstition that a death would occur in the family when the clock struck thirteen. However, a clock striking thirteen has been lucky for at least one person. A soldier named James Hatfield was facing court-martial for sleeping on his watch. However, he was able to prove that he was awake by saying that the clock on St. Paul's Cathedral had struck thirteen instead of twelve. As a number of other people had noticed this aberration, the young soldier was released.

The thirteenth day of the month is believed to be unlucky, but there is one day that is even unluckier. Friday the 13th combines two superstitions, creating a day that many people still dread. Business drops off, and many important events, such as weddings and house purchases, are delayed if the date chosen happens to be Friday the 13th. Children born on Friday the 13th are expected to be unlucky throughout life. (However, another superstition claims that it's lucky to be born on Friday the 13th.) Also, you mustn't cut your hair on Friday the 13th. If you do, someone in your family will die. If you wear black on Friday the 13th, you will soon be wearing it again, at a funeral.

Gamblers, amongst the most superstitious people of all, consider thirteen a lucky number. Lucky Thirteen is a popular number for gamblers to play, and is even more popular on Friday the 13th. However, it's still hard to find a hotel in Las Vegas with a thirteenth floor.

Richard Wagner (1813–1883), the famous German composer, liked the number thirteen. His full name was Wilhelm Richard Wagner, but the world knew him as Richard Wagner, a name comprising thirteen letters. He was born in 1813 and composed thirteen operas, including *Tannhäuser*, which was completed on March 13.

Woodrow Wilson (1856–1924), the twenty-eighth president of the United States, is another example of someone who liked the number thirteen. He regularly announced important decisions on the thirteenth day of the month. As a young adult he stopped using his first name, Thomas, and for the rest of his life was known as Woodrow Wilson, a name consisting of thirteen letters.

About 120 years ago, a group of British journalists formed the London Thirteen Club. Their aim was to disprove the idea that thirteen was an unlucky number. They met on the thirteenth of the month, sat thirteen at a table, and deliberately broke as many superstitions as possible. None of them came to any harm as a result, but their activities appear to have done nothing to quell the fear that many people have about thirteen.

There is a positive side to number thirteen. A baker's dozen consists of thirteen items. There are approximately thirteen weeks in each season of the year, and thirteen stripes in the United States flag (symbolizing the thirteen original colonies).

The Great Seal of the United States can be seen on the back of a one-dollar bill. The seal contains several thirteens in it. The eagle's shield contains thirteen stripes. The eagle's left talon holds thirteen arrows, and the right talon holds an olive branch of thirteen leaves and thirteen berries. There is a circle above the eagle's head containing a constellation of thirteen stars. The Latin motto in the eagle's beak reads *E Pluribus Unum*, and this comprises thirteen letters.

The reverse side of the Great Seal is also shown on the reverse of the dollar bill. It depicts a pyramid built from thirteen layers of stone. The Latin phrase above the pyramid reads *Annuit Coeptis*, again containing thirteen letters. The repetition of the number thirteen in the seal relates to the thirteen original colonies, and symbolizes renewal, regeneration, and a new world.

See *actors and actresses, black, business, cat, clock, death, Friday the 13th, gambling, hair, phobias, primroses, table, wedding, wedding anniversaries.*

Thread: It is considered lucky to find a loose piece of thread on your clothing. If you want to know the name of your future lover, you should drop a length of thread onto the floor and see what initial it forms.

Thread can be tied around a finger of the left hand to ensure that you remember something.

You can stop a bleeding nose by tying a piece of thread around your little finger.

You can also eliminate warts by tying a thread three times around a finger before dropping the thread to the ground. The warts will be magically transferred to whoever picks the thread up.

See *finger, hand, nose, red, warts.*

Three: Three has always been considered a mystical number. This is because the miracle of birth turned a couple (two) into three. The Greek Philosopher Pythago-  ras (fl. sixth century BCE) considered three to be the perfect number. Consequently, three meant life and the continuation of the species. This was demonstrated in pagan Europe whenever a chieftain died. All the fires of the tribe were extinguished, except for the chieftain's fire. As the tribe looked on, the shaman relit all the fires, three at a time, from the chieftain's fire.

In the time of King Vladimir I (956–1015 CE), the first Christian ruler of the Russians, three candles were lit from one taper at funerals to light and guide the deceased into the next world.

Russian soldiers brought this superstition to the Crimean War as the belief that if three cigarettes were lit from a single match, one of the three soldiers would be killed. This belief became firmly established in the Boer War, and has appeared in

every war since. There is a definite logic to this superstition. Keeping a match alight long enough to light three cigarettes gives snipers plenty of time to aim and fire.

Despite this, three is considered a lucky number. Three is the number of the Trinity. We give people "three cheers." Indian philosophy discusses the three worlds of heaven, sky, and earth. In ancient Greece, the medium at Delphi, known as the Pythia, stood on a three-legged stool.

The superstition that "things happen in threes" still continues. If people attend two weddings (or funerals) in quick succession, they usually expect a third one to occur in the near future.

The lucky nature of three is exemplified in the expression "third time lucky." People tend to believe that something will succeed after two attempts have ended in failure. This might also explain why three demands are often made to get a bill paid.

Although three is considered lucky, bad things are also believed to occur in threes. If a famous person dies, people immediately expect two more to occur within a short period of time. If two plates are broken in a house, the owners will often deliberately break a third item, as they believe breakages occur in threes. A drowning person is believed to surface three times before drowning. Wiccans perform white (good) magic, rather than black (evil) magic, because they believe everything they send out will be returned threefold.

See *candle, fire, plate, washing, Wicca.*

Thumb: The thumb is a sign of independence. Small babies reveal their dependence by holding their thumbs inside their fists. You can hold your thumbs this way to ward off ghosts and witches. This also cures hiccups.

An itching thumb is a sign that visitors will shortly arrive. These visitors are not necessarily welcome guests.

A superstition dating from Roman times says it's unlucky to accidentally prick your thumb with a pin or needle. William Shakespeare referred to this in *Macbeth* when the second witch says,

> By the pricking of my thumbs,
> Something wicked this way comes.
> (Act 4, scene 1)

The well known thumbs-up gesture dates back to Roman times. When a gladiator fell, the audience decided if he would live (by holding their thumbs up) or die (by holding their thumbs down). Today, the thumbs-up gesture is a sign of approval or a way to congratulate some-one. Thumbs down indicates disapproval or failure.

In palmistry, long thumbs indicate drive and energy. Thumbs that are rigid and do not bend backward easily reveal a stubborn person. Alternately, someone who has thumbs that bend back easily is assumed to be easily pushed into making a decision.

See *ghost, hiccups, needle, palmistry, pin, white, witch.*

Thunder: The sound of thunder struck fear into the hearts of primitive people, as they thought that it represented the displeasure of the gods.

The sound of thunder is interpreted in different ways depending on the day of the week. Thunder on Monday is said to predict a woman's death. On Tuesday, it is an indication that the next harvest will be a good one. On Wednesday, it shows that a person of low repute will die. On Thursday, it is an indication of a good, abundant harvest. On Friday, it indicates an upcoming battle. On Saturday, it predicts a major health scare, such as an epidemic. On Sunday, it shows that an intellectual or authority of some repute will die.

Ringing church bells is reputed to be a good method of eliminating thunder and lightning.

It is a good omen to hear thunder in the distance as you are leaving on a trip.

It is extremely lucky to hear thunder when the sky is cloudless.

See *bell, days of the week, lightning, milk, November, oak, rainbow, September, sky, weather.*

Thunderstorm: A superstition from the Deep South says that you will never be struck by lightning if you own a feather bed.

See *lightning, feather.*

Tiger's Eye: The tiger's eye is sometimes called the "stone of independence," as it makes its wearers self-reliant and confident. However, this is not always considered a good thing, as tiger's eye also gives a desire for independence, which can lead to relationship break-ups.

In many parts of the world, the tiger's eye is considered an effective amulet against the evil eye.

See *amulet, evil eye, gemstones.*

Tinnitus: Tinnitus is a constant ringing sound in the ears. If you feel that you are suffering from tinnitus because someone has placed a spell on you, you can stop it by calling out the names of everyone you know. When you recite the name of the person who placed the spell on you, the tinnitus will stop. You can then get even if you wish. However, a preferable solution is to untie your shoelaces, and then retie them again.
See *shoelaces, spell.*

Toast: The word "toast" dates back to Elizabethan times, when a small piece of toasted bread was placed into a tankard before the ale or wine was put in. The toast absorbed any sediment, and people felt it improved the taste.

It is considered lucky to accidentally spill a small amount of liquid while making a toast. It is bad luck for a glass to break while making a toast. This means that one of the people present will shortly die.

The sound produced by clinking glasses together is thought to ward off any evil forces that might not approve of the toast. Not everyone is entirely in favor of toasts. In his *Letters to his Son,* Lord Chesterfield (1694–1773) commented on the custom of drinking to someone's health:

> As for instance, the very absurd though almost universal custom of drinking people's health. Can there be anything in the world less relative to any other man's health than my drinking a glass of wine? Common sense, certainly, never pointed it out, but yet common sense tells me I must conform to it.[58]

See *bread, glass, pearl, wassailing, wine.*

Toes: Everybody has stubbed his or her toes at one time or another. However, few people nowadays know that it is good luck to stub the toes of your right foot, but bad luck to stub the toes on your left foot.
See *foot.*

Tomato: An old tradition says that it was a tomato, rather than an apple, that Eve offered to Adam in the Garden of Eden. This might explain why the tomato is sometimes called *pomme d'amour,* or "love apple."

The tomato used to be considered an aphrodisiac, and young women were scared to eat it, at least until they were engaged to be married.

A single woman in search of a husband can speed up the process by wearing a sachet of dried tomato seeds around her neck.

A large red tomato can be placed in a window to ward off any evil spirits. Alternatively, it can be placed on a mantelpiece to attract money into the home. I've been told that the plastic tomatoes that are used to hold tomato sauce work just as well as the real thing. Tomato sauce is also believed to provide good health and prosperity.

Pincushions in the shape of a tomato are believed to attract good luck.

See *aphrodisiac, apple, Good Friday, money.*

Tommy Knocker: Tommy Knockers are the spirits of dead miners. People who have seen them say that they are less than a foot tall. They help living miners by providing advance warning of a disaster by knocking on the walls of the mines. They also help miners find new veins of coal.

Unfortunately, Tommy Knockers are not always kind, and can be spiteful if they feel they are not appreciated. They have been blamed for many cave-ins, and the survivors swear they've heard them laugh when it occurred. Consequently, many miners leave them part of their lunch to keep them happy. Some also make clay figurines of Tommy Knockers to provide them with company.

See *miners.*

Tongue: If you happen to bite your tongue while talking, it is a sign that you are about to lie. You can get rid of warts by licking them with your tongue when you first wake up in the morning. If a blister, ulcer, or spots occur on a tongue, it shows that the person has been lying.

Men who carry a piece of a cat's tongue with them apparently never have to be concerned about wives who talk too much. Carrying the tip of a calf's tongue will bring good luck. Carrying it inside a wallet or purse ensures that the person will never run out of money. The tongue of a toad is extremely useful, as it makes the person sexually attractive to others.

See *cat, ears, handkerchief, money, swallow, warts.*

Toothache: Toothache was a constant problem in the days when few people knew anything about dental care and dentists were hard to find. There were no pain-killing drugs then, either, which meant that people sought help only as a last resort. Consequently, a large number of superstitious cures developed, each promising relief from pain.

One method of avoiding toothache was to carry a few teeth from a horse with you at all times. An alternative was to extract a tooth from a corpse and carry it in a small bag around your neck.

It was possible to transfer the pain on to something else. Consequently, sufferers from toothache could rub their gums with a nail and then hammer the nail into an oak tree.

Another cure for toothache was to crush ladybugs to make a juice that was rubbed on the gums. A more dangerous, and sometimes fatal, method was to inhale the fumes created by burning henbane. Henbane is a poisonous plant, and is also believed to attract evil spirits. Consequently, the toothache needed to be extremely bad for anyone to attempt this particular method.

You can extract a tooth without needing to visit the dentist by making a powder out of dried worms (preferably obtained during their mating season) and applying this to the infected tooth. It will, apparently, immediately fall out of your mouth.

See *corpse, Friday the 13th, garlic, ladybug, nail, oak, teeth.*

Tooth Fairy: The story of the tooth fairy began in Germany. Originally, it was a "tooth rat" that took the baby tooth to its lair. The origin of this superstition was the fear that primitive people had about nail clippings and hair getting into the wrong hands, which rendered them vulnerable to evil spells and possession. If a baby tooth got 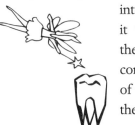 into the wrong hands, it was thought that the new tooth would contain the qualities of whoever possessed the old one.

The tooth fairy ended the old superstition. Losing a tooth became a good thing for a child to do, as he or she would receive a gift from the tooth fairy.

See *hair.*

Topaz: During Roman times, topaz was considered a stone of strength, providing protection from any dangers while traveling. Emperor Hadrian wore a topaz ring to provide protection and strength.

In the Middle Ages, topaz was attached to the left arm to protect its owner from any curse and to ward off the evil eye. People also believed that wearing it increased body heat, which enabled people to relieve a cold or fever.

In the Christian tradition, topaz is believed to cure eye problems and sometimes even blindness. Some authorities claim that St. Matthew used a topaz to cure himself of an eye disease.[59]

Today, topaz is used to relieve anxieties, fears, stress, and insomnia. Topaz is the birthstone for November.

See *birthstone, colds, eye, evil eye, gemstones, ring, wedding anniversaries.*

Touch Wood: See *knock on wood.*

Travel: St. Christopher is the patron saint of travelers, and many people carry a St. Christopher medal with them to provide good luck and protection while they are traveling. Other people carry a variety of other good luck charms, such as a four-leaf clover, to ensure their safety.

Starting a trip on a Friday is considered unlucky. Friday the 13th is even more fraught with possible danger. The chances of staying in a hotel with a thirteenth floor are slim, as most hotels number this floor fourteen. This averts any possibility of guests complaining that their misfortune was the hotel's fault for putting them on the thirteenth floor.

When starting a trip, do not look back at your home. This creates bad luck that will last until you return home again. It's also unlucky to start a trip, and then have to return to pick up something that has been forgotten.

It is bad luck to wave goodbye to someone and then continue to watch until the person moves out of sight. This increases the chance that you'll never see them again.

See *charms, clover, Friday, Friday the 13th, itching, luck, St. Christopher.*

Tree: The folklore of trees contains numerous superstitions. Evergreen trees symbolize immortality, while trees that change with the seasons depict life, death, and rebirth. This made trees seem supernatural, and it isn't surprising that people believed gods lived in them. Pagan religions believed every tree had its own host spirit.

Veneration of trees was common throughout the world, and the death penalty was used to ensure that no one cut any down.

Trees were also used as oracles. Two of the most famous oracles were the oak trees at Dodona, and the laurels at Delphi. The laurels withered and successfully predicted Nero's death.

Touching or knocking on wood is one of the most common superstitions today.

Planting a tree is commonly done to commemorate the birth of a child or as a tribute to someone's life and achievements.

See *apple, ash, bay, birch, blossom, Christmas tree, earth, fairies, knock on wood, leaf, lightning, menstruation, oak, petrified wood, rowan, wood.*

Turquoise: Four gold and turquoise bracelets were discovered on the arm of the mummy of the Egyptian Queen Zer. These bracelets are seventy-four hundred years old. Turquoise is the birthstone for December, which shows how it is still just as popular today.

Turquoise is the most popular amulet stone in the world, and has been used to provide good luck for thousands of years. It also provides protection from a large variety of illnesses and other problems. It is a popular stone of love, and is said to lose its color when love fades. In William Shakespeare's *The Merchant of Venice*, Leah gives Shylock a turquoise ring to win his love (Act 3, scene 1).

The tradition of attaching turquoise amulets to horses probably began in Persia, and is still a common practice in Arab countries. Horses were thought to pull the sun through the heavens. Because the blue of the turquoise reminded people of the sky, it became an amulet worn by horses to ensure sure-footedness and to protect the horses from overheating and exhaustion. These horse amulets protected both the horse and the rider.

See *amulet, birthstone, gemstones, horse, love, sky.*

Turtledove: It is extremely fortunate if a pair of turtledoves nests close to your home. This means no one in your family will suffer from rheumatism.

You can cure pneumonia by placing a dead turtledove on the chest of someone suffering from it.

See *dove, rheumatism.*

Twelfth Night: January 6 is Twelfth Night, the last day of the Christmas season. All Christmas decorations should be taken down on this day. It is bad luck for the family to leave the decorations up after this day, or to take them down earlier.

It is good luck to keep a sprig of holly until the following Christmas. This ensures that the luck of the family will last for at least one more year.

See *Christmas, holly, wassailing.*

Twins: Twins are believed to possess special powers, such as clairvoyance or the gift of seeing into the future. This is because at one time they were believed to be the fruit of a union between a god and a mortal.

Ancient people found the concept of twins a difficult one to accept. Sometimes it was considered bad luck to have twins, and one of the babies would be drowned. This was always the girl if the twins happened to be a boy and girl. However, twins were looked upon more favorably in Egypt and Rome, both of which had twin gods. The Egyptians worshipped Osiris and Set, and the Romans had Romulus and Remus. The expression "by jiminy" was originally a Roman oath that referred to the astrological sign of Gemini, the twins.

Twins were believed to occur if the husband accidentally spilled pepper while his wife was pregnant. However, he could prevent this from happening by tossing some of the pepper over his left shoulder. A

less pleasant belief was that, as a man could supposedly only father one child at a time, the extra child must be a result of his wife's infidelity, or perhaps the work of evil spirits.

Common beliefs about twins are that they possess only one soul, are not as strong as one child, and if one twin dies the survivor will gain additional energy and healing powers. If twins get married on the same day, they should use different churches.

See *church*.

Two: Two is considered a lucky number, as it symbolizes a couple. It also symbolizes a wide range of opposites, such as good and evil, love and hate, male and female, and life and death. These all depict balance in the universe.

The old saying "two are better than three" means that youth is better than old age. A young person stands on two feet, but an elderly person needs a walking stick for support.

See *numbers*.

Two-dollar Bill: Gamblers probably started the superstition that two-dollar bills bring bad luck. This is because the "two" is the lowest card in a deck of playing cards, and "deuce" is a slang name for the devil.

One way to avert any bad luck if you receive a two-dollar bill is to tear off one of the corners. The next person to receive the bill should also tear off a corner. When all four corners have been removed, the bill should be destroyed. An alternative, and less expensive, method is to kiss the bill. This is because saliva effectively wards off the devil.

See *devil, gambling, kiss*.

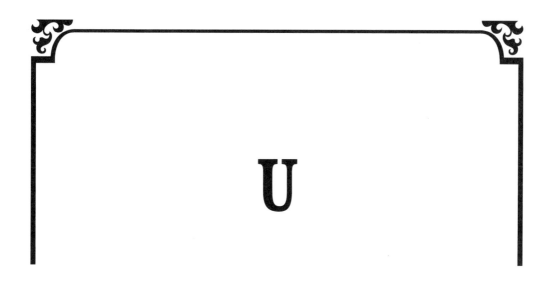

U

Umbilical Cord: The umbilical cord was considered an integral part of the newborn child. Because of this, it had to be disposed of carefully, as it was important that it didn't fall into the hands of anyone who might use it to cast a spell on the child. The umbilical cord could not be burned, as this would cause the child to die in a fire. Neither could it be thrown into water, as this would cause the child to drown. One solution was to bury it under a rose bush, which would give the child a rosy complexion. If a boy's umbilical cord was buried by a grapevine, he would grow up with a fondness for the good things in life. Instead of disposing of it, the umbilical cord could be dried and hung around the child's neck in a small bag. This turned it into a protective amulet.

Barren women were advised to obtain a small piece of umbilical cord to act as a charm.

An old belief cautioned women against spinning or sewing while pregnant, as this might cause the baby to be strangled by the umbilical cord.

See *amulet, charms, children, fire, prenatal influences, rose, sewing, water.*

Umbrella: Umbrellas were not used to protect people from rain until the eighteenth century. Prior to that, they were used as sunshades. The word "umbrella" comes from the Italian *ombrella*, which means "little

shade." The pharaohs of Egypt used them as sunshades thousands of years ago. When umbrellas were first made commercially in England in the late eighteenth century, they were often decorated with acorns to protect the owner from lightning.

A common superstition is the belief that opening an umbrella inside a house causes bad luck. The origin of this is that the umbrella acts as a shield against the sun or rain outdoors. To open it indoors offends the spirit of the umbrella, who will cause bad luck to occur as a result. It is also bad luck to lay your umbrella down on a bed.

Opening an umbrella outdoors when it is not raining is said to cause it to rain. Carrying an umbrella is a sure way of ensuring fine weather.

Another superstition is that if you drop your umbrella, someone else should pick it up. Single ladies risk never finding a partner if they pick up their own umbrellas.

See *acorn, lightning, luck, rain, sun, theater.*

Underwear: An old belief suggests that any woman who wants to get married should obtain a piece of underwear from a recently married woman. If she does, she will be married within a year.

It is also thought that a woman can attract a man by placing a few valerian leaves in her panties or bra.

If a young woman places one of her petticoats under her pillow, she will dream of her future husband.

If a young woman's panties slip down without cause, it is a sign that she is thinking of her lover. If her nightdress rides up at night, it is a sign that he is thinking of her.

If you are experiencing a run of bad luck, you should wear your underwear back to front until your luck changes.

Unicorn: The unicorn is a mythical animal that looks like a horse with a large horn on its forehead. It is considered a symbol of meekness, chastity, and virginity. Ctesias of Cnidos, a Greek doctor, was the first person to mention unicorns in a book he wrote about 398 BCE.

Legend says that only a virgin can catch a unicorn. She can then tame it, but only if she is holding a mirror. If the girl proves not to be a virgin, the unicorn will kill her.

Early Christians symbolized the virgin as Mary, mother of Jesus, and the uni-

corn as Christ. The single horn symbolized the union of Father and Son. People who hunted the unicorn symbolized the Holy Spirit.

The unicorn's horn was believed to be an antidote to any poison. An old story tells of animals waiting by a pond that had been poisoned by snake venom. The unicorn arrived and made a sign of the cross over the pond with his horn, and this instantly restored the pond to its normal state. Because of this legend, the horn has sometimes symbolized the cross of Jesus. The snake, of course, symbolizes the devil, and the poisoned water depicts the sins of the world.

Powdered horn from a unicorn is believed to be an extremely powerful aphrodisiac.

See *aphrodisiac, chastity, cross, devil, horn, mirror, snake, virginity, water.*

Urine: Urine retains a supernatural connection with the body, and care must be taken that it doesn't fall into the hands of witches or other people who might use it to cast spells against the person. Spitting into the urine is said to be an effective way of preventing this from occurring.

Urine is believed to have powerful healing properties. Washing your hands in urine protects you from witches and the evil eye. Urine also heals snakebites and ear infections. It is interesting to note that urea, the solid component of urine, is extremely salty. Consequently, when urine is placed on an open wound, the salty urea absorbs the liquid from the wound and acts as an antiseptic.

Urine can also apparently determine the future well being of someone suffering from a fever. Nettle leaves should be placed in the person's urine. If the leaves stay green, the patient will survive. If they dry out quickly, the patient is doomed.

See *evil eye, spell, spitting, witch.*

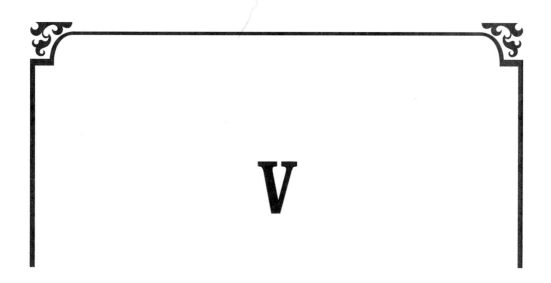

V

Valentine's Day: See *St. Valentine's Day.*

Vampires: A vampire is the dead body of a criminal who is somehow continuing to live in the grave. Vampires come out at night, in the form of bats, and suck blood from the living. This enables them to live forever, as the blood prevents their bodies from decomposing. Victims of a vampire bite ultimately become vampires themselves. There are only three ways to kill a vampire: burn it, decapitate it, or thrust a wooden stake through its heart.

F. W. Murnau, the German filmmaker, was the first person to depict a vampire on screen, in *Nosferatu* in 1922. Bram Stoker's famous novel *Dracula* has been filmed thirty times in fifty years.

See *blood, garlic, grave, heart.*

Vervain: Vervain is an herb that is sometimes called the "enchanter's plant." It has been used for magical purposes for thousands of years. The ancient Romans believed it promoted fertility, and kept it in their homes to ward off evil. The Persians believed that people carrying it would receive friendship and affection from everyone they came across. Vervain was so sacred to the Druids that anyone who picked one had to immediately place a honeycomb on the spot.

Vervain is still used in magical rituals, and is also worn to protect people from nightmares and lightning.

Vervain also works as an aphrodisiac. All you need to do is place a few seeds of vervain into a small bag and wear it around your neck.

A tea made from vervain will cure insomnia.

See *aphrodisiac, insomnia, lightning, nightmare.*

Violet: The violet symbolizes modesty. In the language of flowers, a white violet symbolizes innocence and a blue violet is a sign of devoted love. Like daffodils, violets bring good luck into the house when in bunches. However, a solitary violet attracts bad luck. It is also bad luck for violets to bloom out of season. This is said to indicate the death of the owner of the land.

In Greek mythology, Venus noticed Cupid's love for white violets, and in a fit of jealousy made them purple.

Violets were banned in France for many years after Napoleon's defeat. This was because he used them as his badge of honor.

See *daffodil, death, flowers, periwinkle.*

Virginity: At one time, virginity was the only truly valuable possession women had. It was believed to possess supernatural qualities. Virgins were thought to be the only people who could tame and feed dragons, serpents, and unicorns. Virgins were said to have the ability to stare at the sun without being affected, and to walk through swarms of bees or wasps without getting stung. Virgins had the power to cure warts and other ailments merely by touching the affected part.

Because virginity was so precious, a variety of tests were done to determine if a woman was still a virgin. The woman was deemed to have lost her virginity if she grew large breasts or forgot to put the salt on the dining room table. If a woman was still a virgin, she would need to urinate immediately after drinking or eating anything that contained a small amount of coal powder.

A strange belief from Central Europe says that a woman regains her virginity after giving birth to seven illegitimate children.

See *bees, coal, salt, serpent, sun, unicorn, warts.*

Virgo: Virgo is the sixth sign of the zodiac. Its symbol is the virgin. Its element is earth, and its gemstone is sapphire. The keyword for Virgo is: I analyze.

Virgoans are modest, down-to-earth people with a shrewd approach to life. They enjoy detailed, precise work and constantly strive for perfection. They can be critical, of both themselves and others, when their high standards are not met. Virgoans enjoy working behind the scenes. They seldom seek the spotlight, but are not afraid to stand up for themselves when their sense of honesty and fair play is affected.

See *astrology, earth, elements, gemstones, sapphire, zodiac.*

Voodoo: Voodoo is a magical religion practiced by many people in the Caribbean and the southern United States. It is an intriguing combination of Roman Catholicism and African magic. Animal sacrifices, spirit possession, sorcery, sex magic, and shamanistic trance are all factors in voodoo.

Voodoo dolls are still made to symbolize someone who is to be cursed. These dolls are then tortured, knowing that the pain will be inflicted on the person they are meant to represent.

Voodoo priests have the power to raise the dead and turn them into zombies.

See *gris-gris, zombies.*

V-Sign: The "V for Victory" sign was popularized by Sir Winston Churchill during the Second World War. It is made by holding up the first and second fingers, with the palm of the hand facing outwards. This gesture was probably first used to mean "victory" by a Belgian refugee, Victor de Lavelaye, who started a campaign to popularize the gesture to motivate the people.

V-sign amulets were popular in ancient Egypt, where they were worn partly to honor Horus. Apparently, Horus was thrust into the darkness by Set, who was evil incarnate. Fortunately, Horus' father, Osiris, the sun god, let down a ladder that Horus used to escape. Horus then used his index and middle fingers to save other people who were also trapped in the darkness.

Christian priests have a long tradition of holding up the same two fingers, though held together, as a sign of blessing.

If the V-sign is made with the hand pointing downwards, it symbolizes the devil's horns.

See *amulet, devil, finger, ladder.*

Vulture: Probably because they eat dead animals, vultures are considered an omen of death in the West. They have an uncanny ability to sense death, sometimes days in advance. Consequently, even the sight of a vulture can cause panic and concern. However, vultures were worshipped in ancient Egypt, and people still believe they possess clairvoyant powers. Vultures mate for life and share nesting duties. They are also dedicated parents.

Legend says that the god Jupiter sent six vultures to Remus and twelve to Romulus to point out the future site of Rome.

In South Africa, the local people eat vulture meat believing that it will give them powers of clairvoyance. In Zimbabwe, voters ate vulture meat believing that this would enable them to pick the winning party in an election.[60] Sadly, as a result of this belief, vultures are now an endangered species.

See *death.*

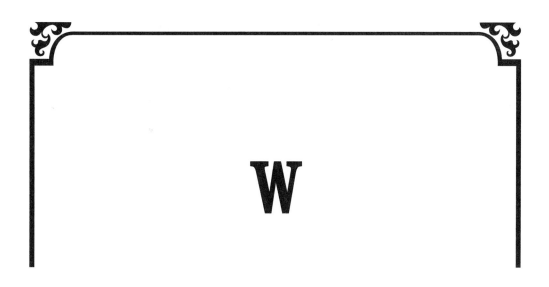

W

Waiter: Waiters are as superstitious as everyone else. Consequently, they consider it an indication of a small tip if a customer sits in a different seat than the one assigned to him or her. It is also considered a bad sign to receive a large tip early on in the shift. This means that all later tips will be small. Breaking a plate or other dish is thought to be bad luck, which may be reflected in the size of the tips.

It is good luck to open the napkin for the customer and to place it on his or her lap. It is also good luck to bring customers anything they might need, such as extra butter or bread, before they ask for it.

See *bread, napkin, plate.*

Walking: The most famous superstition of all is the advice that you should not walk under a ladder. This dates back to ancient Egyptian times, when people believed you might see a god walking up or down the ladder while you walked under it.

When walking with a friend, you should both walk on the same side of an obstruction in your path. If you separate and walk on either side of it, you will both experience bad luck. Fortunately, the bad luck can be averted if either of you says the magical words "bread and butter."

It is also bad luck to trip over a curb or anything else that gets in your way. Again, the bad luck can be averted if you retrace your steps and pass over the obstruction again without tripping.

Many people dislike walking on the cracks in pavement, as they think bad luck will occur if they do. This comes from the old belief that the cracks lead directly to a grave. A children's chant grew out of this superstition:

> Step on a crack,
> break your mother's back;
> Step on a line,
> break your mother's spine.

Walking backwards is also believed to attract bad luck. Walking on a grave is extremely dangerous, and always brings bad luck.

See *bread and butter, grave, ladder.*

Walnut: Walnut trees are considered a safe haven for witches and evil spirits. This might be because walnut trees provide protection from lightning. Apparently, a witch is unable to move if someone places a walnut under the chair she is sitting on.

You will receive pleasant dreams about your future lover if you fall asleep under a walnut tree. However,

this is a risky undertaking, as you may never awaken from your sleep.

In ancient Greece and Rome, stewed walnuts were used to encourage fertility. However, the opposite belief was held in Romania. If a bride wanted to remain childless for a period of time, she had to place one roasted walnut, for each year she wanted to remain childless, in her bodice before she got married. After the ceremony, she had to bury the walnuts.

Walnuts have been used to cure sore throats and even to thicken thinning hair. Native Americans used the bark of black walnut trees as a laxative.

See *bride, chair, dreams, fleas, hair, lightning, Midsummer's Eve, witch.*

Wand: A wand is a symbol of power and authority. Wands give authority to magicians, sorcerers, wizards, druids, and fairies. In Celtic mythology, a druid could transform a person into an animal, such as a bird or boar, by touching the person with a wand. In Greek mythology, Hermes, the magician, had a golden wand with which he could raise the dead. Magic wands are frequently cut from ash or hazel trees, and are frequently inscribed. In magic, the wand symbolizes the element of air.

See *air, ash, birds, elements, fairy, magic.*

Warlock: Traditionally, a warlock was a male witch. However, the word "warlock" comes from *waerloga*, an Old English word that means "oath breaker." Consequently, in modern Wicca, a warlock is someone who has broken an oath or betrayed the Craft in some manner.

See *witch.*

Warts: Warts are viral infections of the skin. Warts were dangerous things to have in Jacobean times, as they were considered marks of the devil and witches were believed to possess them. Obviously, there were extremely good reasons for getting rid of them in those days.

Superstition provides many suggested remedies for getting rid of warts. These range from spitting on them every morning, to burying a bag that contains as many stones as you have warts. One intriguing method is to secretly rub the warts against a man who has fathered a child out of wedlock. However, it is important that he is not aware of what you are doing. Another cure is to steal a piece of meat, rub it on the wart, and then bury it. Alternatively, you can rub the wart while a funeral procession passes by. The wart will disappear after it has rained nine times.

Talking to the warts and telling them to shrink is one remedy that seems to work. An interesting experiment conducted by several psychologists, headed by Dr. Nicholas P. Spanos, professor at Carleton University in Ottawa, Canada, in 1990, demonstrated how effective hypnosis was in curing warts. Ten volunteers were hypnotized and told that their warts were shrinking. Another ten had their warts painted with salicylic acid. A third ten were given a placebo, and a final ten received no treatment whatsoever. After six weeks, six of the ten hypnotized volunteers had lost at least one wart each. Three of the final group, and one of the volunteers who had received a placebo, also lost warts. Interestingly, none of the volunteers who used salicylic acid lost any warts.[61]

Of course, none of this is necessary if you avoid getting warts in the first place. A good way to start is to avoid handling toads. Because their skin is wart-like, they are considered a prime cause of warts. Additionally, you should never wash your hands in water that has been used to boil eggs.

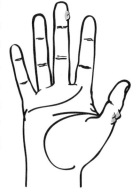

See *abracadabra, charmers, devil, eggs, Good Friday, holy water, numbers, pea, thread, tongue, virginity.*

Washing: You should not do any washing on Good Friday or New Year's Day. Good Friday is particularly ill omened, as a washerwoman swore obscenities at Christ as he was carrying the cross. A Scottish tradition says that you will wash a member of your family away if you wash your clothes on New Year's Day.

If you avoid washing a child's right hand during his or her first year of life, the child will be able to gather and retain wealth more easily in later life.

It is bad luck for two people to wash in the same water at the same time. The remedy is for one of them to spit in the water.

At one time, people felt they could cure an illness by thoroughly washing the ill person and then throwing the water out of the house. The illness was believed to leave with the water.

You need to carefully dispose of water you have washed in, as it contains part of your soul. Anyone who gets hold of this water could gain a magical influence over you.

It is considered bad luck to break any crockery while washing the dishes. Because breakages occur in threes, you can avert the next two breakages by deliberately breaking two pieces of old china.

An old superstition says that if a single woman gets wet while washing clothes, she will marry a drunkard.

See *cross, clothes, Good Friday, hand, miners, three, water.*

Wasp: It is good luck for a wasp to fly into a house. If necessary, gently guide the wasp back out again after it has done some exploring. A common superstition says that wasps are capable of killing cows.

See *cow.*

Wassailing: Wassailing means to toast someone, especially at large celebrations where huge amounts of food and alcohol are consumed. The word "wassail" comes from *Waes Haeil*, which means "be thou well." Wassailing is a popular custom, particularly in Devon and Somerset, where cider apples grow.

The wassail bowl is a cup from which toasts of steaming spiced apple cider were drunk, especially on Christmas Eve and Twelfth Night. A milk can of cider was placed in the center of the orchard, and the wassail bowls were filled from this. The participants took their cups of liquor to one of the trees, drank some of it, and then splashed the rest of the liquid onto the tree trunk while saying,

Here's to thee, old apple tree,
Hence thou mayest bud,
and whence they mayest blow,
And whence thou mayest
bear apples enow!
Hats full! Caps full!
Bushel, bushel-sacks full!
And my pockets full, too! Huzza!

Frequently, rifles were fired to scare off any evil spirits. It is a good idea to visit the barn and wassail the animals before wassailing your plants, fields, and bees.

See *apple, bees, Christmas Eve, taboo, toast, Twelfth Night*.

Water: Water is one of the essentials of life, and people have always had great faith in its healing, curative, cleansing, and magical powers.

Running water is believed to be especially powerful, and at one time it was believed that enchantments could not withstand it. In Robert Burns' famous poem "Tam o' Shanter," Tam, a farmer, was unable to escape from the witches who were chasing him until he was halfway across the bridge over the River Doon.

It is considered bad luck for two people to wash in the same water together. However, you can avoid this bad luck by making the sign of the cross over the water you are sharing.

You mustn't sing in the bath if you bathe in the morning. If you do, you'll be sad before evening.

If a single girl splashes herself unnecessarily while bathing, she'll end up with a drunkard for a husband.

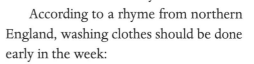

It is also considered bad luck to throw any water outside the house after dark, as you lose the water's protection. Dreaming of water is also considered unlucky.

According to a rhyme from northern England, washing clothes should be done early in the week:

They that wash on Monday
have the whole week to dry.
They that wash on Tuesday
are not so much arye.
They that wash on Wednesday
will get their clothes so clean.
They that wash on Thursday
are not so much to mean.
They that wash on Friday
wash for their need.
But they that wash on Saturday
are dirty folks indeed.

Water was one of the four elements of the ancient Greeks. The three water signs of the zodiac are Cancer, Scorpio, and Pisces. In Wicca, a water elemental is one of the four nature spirits that activate spells.

Water symbolizes emotions, intuition, and the cycle of birth, death, and rebirth.

See *air, Cancer, cross, earth, elemental, elements, fire, knife, petrified wood, Pisces, rain, Scorpio, spell, umbilical cord, unicorn, washing, well, Wicca, witch, zodiac.*

Waves: Waves follow a cycle of nine, and every ninth wave is believed to be the largest in the cycle.

See *nine, water.*

Weather: In previous times, people were highly dependent on the weather, and it was important to be able to predict times of good or bad weather. Apart from the effect weather has on crops, people wanted the weather to be sunny while a couple was getting married, and rainy during a funeral. Consequently, a variety of magical incantations and rituals were conducted in the attempt to influence the weather. One of the most famous of these is the old children's nursery rhyme,

> Rain, rain, go away,
> Come again another day.

Omens and signs were looked for in attempts to predict the weather. Almost everyone knows the old rhyme,

> Red sky at night,
> Shepherd's delight.
> Red sky in the morning,
> Shepherd's warning.

It is considered a sign of rain if spiders leave their webs and hide in sheltered spots. The weather is about to deteriorate if swallows start flying low.

It is said that you can determine the temperature by counting the number of chirps a cricket makes in fifteen seconds. If you add thirty-seven to this total, you will have the temperature in Fahrenheit.

Many people predict the weather by observing the groundhogs on Groundhog Day (February 2). If the groundhog can see his shadow, he goes back to sleep for another six weeks, as this as a sign that the cold weather is not yet over.

See *ants, April, August, bell, crickets, February, December, drowning, Easter, funeral, grass, Groundhog Day, January, July, June, lightning, March, May, nine, November, October, rain, rainbow, September, sky, snow, spider, swallow, thunder.*

Wedding: The word "wedding" comes from the Anglo-Saxon word *wed*, or pledge. In Anglo-Saxon times, young children were sometimes betrothed to each other. The future bridegroom gave a pledge, or "wed," to the bride, promising that he would marry her. As part of this pledge, he gave her a ring that she wore on her right hand until the wedding, when it was placed on her left hand.

The Romans considered June the best month for a wedding, especially if the wedding coincided with a full moon or the conjunction of the moon and sun. May was considered the worst month, as the spirits related to this month were not conducive to happy relationships. May was also the month in which they honored the dead.

In medieval times, it was considered bad luck for the bridal party to come across a monk, priest, dog, hare, lizard, or snake while on their way to the church. It was, however, good luck to come across a spider, toad, or wolf.

Every bride knows the old superstition about what to wear:

> Something old,
> Something new,
> Something borrowed,
> Something blue.

Few people know the reasons behind this saying. But magic is extremely powerful when attached to a highly charged occasion, such as a wedding. Consequently, the clothing worn by the bride has to be selected with great care, as it is seen to have the power to affect her entire future. Getting married means leaving the past behind and entering a whole new stage of life.

The bride has to wear something old, as this provides her with a sense of security. Wearing something new provides her with good luck and happiness, as people are made happy by buying something new for themselves. The "something borrowed" has to be borrowed from a woman who has worn the object at a time of great happiness. Sympathetic magic ensures that this happiness transfers itself to the bride. Protective magic is involved with the "something blue." Heaven was considered to be up in the sky, which on a good day appears to be blue. Consequently, blue became associated with purity and the divine. Wearing something blue effectively protects the bride from jealousy and any other form of negativity on her special day.

The bouquets carried by Roman brides contained garlic, chives, and other herbs. They symbolized fertility and also scared away evil spirits. Gradually, bouquets became purely ornamental, but the choice of flowers remained important. Ivy or myrtle ensured good luck, apple blossoms signified a happy future, and the rose represented undying love.

The Victorians believed that it was good luck to be married on the same day of the week that the groom was born on. They also believed that the wedding ceremony should be held between the half hour and the hour. The rising minute hand symbolized an increase in the couple's luck.

It is considered good luck if the wedding party consists of an even number of people. Another old superstition says, "Happy is the bride whom the sun shines on." At one time, weddings took place outside the church door, rather than inside the church itself. Naturally, under those conditions, the bride would be extremely happy to be married on a sunny day. Weddings continued to be held outdoors until the reign of King Edward VI (1537–1553).

The bride and groom should leave the church after the ceremony through the same door that they came in. It is thought to be bad luck to leave by another door, because coffins are taken out of the church by a different door.

See *bride, candle, cat, children, church, coffin, dog, engagement, flowers, garlic, glass, hare, ivy, knife, lizard, magic, mari-* *gold, mirror, plate, ring, rose, sky, sleep, snake, spider, spoon, thirteen, widow, wolf.*

Wedding Anniversaries: Wedding anniversaries are major milestones in life and provide a good reason for family celebrations. A variety of items have gradually become connected with each anniversary, and gifts made from these objects are given as anniversary presents.

1st anniversary: paper

2nd anniversary: cotton

3rd anniversary: linen or leather

4th anniversary: book or flowers and fruit

5th anniversary: wood

6th anniversary: iron

7th anniversary: copper or bronze

8th anniversary: leather

9th anniversary: pottery

10th anniversary: tin or aluminum

11th anniversary: steel

12th anniversary: silk or linen

13th anniversary: moonstone.

14th anniversary: moss-agate

15th anniversary: rock-crystal or glass

16th anniversary: topaz

17th anniversary: amethyst

18th anniversary: garnet

19th anniversary: hyacinth

20th anniversary: china

21st anniversary: brass

22nd anniversary: copper

23rd anniversary: sapphire

24th anniversary: music or musical instrument

25th anniversary: silver

26th anniversary: star sapphire

27th anniversary: sculpture

28th anniversary: orchids

29th anniversary: furniture

30th anniversary: pearl

31st anniversary: clock or watch

32nd anniversary: conveyance

33rd anniversary: amethyst

34th anniversary: opal

35th anniversary: coral

36th anniversary: bone china

37th anniversary: alabaster

38th anniversary: beryl or tourmaline

39th anniversary: cat's eye

40th anniversary: ruby.

45th anniversary: alexandrite

50th anniversary: gold

52nd anniversary: star-ruby

55th anniversary: emerald

60th anniversary: diamond

65th anniversary: star-sapphire, gray

67th anniversary: star-sapphire, purple

70th anniversary: platinum

75th anniversary: diamond

It is interesting to note that all the anniversaries that reduce down to thirteen (13, 26, 39, 52, and 65) have gemstones with the appearance of moving light. This is to counteract the negative effects of the thirteen.

See *thirteen*.

Wedding Cake: In Roman times, the guests broke a cake made of meal over the bride's head to wish her luck. They would then sprinkle the crumbs over their own heads to ensure their good luck also.

The wedding cake symbolizes fruitfulness, fertility, abundance, and good luck for everyone who eats it. Consequently, the cake should be rich and tasty. Superstition says that if the cake is a failure, the marriage will be too. The bride should not play any part in the making of the cake, and should not sample it before the wedding reception.

The bride should be the first person to cut the cake to ensure a happy marriage. Nowadays, the groom places his hand over hers, and they cut the first slice of the wedding cake together to ensure good luck and a long and happy life together.

The bride should keep a tier of the cake for use as a future christening cake. This ensures that children will come along in time.

An old tradition says that the bride should place a piece of the wedding cake under the marriage bed to ensure the faithfulness of both parties.

An old superstition says that a young girl should pass a small piece of wedding cake through a wedding ring before placing it in her left stocking. If she then places this stocking under her pillow before going to bed, she will dream of her future husband. All of this is made much easier

for a single girl today. If she is given a piece of wedding cake in a small box, she should place this under her pillow.

See *bed, bride, cake, children, christening, marriage, wedding ring.*

Wedding Dress: Traditionally, brides were married in white to symbolize purity, chastity, and innocence. However, white symbolized joy to the ancient Greeks, who sometimes even painted their bodies white before getting married.

Silk is believed to be the most fortunate material for a wedding dress. Satin is a sign of bad luck, while velvet indicates poverty and life-long struggle.

The bride should not try on the dress before the wedding day. As this superstition can create problems, a loophole was developed. The bride may try on the dress, as long as she does not wear everything she's planning to wear on her wedding day. If she

leaves off a shoe or a glove, everything will be all right. Even so, she must not look at herself in a full length mirror.

It is important that the bridegroom does not see the wedding dress until he meets his bride at the altar.

See *bride, glove, mirror, pin, shoe.*

Wedding Ring: The wedding ring symbolizes eternity. The ring is placed on the third finger of the left hand because the ancient Egyptians believed a love vein ran directly to the heart from this finger. If the ring was removed, the love was believed to escape. Consequently, a wedding ring should never be taken off unless you are using it to ward off a witch.

It is bad luck to drop the wedding ring during the wedding ceremony. If the groom

drops it, he will die before his bride. If she drops it, she will be the first to die.

If you turn a wedding ring around three times while making a wish, your wish will come true.

It was the Egyptians who first made wedding rings from gold. This demonstrated that the husband entrusted his wife with his valuable possessions.

At one time it was uncommon for a man to wear a wedding ring. However, fashions change, and nowadays most men wear one.

See *eye, finger, gold, hand, heart, ring, wedding cake, wish, witch.*

Wednesday: A charming superstition says that it never rains on Wednesday because this is the day on which God created the sun.

It is considered bad luck for the new moon to fall on a Wednesday. All important decisions should be delayed until after the next new moon.

See *sun, moon.*

Weeds: Weeds are the bane of every gardener. According to superstition, God was so upset with Adam's disobedience that he cursed the earth with weeds. No matter how hard you work in your garden, God's disapproval of Adam means that you will never be free of weeds.

See *earth.*

Well: Wells used to be essential to every community, and a number of superstitions have grown up around them. Every well was believed to have a guardian spirit who had to be treated with courtesy and respect. Some wells became famous for their healing properties. Others were renowned for their divination abilities, as they made strange sounds when disaster threatened.

Wells should be offered a piece of bread at the New Year to ensure that they do not run dry during the next twelve months. It was said that anyone who drank from the first bucket of water drawn from a well on January 1 would enjoy good luck all year. People who regularly drink water from a well will grow up to be tall and strong.

See *bread, divination, New Year, water, wishing well.*

Werewolf: The werewolf is a popular superstition that goes back to Greco-Roman times. It was particularly popular in medieval times. Werewolves were people who had been turned into wolves by some magical enchantment. The people most vulnerable to this were those born on Christmas Eve or born out of wedlock. Some people were also believed to be able to

turn themselves into wolves. You could sometimes recognize these people because their eyebrows met over the nose, they were hairy, and they had fingernails that looked like claws and small, slightly pointed ears.

Werewolves were frightening animals, as they roamed the countryside in search of human flesh. They particularly enjoyed eating young babies. When they were extremely hungry, werewolves dug up corpses to eat.

A silver bullet is said to be the only way to kill a werewolf. However, a werewolf can be cured if you know the person's first name. All you need do is call out the person's name three times while he or she is in the body of a wolf. The risk in doing this is that if you get the name wrong, you might find yourself transformed into a wolf.

See *Christmas Eve, corpse, eyebrow, fingernail, moon, nose, silver, wolf.*

Whistle: During the Middle Ages, sailors believed they could produce a wind by whistling. A gentle whistle would produce a breeze, and a loud one would produce a gale. Even today, many sailors still whistle for a wind. However, this needs to be done carefully. Vigorous, loud whistling might create storms. Consequently, whistling at sea is considered bad luck when weather conditions are favorable. Whistling only becomes good luck when the ship is becalmed and a wind is desired.

Whistling was once considered something that only males did. It was bad luck to see or hear a woman whistle, as it could produce all kinds of bad luck including gale-force winds from the wrong direction. Small girls were told they'd grow a beard if they whistled. An American rhyme cautions,

> Whistling girls and crowing hens
> Always come to some bad ends.

Nowadays, whistling at a girl is considered a vulgar way of attracting attention from the opposite sex. Originally, whistling in this way was believed to magically captivate the girl, who would then become attracted to the whistler.

Actors and actresses believe it is unlucky to whistle backstage.

There has always been doubt about the effectiveness of whistling, from a superstition point of view. The expression "you can whistle for it" comes from this. When someone tells you this, you are unlikely to get whatever it is that you want.

See *actors and actresses, beard, miners, sailors, ships, snapping fingers, stairs, storm, theater, wind, women.*

White: White symbolizes purity, innocence, virginity, holiness, and hope. It is also considered a protective color, which might partly explain why it is such a popular choice for wedding dresses. White is the color of mourning in much of the East. This is because the deceased are thought to be moving into a better world.

Despite these positive meanings, there are a few superstitions involving the color white. You should, for instance, always spit when you see a white cat, dog, hare, or horse. You might also want to lick one of your thumbs and stamp it into the palm of your other hand. This stamps out the devil and enables you to avert any potential bad luck.

Lilies and lilacs should not be kept indoors, as they are closely associated with funerals. You can bring them indoors, though, as long as they are accompanied by flowers of any other color except red.

People used to believe that hair could turn white or grey overnight. Extended periods of stress or

worry can turn hair grey, but it always takes time.

See *cat, devil, dog, fishing, funeral, hair, hand, hare, horse, lilac, lily, red, thumb, wedding dress.*

Whooping Cough: Until relatively recently, a popular cure for whooping cough was to sew a live caterpillar into a cloth bag that was hung around the neck of the sufferer.

Wicca: The word "wicca" comes from the Celtic *wicce*, which means "wise." Wicca is the term given to modern-day witchcraft. However, Wicca could be described more accurately as a neo-pagan religion. It is based on ancient pagan traditions, but in its present form dates back to the 1950s, when witchcraft experienced a huge revival led largely by Alex Sanders (1926–1988) and Gerald Gardner (1884–1964). These two men combined a number of beliefs into an organized, consistent system. There are many schools of Wicca today, which practice white magic and the pagan nature religion of goddess worship.

Wiccan beliefs include practicing the Wiccan Rede and the Threefold Law. *Rede* is an Old English word meaning "advice" or "counsel." The Wiccan Rede says, "And as it harm none, do as thou will." In other words, you can do whatever you wish as long as it harms no one. The Threefold Law says that whenever you send out a spell, the energy returns three-fold. This is a strong incentive to send out only positive thoughts or spells, and is based on the law of karma.

Many Wiccans call themselves witches and practice white magic, casting spells for healing, prosperity, and the environment. Most Wiccans conduct rituals, either on their own or in groups, to honor and sanctify the earth. Many Wiccans are solitary practitioners, either by preference or circumstance. They are called "hedge witches." This comes from the days when witches planted hawthorns around their homes to create a sacred boundary.

See *ankh, ash, earth, elemental, familiar, hawthorn, magic, spell, water, witch, witchcraft.*

Widdershins: The word "widdershins" comes from two Old English words: *vithr* (against) and *sinni* (movement). It means backwards or reverse. The word is still sometimes used in Scotland and northern England. Nowadays, it is used in magic when someone has to do something in an counterclockwise direction. If a spell asks that a number of candles be lit in a clock-

wise direction, they may well be put out at the end of the ritu-

al in an counterclockwise direction, known as widdershins.

It was considered unlucky to do anything widdershins. Even stirring food in a pot had to be done in a clockwise direction. Muslims pass food around a table in a clockwise direction. They will politely decline food that is offered to them widdershins, by someone unaware of this tradition.

Acting in a widdershins fashion is also guaranteed to attract attention from ghosts and evil spirits. Consequently, you should ensure that you always walk around a church or haunted house in a clockwise direction.

All of this began when people started watching the movement of the sun across the sky. They noticed that it rose in the east and set in the west. They felt that if they followed the sun's direction, they would be assured of success. To go in the opposite direction was bound to result in problems, failures, and bad luck.

See *candle, church, ghost, magic, sky, spell, sun.*

Widow: Widows have always been considered unlucky, and at one time people avoided inviting them to weddings in case their presence affected the future happiness of the bride and groom. The spirit of the widow's first husband is thought to never totally disappear, and is believed to haunt the widow and her next husband. Not surprisingly, this can create disagreements and stress in the new relationship. One possible remedy for this is for the groom to make as much noise as possible during the wedding, to drive away the first husband's spirit.

See *bride, wedding.*

Widow's Peak: A widow's peak is a V-shaped hairline, which ends in a point on the forehead. When Anne of Brittany (1476–1514) lost her husband King Charles VIII, her hat designer created a striking black V-shaped bonnet for her to wear as part of her mourning clothes. One year later, she married King Louis XII, and the superstition began that if you have a widow's peak, you will lose your first husband early and quickly remarry.

Will: An old superstition says that it's unlucky to make a will, as this is likely to speed up your demise. The will used to be read over the person's coffin, presumably to give the deceased an opportunity to protest if the relatives seemed unhappy with it.

See *coffin.*

Willow: The willow tree has always been associated with melancholy, sorrow, tragic love affairs, and mourning. Sometimes, people would wear a sprig of willow while mourning, believing that this would help relieve their pain.

One superstition says that willow catkins should not be brought inside, as they will bring sorrow with them. May Day is the only day on which willow can be brought indoors.

Touching a willow tree brings good luck. A frond of willow is effective at warding off witches and the evil eye. Magic wands are often made of willow.

Because willow trees are believed to gossip, you should not discuss important secrets near them. If you do, the secrets will quickly be spread by the wind.

See *evil eye, magic, May Day, wind, witch.*

Wind: Sailors had a vested interest in encouraging the wind when they were becalmed. Scratching the mast of the ship was one method. An alternative method, though fraught with danger, was to whistle softly. Whistling loudly risked causing a gale. They could also pay the elements for a wind by tossing a coin overboard.

See *coin, elements, sailors, ships, sky, whistle, willow.*

Window: People are at their most vulnerable while asleep. This was considered an especially dangerous time, as for thousands of years people believed that evil spirits and demons roamed the earth at night. Even the Bible confirmed "the terror by night" (Psalm 91:5). Consequently, people kept their windows securely closed and shuttered at night to prevent the evil spirits from coming in.

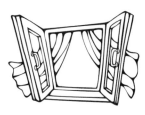

It is said that windows should be kept open when someone in the house is dying. This enables the soul to leave the body and go to heaven without any impediments in the way. Windows should also be kept open during a violent storm, as this allows any lightning that enters the house to leave.

See *lightning, storm.*

Wine: Wine has been a popular drink for thousands of years. Ancient people believed that wine contained spirits who became active when the wine was drunk. You could actually feel the effects of this spirit as you became intoxicated. Consequently, it was considered bad luck to spill any wine, as this was a sign that some misfortune was on its way. Fortunately, there is a remedy. You could rub some of the spilled

wine behind your ears, using the middle finger of your right hand.

Some people still regard sparkling wines with suspicion. If any is spilt, you must touch your ear with it and make a wish.

Wine should be passed around the table in a clockwise direction, using your right hand. This brings good luck to everyone at the table.

Pouring a glass of wine into the sea will immediately calm a storm.

Wine is believed to cure many ailments, including migraine, colds, fevers, and rabies. In the case of rabies, a few hairs from a rabid dog must be added to the wine. Consecrated wine is thought to be particularly good in curing children's health problems.

See *colds, dog, ear, finger, grape, hair, hand, rosemary, ships, storm, toast.*

Wish: When you make a wish, you are asking fortune to smile on you and grant whatever it is that you are asking for. Some times are better than others for making wishes. When you experience an itchy palm, it is a good time to make a wish. You can also make a wish while stirring the Christmas pudding, or putting on new clothes for the first time. You should definitely make a wish when tossing coins into a wishing well or pulling on a wishbone. Seeing the first evening star is another good time, and you should make your wish immediately after reciting,

> Star light, star bright,
> First star I see tonight.
> I wish I may, I wish I might,
> Have the wish I wish tonight.

The most popular time to make a wish is when you are blowing out the candles on your birthday cake.

See *candle, Christmas, clothes, coin, fairy ring, rainbow, robin, sage, shoelaces, wedding ring, star, wishbone, wishing well.*

Wishbone: It would be hard to find someone who hasn't pulled on a wishbone, hoping that the wish will come true. The origin of this custom is lost, but it's connected with the importance poultry has always had to mankind. The cock's crow announced morning to everyone within earshot, and the clucking of a hen meant that she was about to lay an egg, the universal symbol of fertility. Because of this, hens and chickens were believed to possess magical powers. This magic extended to their bones. The wishbone's proper name is fercula. The fercula was chosen because its shape resembled the human groin, and it became a symbol of fertility and the perpetuation of the species.

Christmas and Thanksgiving are the most popular times of year for pulling a wishbone. This is doubtless because large birds, such as turkeys, are eaten at this time.

The only person who should not pull on a wishbone, according to a north of England belief, is a young, single woman. She should hang it over her front door on New Year's Day. The first man to enter the house after it has been put up will become her husband.

It is said that the person who breaks off the larger piece of the wishbone will have the wish granted, as long as he or she does not talk or laugh while pulling on the bone, and does not reveal the wish to anyone afterwards.

See *Christmas, cock, eggs, wish.*

Wishing Well: A wishing well is a pond or well that people throw coins or stones into, believing that any wish they make will be granted. This is one of the most ancient of superstitions. On the night of a full moon, a young girl can toss a coin into a wishing well and see an image of her future husband in the water.

See *coin, moon, well.*

Witch: Shamans, witch doctors, witches and sorcerers were the first people who attempted to appease the gods and make sense of the world. The word "witch" comes from the Saxon *wica*, which means "wise one."

There have always been witches. The ancient Assyrians, Babylonians, Hebrews, Greeks, and Romans all mention them in their writings. In Greco-Roman times, witches were renowned for their healing skills using herbs and magic potions. However, even then, not everyone approved of witches. Pliny, Ovid, and Plutarch all wrote negatively about witches.

Witches are even mentioned in the Bible: "Thou shalt not suffer a witch to live" (Exodus 22:18). However, the witches mentioned in the Bible are generally considered diviners, rather than witches as we know them.

Unfortunately, over time witches began to be viewed as unpleasant people who cast evil spells and deliberately hurt others. Persecution of witches began when the Christian Church started fostering the belief that witches were in league

with the devil. Witches were also said to copulate with demons, conduct wild orgies, and indulge in many other forms of diabolical and depraved behavior.

This belief led to many horrific injustices, and countless innocent men and women were accused of practicing witchcraft and then burned at the stake. The European witch craze began in the mid-fifteenth century, and lasted almost 250 years. Between 1484 and 1685, about one thousand people were hanged or burned as witches in Great Britain. In North America, more than thirty people were convicted of witchcraft at the famous trials at Salem, Massachusetts in 1692.

Witches were believed to be able to cast spells, change form or shape at will, and pass the evil eye on to anyone they disliked. As witches were thought not to have a soul, they made no reflection in a mirror. Witches could also recite the Lord's Prayer backwards, and were thwarted by anything made of iron. People believed that witches possessed "devil's marks," which were warts, moles, or other markings on their skin, usually in the area of the armpits.

Witches were considered responsible for all the bad things that occurred in a community. If a calf died, or the crops failed, or a child was stillborn, a witch must have caused it to happen. Even storms and murders were blamed on witchcraft. A wide variety of amulets and other forms

of protection were used to protect people, homes, and property from witches.

Witches could not usually hurt you unless they had a small part of you to work with. Consequently, it was extremely important to carefully dispose of nail clippings, cut hair, blood, urine, and saliva in order to prevent it from getting into the hands of a witch.

Even today, many people are scared of witches. This isn't surprising when you think of the stereotypical image of a witch. Movies and children's books still perpetuate the picture of a hideous hag with a warty nose, pointed chin, and black hat, who lives alone with a black cat and casts evil spells.

Witches today practice a pagan religion and consider themselves servants of the Goddess (and, sometimes, the Horned God). They are natural healers and believe in the sanctity of all life.

See *amulet, baby, blood, bread, cat, chimney, church, coven, crossroads, devil, evil eye, fingernail, fox, Friday, garlic, hair, hare, holy water, iron, ladybug, Macbeth, mirror, moles, onion,* *rabbit's foot, right side, rosemary, rowan, ships, spell, storm, urine, warts, water, Wicca, willow, witchcraft, women.*

Witchcraft: Witchcraft is the art and practices conducted by a witch. Because witchcraft is interpreted differently in different cultures, it is impossible to give a simple definition. Witchcraft is also called the Craft, the Way of the Wise, and the Old Religion, and claims a direct lineage with prehistoric fertility religion.

Until the twentieth century, the term witchcraft alluded to a number of elements that are not included in modern-day Wicca. In his famous book *The Discoverie of Witchcraft*, Reginald Scot (c.1538–1599) covered topics such as alchemy, astrology, ceremonial magic and demonology, indicating that the witches of his time practiced a variety of forms of magic. For most people, the term "witchcraft" represented a negative form of magic that was utilized to harm an enemy. Consequently, different forms of psychic protection, such as charms, were used to protect people from these negative forces.

In the twentieth century, a new form of witchcraft, known as Wicca, has grown in popularity. Wicca claims its origin in pre-Christian pagan religions. Wicca is one of the fastest growing religions in the world.

See *astrology, charms, holly, Macbeth, magic, prayer, spell, spitting, Wicca, witch.*

Wolf: Ever since a she-wolf suckled Romulus and Remus, people have been fascinated by wolves, and a number of superstitions have developed around them.

Hanging a wolf's tail above a barnyard door ensures that other wolves keep well away. A necklace of wolves' teeth protects children from harm.

But wolves are usually associated with evil and have always been feared. They are thought to be one of the devil's favorite disguises. If a wolf sees you before you see it, you will immediately become dumb.

It is not a compliment to call a man a "wolf," as this means that he has a predatory approach toward women. Likewise, a "wolf in sheep's clothing" is someone who appears kind and gentle, but is in fact dangerous.

It is not a good idea to say the word "wolf" out loud, especially in December. This will increase your likelihood of being confronted by one.

See *devil, lycanthropy, wedding, werewolf.*

Women: There are many more superstitions relating to, or involving, women than men. This is probably due to factors such as menstruation and childbirth, which are mysteries to men.

Goddess worship was widely practiced twenty-five thousand to forty thousand years ago. The veneration paid to women at that time is revealed in the fact that, for every one male figurine found, ten goddess figurines have been discovered.

Unfortunately for women, this golden age didn't last. When Adam and Eve were banished from the Garden of Eden, the blame was laid entirely on Eve. This denigration of women continued, and reached its zenith with the witch hunts in Europe and America.

Fear of women and the magic they can do still applies in certain areas. Sailors do not like women to be on the wharf when a ship leaves. Women mustn't wave goodbye to their husbands as they leave for their ship, and they mustn't wash clothes on the day the ship leaves port. It is bad luck for a man to hear a woman whistle or to see a cross-eyed woman.

See *clothes, cross-eyed, magic, menstruation, sailors, ships, whistle, witch.*

Wood: Knocking on wood, or touching wood, is one of the most popular superstitions concerning good luck. In the

United States, people knock on wood, but in the United Kingdom touching wood is more common. It is usually performed after making a highly optimistic remark, and is done to appease the fates who might prevent the good luck from occurring. You should touch or knock on wood with your right hand. If you are knocking on wood, you should do it three times to ensure that any bad luck is averted.

This belief goes back to prehistoric times, when people worshipped the gods who lived in the trees. These gods were responsible for the seasonal changes in trees that symbolized birth, death, and resurrection. The tree gods were happy to help humans who approached them in a respectful manner. Consequently, people touched trees when asking for favors, and touched them again once the request had been granted.

As a result of this, many charms and amulets were made from wood to enable people to touch it more easily. The wooden crosses that medieval Christians wore are a good example of this.

See *amulet, boasting, charms, cross, fairies, knock on wood, luck, petrified wood, sugar, tree, wedding anniversaries.*

Words: The Bible says, "In the beginning was the Word, and the Word was with God, and the Word was God" (John 1:1). Words possess magical powers, and frequently act as charms. It was believed that injuries and sores could be cured by repeating healing words nine times while using a finger to circle the affected part. Alternatively, the healing words could be said silently, while the mouth covered the afflicted part of the body.

Every word possesses magic. The word "home" has much more power associated with it than the word "house." The words "I love you" are full of magic. Emotional words possess enormous magic. Think of love, hate, revenge, and grief.

The names we are given at birth also possess incredible power. In *The Golden Bough: A Study in Magic and Religion,* James Frazer wrote that the North American Indian "regards his name not as a mere label, but as a distinct part of his personality ... and believes that injury will result from malicious handling of his name as from a wound inflicted on any part of his physical organism."[62] Consequently, knowing someone's name increases your power, while it weakens theirs.

The magical power associated with words is well exemplified in the story *Rumplestiltskin* by the Brothers Grimm. This tells the story of a little manikin who teaches the miller's daughter how to spin straw into gold in exchange for her first child. This bargain enables her to marry the king. However, when the baby is born, she is so heartbroken that the manikin

gives her three days in which to guess his name. Her guesses are wrong for two days, but on the third day, one of the queen's servants hears the manikin singing,

Little dreams my dainty dame
Rumplestiltskin is my name.

When he learns that she knows his name, the manikin is furious and kills himself with rage. The king, queen, and baby live happily ever after.

See *abracadabra, airplane, charms, finger, lying, magic, nine.*

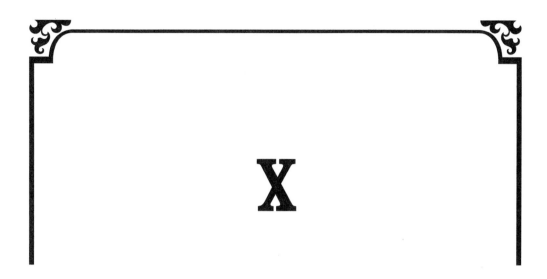

X

X in the Palm of My Hand: Many people believe they can determine the number of children a person will have by counting the number of crosses they find in the palm of the person's hand. Palmists do not accept this belief. They determine the number of children by counting the fine vertical lines beneath the little finger. In a woman's hand these lines indicate the potential, rather than the actual, number of children she will have. In a man's hand they indicate the number of children he will be close to.

Xmas: Many years ago, I was told that spelling the word "Christmas" as "Xmas" was invented by Pagans, as it effectively took "Christ" out of Christmas.

X-Ray: A comparatively modern superstition says that you will attract bad luck if you smile while having your X-ray taken.

X-Roads: See *crossroads*.

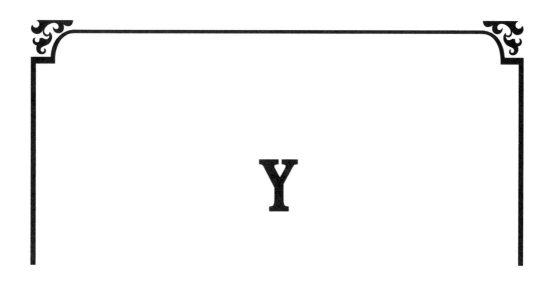

Y

Yarrow: In Christian tradition, yarrow is said to be the first herb that the baby Jesus touched. Consequently, yarrow has the power to avert evil spirits.

In ancient times, yarrow was called the herb of Venus. Because of this association, yarrow is often used to attract love.

See *love*.

Yawning: People cover their mouths when yawning. Most have no idea that this example of good etiquette is derived from an ancient belief that evil spirits can enter the body while a person is yawning. Covering the mouth prevented this from happening. Yawning for too long a time was also considered dangerous, as this enabled the soul to leave the body. Breath has always played a major role in magic, and this superstition derives from that.

See *breath, magic*.

Yellow: Yellow is considered an extremely unlucky color. It is related to cowardice and illness. As leaves turn yellow before falling from the tree, yellow can also symbolize death.

See *death, leaf*.

Yew: The yew is a long-living evergreen tree that has become associated with life after death. As a result, it is frequently found in graveyards throughout the British Isles and parts of Europe. In Elizabethan times it was considered an unlucky plant. William Shakespeare alluded to this attitude in *Twelfth Night* when Feste said, "Come away, come away death…My shroud of white, stuck all with yew" (Act 2, scene 4). The Elizabethans tossed sprigs of yew into graves to ensure that the spirits of the dead did not come back to haunt the living.

The yew is also renowned for protecting homes and other buildings from witches and evil spirits. It is believed that you are likely to die within twelve months if you trim or cut down a yew tree.

At one time, it was considered dangerous to carry a sprig or branch of yew into the home. However, another superstition has a different slant on this. An unmarried woman can pick a sprig of yew from a graveyard she hasn't visited before and place it under her pillow. This enables her to see her future partner in her dreams.

See *death, grave, graveyard, witch.*

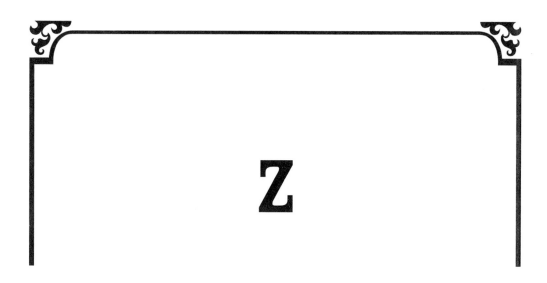

Z

Zoanthropy: Zoanthropy comes from the Greek word *zoion*, which means "an animal." Zoanthropy is the belief that humans can be transformed, or transform themselves, into animals and temporarily acquire the characteristics of the particular animal.

See *lycanthropy, werewolf*.

Zodiac: The concept of the zodiac goes back at least four thousand years. It is an imaginary wheel in the sky that divides the  year into twelve constellations, or signs. The sun, moon, and other planets appear to travel around this imaginary circle. The zodiac signs are determined by people's dates of birth, and most people know which sign of the zodiac they belong to. The signs are:

Aries: March 21–April 20
Taurus: April 21–May 20
Gemini: May 21–June 20
Cancer: June 21–July 20
Leo: July 21–August 20
Virgo: August 21–September 20
Libra: September 21–October 20
Scorpio: October 21–November 20
Sagittarius: November 21–December 20
Capricorn: December 21–January 20
Aquarius: January 21–February 20
Pisces: February 21–March 20

Each zodiac sign gives some idea as to the character and disposition of the people born under it. Because the signs have certain characteristics in common, they can be arranged into groups. People born under fire signs (Aries, Leo, and Sagittarius) are considered enthusiastic, independent self-starters. The earth signs (Taurus, Virgo, and Capricorn) are reliable, dependable, and conservative. The air signs (Gemini, Libra, and Aquarius) are idealistic, intellectual communicators. The water signs (Cancer, Scorpio, and Pisces) are intuitive, emotional, and receptive.

See *air, astrology, earth, fire,* individual zodiac signs, *moon, sun, water.*

Zombie: Zombie means "living dead." A zombie was originally a god in different countries in Africa, particularly the Congo. However, the term has become an integral part of voodoo magic, and describes

a corpse that has been enchanted and brought back to life by having part of its soul temporarily restored by a magician or sorcerer. This person then has control over the zombie, who is kept in a semi-conscious state.

The only people who can become zombies are those who have had an unnatural death. The only way to prevent such people from becoming zombies is by symbolically killing them a second time. This thwarts the sorcerer, who will be unable to revive the corpse.

The term "zombie" is sometimes given to a person who looks or acts differently from the norm, or who appears to be only half alive.

See *corpse, death, voodoo.*

NOTES

Introduction:

1. "The Way We Were," *Sunday Star Times* (Auckland, NZ, December 31, 2006): A12.

2. B. F. Skinner, "'Superstition' in the Pigeon," *Journal of Experimental Psychology* 38 (1948): 168–172.

3. *Encyclopaedia Britannica, Micropaedia Vol. IX*, 15th ed. (Chicago: Encyclopedia Britannica, 1983), 683.

4. Kurt Koch, *Occult ABC*, 1st American ed. (Literature Mission Aglasterhausen, Germany, 1978; distributed by Grand Rapids International Publications, Grand Rapids, MI), 239.

5. Ananda K. Coomaraswamy, *What Is Civilization? And Other Essays* (Oxford: Oxford University Press, 1993), 102.

6. Mark Henderson, "Evolution Keeps Us Superstitious. Now That's Lucky," *The Times* (London, September 5, 2006): 31.

7. Francis Bacon, "Of Superstition," *Essays or Counsels, Civil and Moral* (1625) (London: Folio Society, 2002), 60.

Actors and Actresses:

8. Nat Segaloff, *The Everything Trivia Book* (Holbrook, MA: Adams Media Corporation, 1999), 149.

Agate:

9. Harriet Keith Fobes, *Mystic Gems* (Boston: Richard G. Badger, 1924), 55.

Aluminum:

10. Albert A. Hopkins, "Aluminum on Trial," *Scientific American* 140 (March 1929): 246–248.

Ambulance:

11. Iona Opie and Moira Tatem, *A Dictionary of Superstitions* (Oxford: Oxford University Press, 1989), 2.

Amethyst:

12. Camillus Leonardus, *Speculum Lapidum* (Venice, 1502). English translation, *The Mirror of Stones* (London, 1750).

Aphrodisiac:

13. Graeme Donald, *Things You Thought You Thought You Knew!* (London: Unwin Paperbacks, 1986), 9.

14. Jonathan Leake and Sian Griffiths, "Truth About Nutrition Is Food for Thought," *The Sunday Times* (London, December 31, 2006).

Apple:

15. C. L. Pullen, "A Rhyme for Divination by Means of Apple-Seeds," *Journal of American Folklore* 2.4 (January–March 1889): 71.

April Fool's Day:

16. Charles Platt, *Popular Superstitions* (London: Herbert Jenkins, 1925), 86.

Baby:

17. R. Chambers, ed., *The Book of Days: A Miscellany of Popular Antiquities*, vol. 2 (London: W & R Chambers, 1866), 39.

Baseball:

18. Kathlyn Gay, *They Don't Wash their Socks! Sports Superstitions* (New York: Avon Books, 1990), 8–9.

Birthstone:

19. Bruce G. Knuth, *Gems in Myth, Legend and Lore* (Thornton, CO: Jewelers Press, 1999), 236.

20. George Frederick Kunz, *The Curious Lore of Precious Stones* (Philadelphia: J. B. Lippincott Company, 1913), 307.

Candle:

21. Cassandra Eason, *Encyclopedia of Magic and Ancient Wisdom* (London: Piatkus Books, 2000), 14.

Charms:

22. Sheila Paine, *Amulets: A World of Secret Powers, Charms and Magic* (London: Thames & Hudson, 2004), 11.

23. Queen Victoria, quoted in *Superstition and the Superstitious* by Eric Maple (London: W. H. Allen & Company, 1971), 178.

Evil Eye:

24. Jean Patterson and Arzu Aghayeva, "The Evil Eye: Staving Off Harm—With a Visit to the Open Market," *Azerbaijan International* (Autumn 2000): 8.

Exorcism:

25. Robert Herrick, *Works of Robert Herrick*, vol. 2, ed. Alfred Pollard (London: Lawrence & Bullen, 1891), 73.

Familiar:

26. Leonard R. N. Ashley, *The Complete Book of Spells, Curses and Magical Recipes* (New York: Barricade Books, 1997), 201.

Film Stars:

27. David Hartnell, *David Hartnell's Hollywood Trivia* (Auckland, NZ: David Bateman, 2003), 105–108.

Grave:

28. William Jones, *Credulities Past and Present* (London: Chatto and Windus, 1880), 268.

Green:

29. Alec Gill, *Superstitions: Folk Magic in Hull's Fishing Community* (Beverley, UK: Hutton Press, 1993), 99.

Groundhog Day:

30. Vergilius Ferm, *A Brief Dictionary of American Superstitions* (New York: Philosophical Library, 1965), 51.

Hand:

31. C. J. S. Thompson, *Amulets, Talismans and Charms* (Edmonds, WA: Holmes Publishing Group, 1994), 16–17.

Hare:

32. Eric Maple, *Superstition and the Superstitious* (London: W. H. Allen & Company, 1971), 12.

Hiccups:

33. Nat Segaloff, *The Everything Trivia Book* (Holbrook, MA: Adams Media Corp., 1999), 211.

Hunchback:

34. Michael Williams, *Superstition and Folklore* (Bodmin, UK: Bossiney Books, 1982), 70.

Immaculate Conception:

35. Ernest Busenbark, *Symbols, Sex and the Stars in Popular Beliefs* (New York: The Truth Seeker Company, 1949), 115.

36. Steve Connor, "Scientists Are Leaping over Lizards," *The New Zealand Herald* (December 22, 2006): A10.

Lapis Lazuli:

37. Bruce G. Knuth, *Gems in Myth, Legend and Lore* (Thornton, CO: Jewelers Press, 1999), 113.

38. George Frederick Kunz, *The Curious Lore of Precious Stones* (Philadelphia: J. B. Lippincott Company, 1913), 92–93.

Lightning:

39. Peter Haining, *Superstitions* (London: Sidgwick & Jackson, 1979), 71.

40. Don Lewis, *Religious Superstition Through the Ages* (London: A. R. Mowbray & Co., 1975), 153.

Lodestone:

41. Bartholomaeus Angelicus, *De Proprietatibus Rerum* (1396), trans. John of Travisa (London: Wynkyn de Worde, 1495), Lib xvi, cap. 43.

Mirror:

42. Peter Haining, *Superstitions* (London: Sidgwick & Jackson, 1979), 61.

Moon:

43. Ken Ring, *The Lunar Code: How the Moon Affects Our Weather on Earth* (Auckland, NZ: Random House New Zealand, 2006).

Nail:

44. Richard Webster, *Amulets and Talismans for Beginners* (St. Paul, MN: Llewellyn Publications, 2004), 1.

Names:

45. Leslie Alan Dunkling, *Our Secret Names: What They Reveal about Ourselves and Others* (London: Sidgwick and Jackson, 1981), 40.

Onyx:

46. M. L. Seymour, ed., *Mandeville's Travels* (London: Oxford University Press, 1968), 167.

47. Camillus Leonardus, *Speculum Lapidum* (Venice, 1502). English translation, *The Mirror of Stones* (London, 1750), 213.

Rabbit's Foot:

48. Robert Latham, ed., *Pepys's Diary*, vol. 2 (London: The Folio Society, 1996), 120.

Rain:

49. John Aubrey and Strattis, both quoted in *The Oxford Dictionary of Nursery Rhymes*, eds. Iona and Peter Opie (Oxford: Oxford University Press, 1952), 360–361.

Ring:

50. George Frederick Kunz, *Rings for the Finger* (Philadelphia: J. B. Lippincott Company, 1917), 123.

51. Henry Cornelius Agrippa of Nettesheim, *Three Books of Occult Philosophy*, ed. Donald Tyson (St. Paul, MN: Llewellyn Publications, 1993), 140–142.

Ruby:

52. John M. Riddle, *Marbode of Rennes' (1035–1123) De Lapidus Considered as a Medical Treatise with Text, Commentary and C. W. King's Translation* (Wiesbaden: Franx Steiner Verlag GMBH, 1977), 68–69.

St. Christopher:

53. Harvey Day, *Occult Illustrated Dictionary* (London: Kaye & Ward, 1975), 129.

Sneezing:

54. Charles Platt, *Popular Superstitions* (London: Herbert Jenkins, 1925), 222.

Star:

55. Napoleon, quoted in *A Treasury of American Superstitions* by Claudia De Lys (New York: Philosophical Library, 1948), 422.

Taboo:

56. Sigmund Freud, *Totem and Taboo* (1913), trans. James Strachey (London: Routledge & Kegan Paul, 1950), 18–19.

Thirteen:

57. Charles Mackay, *Extraordinary Popular Delusions and the Madness of Crowds* (1841) (Manchester, UK: George Routledge & Sons, 1892), 256–257.

Toast:

58. Lord Chesterfield, *Letters to his Son* (London: W. & R. Chambers, 1884), letter of September 22, 1752. First published as *Letters written by the Earl of Chesterfield to his Son, Philip Stanhope, together with several other pieces on various subjects.*

Topaz:

59. Harriet Keith Fobes, *Mystic Gems* (Boston: The Gorham Press, 1924), 102.

Vulture:

60. Robin McKie, "Survival Now a Lottery for Graceful Scavengers," *The New Zealand Herald*, July 24, 2006.

Warts:

61. Carol Ann Rinzler, *Feed a Cold, Starve a Fever: A Dictionary of Medical Folklore* (New York: Facts on File, 1991), 204–205. First published by Thomas Y. Crowell in 1979 as *The Dictionary of Medical Folklore.*

Words:

62. James Frazer, *The Golden Bough: A Study in Magic and Religion* (abridged edition) (London: Macmillan and Company, 1922), 244.

BIBLIOGRAPHY

Andrews, Tamra. *Nectar & Ambrosia: An Encyclopedia of Food in World Mythology*. Santa Barbara: ABC-CLIO, 2000.

Ashley, Leonard R. N. *The Wonderful World of Superstition, Prophecy and Luck*. New York: W. W. Norton and Company, 1984.

Beck, Horace P. *The Folklore of Maine*. Philadelphia: J. B. Lippincott Company, 1957.

Benitez, Armando. *Sheer Superstition: Outmaneuvering Fate*. Charlottesville, VA: Hampton Roads Publishing Company, 2000.

Bonnerjea, Biren. *A Dictionary of Superstitions and Mythology*. London: Folk Press, 1927.

Brasch, R. *How Did It Begin? Customs and Superstitions and Their Romantic Origins*. New York: David McKay Company, 1965.

Brown, Raymond L. *A Book of Superstitions*. Devon, UK: David & Charles, 1970.

Brown, W. J. *The Gods Had Wings: Legends, Folklore and Quaint Beliefs about Birds*. London: Constable and Company, 1936.

Caradeau, Jean-Luc, and Cécile Donner. *The Dictionary of Superstitions*. New York: Henry Holt and Company, 1987.

Cashford, Jules. *The Moon: Myth and Image*. London: Cassell Illustrated, 2002.

Chambers, R., ed. *The Book of Days: A Miscellany of Popular Antiquities* (two volumes). London: W. & R. Chambers, 1866.

Chaundler, Christine. *Every Man's Book of Superstitions*. New York: Philosophical Library, 1970.

Cohen, Daniel. *Superstition*. Mankato, MN: Creative Education Press, 1971.

Colin, Didier. *Dictionary of Symbols, Myths and Legends*. Trans. Wendy Allatson and Sue Rose. London: Hachette Illustrated UK, 2000.

Cowan, Lore. *Are You Superstitious?* London: Leslie Frewin Publishers, 1968.

De Lys, Claudia. *A Treasury of American Superstitions*. New York: Philosophical Library, 1948.

Di Stasi, Lawrence. *Mal Occhio: The Underside of Vision*. San Francisco: North Point Press, 1981.

Dorson, Richard M. *American Folklore*. Chicago: The University of Chicago Press, 1959.

Dossey, Donald E. *Holiday Folklore, Phobias and Fun*. Los Angeles: Outcomes Unlimited Press, 1992.

Dunkling, Leslie Alan. *Our Secret Names: What They Reveal about Ourselves and Others*. London: Sidgwick and Jackson, 1981.

Ferm, Vergilius. *A Brief Dictionary of American Superstitions*. New York: Philosophical Library, 1965.

Fielding, William J. *Strange Superstitions and Magical Practices*. Philadelphia: The Blakiston Company, 1945.

Fowler, Marian. *Hope: Adventures of a Diamond*. New York: The Ballantine Publishing Group, 2002.

Frazer, James. *The Golden Bough: A Study in Magic and Religion* (abridged edition). London: Macmillan and Company, 1922.

Freud, Sigmund. *Totem and Taboo*. London: Routledge & Kegan Paul, 1950.

Gay, Kathlyn. *They Don't Wash Their Socks! Sports Superstitions*. New York: Avon Books, 1990.

Gill, Alec. *Superstitions: Folk Magic in Hull's Fishing Community*. Beverley, UK: Hutton Press, 1993.

Haining, Peter. *Superstitions*. London: Sidgwick & Jackson, 1979.

Hazlitt, W. C. *Dictionary of Faiths and Folklore*. London: Reeves and Turner, 1905.

Heaps, Willard A. *Superstition!* New York: Thomas Nelson, 1972.

Hill, Douglas. *Magic and Superstition*. London: The Hamlyn Publishing Group, 1968.

Hole, Christina. *A Dictionary of British Folk Customs*. London: Granada Publishing, 1979.

Igglesden, Charles. *Those Superstitions*. London: Jarrolds Publishers, 1932.

Jahoda, Gustav. *The Psychology of Superstition*. London: Penguin Books, 1969.

Johnson, Clifton. *What They Say in New England and Other American Folklore*. Boston: Lee and Shepherd, 1896. (Reprinted by Columbia University Press, New York, 1963.)

Jones, William. *Credulities Past and Present*. London: Chatto and Windus, 1880.

Kendall, Leo P. *Diamonds Famous and Fatal: The History, Mystery and Lore of the World's Most Precious Gem*. Fort Lee, NJ: Barricade Books, 2001.

Kunz, George Frederick. *The Curious Lore of Precious Stones*. Philadelphia: J. B. Lippincott Company, 1913.

Lachenmeyer, Nathaniel. *13: The Story of the World's Most Popular Superstition*. New York: Thunder's Mouth Press, 2004.

Lasne, Sophie, and André Pascal Gaultier. *A Dictionary of Superstitions*. New York: A. S. Barnes and Company, 1984.

Leach, Maria. *The Luck Book*. Cleveland, OH: World Publishing, 1964.

Lewis, Don. *Religious Superstition through the Ages*. London: A. R. Mowbray & Company, 1975.

Lin, Henry B. *What Your Face Reveals: Chinese Secrets of Face Reading*. St. Paul, MN: Llewellyn Publications, 1999.

Lorie, Peter. *Superstitions*. New York: Simon & Schuster, 1992.

Maple, Eric. *Superstition and the Superstitious*. London: W. H. Allen & Company, 1971.

Meerloo, Joost A. M. *Intuition and the Evil Eye*. Wassenaar, Netherlands: N. V. Servire Publishers, 1971.

Miller, Carey. *Superstitions*. London: Piccolo Books, 1977.

Morris, Desmond. *Body Guards: Protective Amulets and Charms*. Shaftesbury, UK: Element Books, 1999.

Opie, Iona, and Moira Tatem. *A Dictionary of Superstitions*. New York: Oxford University Press, 1993.

Paine, Sheila. *Amulets: A World of Secret Powers, Charms and Magic*. London: Thames & Hudson, 2004.

Perl, Lila. *Blue Monday and Friday the Thirteenth*. New York: Clarion Books, 1986.

Pickering, David. *Dictionary of Superstitions*. London: Cassell & Company, 1995.

Planer, F. E. *Superstition*. London: Cassell & Company, 1980.

Platt, Charles. *Popular Superstitions*. London: Herbert Jenkins, 1925.

Plimmer, Martin, and Brian King. *Beyond Coincidence*. Cambridge, UK: Icon Books, 2004.

Potter, Carole. *Knock on Wood and Other Superstitions*. New York: Sammis Publishing Company, 1983.

Rachleff, Owen S. *The Secrets of Superstitions: How They Help, How They Hurt*. Garden City, NJ: Doubleday & Company, 1976.

Radford E., and M.A. Radford. *Encyclopedia of Superstitions*. Edited and revised by Christina Hole. London: Hutchinson & Company, 1961. (First published 1948.)

Randolph, Vance. *Ozark Superstitions*. New York: Columbia University Press, 1947.

Read, Carveath. *Man and His Superstitions*. London: Cambridge University Press, 1925.

Ring, Ken. *The Cat Omen Book*. Auckland, NZ: Milton Press (NZ), 1999.

———. *Moon and Weather Lore*. Auckland, NZ: Milton Press (NZ), 2002.

———. *The Lunar Code: How the Moon Affects Our Weather on Earth*. Auckland, NZ: Random House New Zealand, 2006.

Rinzler, Carol Ann. *Feed a Cold, Starve a Fever: A Dictionary of Medical Folklore*. New York: Facts on File, 1991. (First published by Thomas Y. Crowell, Publishers, in 1979 as *The Dictionary of Medical Folklore*.)

Room, Adrian, ed. *Brewer's Dictionary of Phrase and Fable*. 16th edition. London: Cassell & Company, 2000. (First published 1870.)

Schwartz, Alvin. *Cross Your Fingers, Spit in Your Hat: Superstitions and Other Beliefs*. New York: Lippincott and Company, 1974.

Shermer, Michael. *Why People Believe Weird Things: Pseudoscience, Superstition, and Other Confusions of Our Time*. New York: W. H. Freeman and Company, 1997.

Simons, G. L. *Sex and Superstition*. London: Abelard-Schuman, 1973.

Spence, Lewis. *Myth and Ritual in Dance, Game and Rhyme*. London: C. A. Watts and Company, 1947.

Sullivan, George. *Sports Superstitions*. New York: Coward McCann, 1978.

Thomas, Daniel L., and Lucy B. Thomas. *Kentucky Superstitions*. Princeton: Princeton University Press, 1920.

Thompson, C. J. S. *The Hand of Destiny: Folklore and Superstition for Everyday Life*. New York: Bell Publishing Company, 1989.

Thurston, Herbert. *Superstition: A Backward Glance over Nineteen Centuries*. London: The Centenary Press, 1933.

Waring, Philippa. *A Dictionary of Omens and Superstitions*. London: Souvenir Press, 1978.

Waterman, Philip F. *The Story of Superstition*. New York: Alfred A. Knopf, Inc., 1929.

Webster, Richard. *Write Your Own Magic*. St. Paul, MN: Llewellyn Publications, 2001.

——. *Amulets and Talismans for Beginners*. St. Paul, MN: Llewellyn Publications, 2004.

——. *Magical Symbols of Love and Romance*. Woodbury, MN: Llewellyn Publications, 2007.

Williams, Michael. *Superstition and Folklore*. Bodmin, UK: Bossiney Books, 1982.

Wright, Ruth and Robert L. Chadbourne. *Crystals, Gems and Minerals of the Bible*. New Canaan, CT: Keats Publishing, 1970.

Zolar. *Zolar's Encyclopedia of Omens, Signs and Superstitions*. New York: Prentice Hall Press, 1989.

Free Magazine

Get the latest information on our body, mind, and spirit products! To receive a free copy of Llewellyn's consumer catalog, *New Worlds of Mind & Spirit*, simply call 1-877-NEW-WRLD or visit our website at www.llewellyn.com and click on *New Worlds*.

LLEWELLYN ORDERING INFORMATION

Order Online:
Visit our website at www.llewellyn.com, select your books, and order them on our secure server.

Order by Phone:
- Call toll-free within the U.S. at 1-877-NEW-WRLD (1-877-639-9753). Call toll-free within Canada at 1-866-NEW-WRLD (1-866-639-9753)
- We accept VISA, MasterCard, and American Express

Order by Mail:
Send the full price of your order (MN residents add 7% sales tax) in U.S. funds, plus postage & handling to:

Llewellyn Worldwide
2143 Wooddale Drive, Dept. 978-0-7387-1277-2
Woodbury, MN 55125-2989, U.S.A.

Postage & Handling:
Standard (U.S., Mexico, & Canada). If your order is:
$24.99 and under, add $3.00
$25.00 and over, FREE STANDARD SHIPPING

AK, HI, PR: $15.00 for one book plus $1.00 for each additional book.

International Orders (airmail only):
$16.00 for one book plus $3.00 for each additional book

Orders are processed within 2 business days.
Please allow for normal shipping time. Postage and handling rates subject to change.

Spirit Guides & Angel Guardians
Contact Your Invisible Helpers

RICHARD WEBSTER

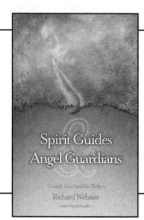

They come to our aid when we least expect it, and they disappear as soon as their work is done. Invisible helpers are available to all of us; in fact, we all regularly receive messages from our guardian angels and spirit guides but usually fail to recognize them. This book will help you to realize when this occurs. And when you carry out the exercises provided, you will be able to communicate freely with both your guardian angels and spirit guides.

You will see your spiritual and personal growth take a huge leap forward as soon as you welcome your angels and guides into your life. This book contains numerous case studies that show how angels have touched the lives of others, just like yourself. Experience more fun, happiness, and fulfillment than ever before. Other people will also notice the difference as you become calmer, more relaxed, and more loving than ever before.

978-1-5671-8795-3

368 pp.

5 ³/₁₆ x 8 $9.95

Also available in Spanish.

To order, call 1-877-NEW-WRLD

Prices subject to change without notice

Michael

Communicating with the Archangel for Guidance & Protection

RICHARD WEBSTER

Michael is considered the greatest angel in the Christian, Judaic, and Islamic traditions. Throughout the ages, he has appeared as a protector, a messenger, a guide, a warrior, and a healer. In *Michael*, Richard Webster presents a thorough history of this famous archangel and offers simple techniques for contacting him.

Readers are treated to a detailed introduction to Michael and his many appearances. The rest of this practical guide provides a variety of methods for connecting with Michael, petitioning his help, and creating a lasting bond. Through easy-to-perform rituals and meditations—some involving candle magic, crystals, and dreamwork—readers will learn how to get in touch with the Prince of Light for courage, protection, strength, and spiritual guidance.

978-0-7387-0540-8

192 pp.

5 ³⁄₁₆ x 8 $11.95

Also available in Spanish.

Color Magic for Beginners

*Simple Techniques to Brighten &
Empower Your Life*

RICHARD WEBSTER

From our clothes to the color of our bedroom walls, we are surrounded by colors that influence our mood, energy level, creativity, and overall well being. Richard Webster offers an astonishing number of ways to use stimulating reds, soothing blues, and every other color of the rainbow to our advantage.

Webster begins with an overall picture of each color's major aspects—its psychological influence, healing qualities, emotional impact, and magical characteristics. From there, readers learn a multitude of color-based techniques involving astrology, the aura, candle magic, chakras, color rituals, crystals and gemstones, feng shui, flower magic, mandalas, meditation, numerology, and visualization. Webster demonstrates how color can be used to attract good luck, heal illness, reduce stress, create harmony in the home, overcome depression, solve problems, and magically enhance one's life in a variety of ways.

978-0-7387-0886-7

264 pp.

5 ³/₁₆ x 8

appendix, bibliog., index $12.95

To order, call 1-877-NEW-WRLD

Prices subject to change without notice

Creative Visualization for Beginners
Achieve Your Goals & Make Your Dreams Come True

RICHARD WEBSTER

Everyone has the natural ability to visualize success, but ordinary methods used to reach fulfillment can be inefficient and unclear. Creative visualization allows anyone to change the direction of his or her life by mentally picturing and altering images of their goals. In his popular conversational style, bestselling author Richard Webster explains the methodology behind creative visualization, and provides readers with the tools and knowledge necessary to achieve their goals in all areas of life, including business, health, self-improvement, relationships, and nurturing and restoring the soul.

Creative Visualization for Beginners includes simple exercises enhanced by real-life situations from the author's personal experiences with creative visualization, and demonstrates how to react when you encounter difficulties along the way. In addition, he gives advice on what to do if you have no predetermined goals in mind, and how to implement positive results while maintaining your natural balance.

978-0-7387-0807-2

240 pp.

5 ³⁄₁₆ x 8

notes, index $12.95

Also available in Spanish.

Praying with Angels
Richard Webster

Reverence for angels spans culture, faith, and time. But can these celestial messengers answer our prayers?

Praying with Angels can help you develop a rewarding, lifelong relationship with these divine creatures. From prayer to dreamwork, you'll explore a myriad of simple ways to communicate with angels. There are practical exercises and meditations to aid in developing angel awareness—an important first step towards angelic communication. Webster also provides a fascinating tour of the angelic kingdom, revealing the role and strengths of guardian angels, angels of the zodiac, elemental angels, and others. This crucial information lays the groundwork to help you select the appropriate angel to contact according to your unique circumstances. *Praying with Angels* also includes rituals and techniques for requesting healing, protection, abundance, and personal guidance.

978-0-7387-1098-3

240 pp.

5 ³⁄₁₆ x 8

bibliog., index $13.95

To order, call 1-877-NEW-WRLD

Prices subject to change without notice

Magical Symbols of Love & Romance
RICHARD WEBSTER

A candlelight dinner, wine, and roses are obvious choices when you want to woo a special someone. But this is only the tip of a colossal heart-shaped iceberg when it comes to expressing love and creating romance.

From pearls to pomegranates, tulips to truffles, vodka to Venus, Richard Webster introduces a wide array of items that signify this ubiquitous, complicated emotion. Going back to prehistoric cave paintings, Greek and Roman myth, and the origin of Valentine's Day, he offers a colorful history of love rituals, spells, charms, and aphrodisiacs. Modern success stories illustrate how individuals have used these powerful symbols to attract a partner, stimulate marriage, or resolve relationship issues. A handy reference and practical guide rolled into one, this book also advises on how to use these symbols in your own life.

978-0-7387-1032-7

240 pp.

5 ³/₁₆ X 8

bibliog., suggested reading, index $12.95

Feng Shui in the Garden
RICHARD WEBSTER

Whether you own an estate with formal gardens or live in a studio apartment with room for a some flowerpots, you can discover the remarkable benefits of using plants to create more ch'i (universal energy) in your life. Wherever you find an abundance of ch'i, the vegetation looks rich and healthy, the air smells fresh and sweet, and the water is cool and refreshing.

The ancient Chinese believed that when you live in harmony with the earth, you become a magnet for health, wealth, and happiness. *Feng Shui in the Garden* shows beginning and expert gardeners alike how to tailor their gardens to bring them the greatest amount possible of positive energy. Select your most beneficial location, layout, flowers, colors, fragrances, herbs, and garden accessories based on proven feng shui principles. Discover the optimum placement of fountains, waterfalls, or swimming pools. Learn how to construct a serene secret garden, even if you live in an apartment!

978-1-5671-8793-9

168 pp.,

5 ¼ x 8 $9.95

To order, call 1-877-NEW-WRLD
Prices subject to change without notice

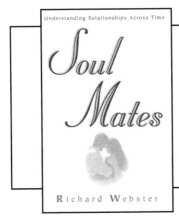

Soul Mates
Understanding Relationships Across Time

RICHARD WEBSTER

The eternal question: how do you find your soul mate—that special, magical person with whom you have spent many previous incarnations? Popular metaphysical author Richard Webster explores every aspect of the soul mate phenomenon in his newest release.

The incredible soul mate connection allows you and your partner to progress even further with your souls' growth and development with each incarnation. *Soul Mates* begins by explaining reincarnation, karma, and the soul, and prepares you to attract your soul mate to you. After reading examples of soul mates from the author's own practice and famous soul mates from history, you will learn how to recall your past lives. In addition, you will gain valuable tips on how to strengthen your relationship so it grows stronger and better as time goes by.

978-1-5671-8789-2
216 pp.
6 x 9 $12.95

Encyclopedia of Natural Magic
JOHN MICHAEL GREER

Natural magic is the ancient and powerful art of using material substances—herbs, stones, incenses, oils, and much more—to tap into the hidden magical powers of nature, transforming your surroundings and yourself.

Not just a cookbook of spells, the *Encyclopedia of Natural Magic* provides an introduction to the philosophy underlying this system. It also gives detailed information on 176 different herbs, trees, stones, metals, oils, incenses, and other substances, and offers countless ways to put them to magical use. With this book and a visit to your local herb store, rock shop, or backyard garden, you're ready to enter the world of natural magic!

978-0-7387-0674-0

312 pp.

7 ½ x 9 ⅛

illus. $16.95

To order, call 1-877-NEW-WRLD

Prices subject to change without notice